MANAGING IN THE AGE OF CHANGE

MANAGING IN THE AGE OF CHANGE

Edited by

Roger A. Ritvo

Anne H. Litwin

Lee Butler

INSTITUTE

IRWIN
Professional Publishing
Burr Ridge, Illinois
New York, New York

Sponsoring editor: Cynthia A. Zigmund
Project editor: Mary Conzachi
Production manager: Bob Lange
Interior designer: Mercedes Santos
Cover designer: Tim Kaage
Art manager: Kim Meriwether
Compositor: Precision Typographers
Typeface: 11/13 Palatino
Printer: Book Press

Library of Congress Cataloging-in-Publication Data

Managing in the age of change / edited by Roger A. Ritvo, Anne H.
  Litwin, Lee Butler.
     p.   cm.
  Includes index.
  ISBN 0-7863-0303-4
  1. Management. 2. Executive ability. I. Ritvo, Roger A., 1944–
  II. Litwin, Anne H. III. Butler, Lee.
  HD31.M29417 1995
  658.4—dc20   94-9331

Printed in the United States of America
1 2 3 4 5 6 7 8 9 0 BP 1 0 9 8 7 6 5 4

Preface

T he more things change, the more they stay the same. How many times have we heard this said? Probably thousands. The premise of this book lies in the fallacy of this assertion when it is applied to the future role of managers. A more accurate reframing of this axiom would be: "The more things change, the more adaptable successful managers must become." The technological explosion, the information highway, total quality management, efficiency experts, management rights, downsizing, and consolidation—these are some of the issues that confront managers each day as they report to work. Solving complex problems in the future will require new skills, not the same old ones.

The rate, direction, and impact of these social, cultural, structural, and technological shifts are issues that remain open to discussion, not whether these shifts will occur. The global marketplace is more than a phrase in the popular literature. When a US insurance company decides to move its claims processing division to Ireland in order to gain the competitive advantage of lower salaries and benefits, the management team must adapt to the culture, language, habits, norms, and holidays of this new workforce.

There are other changes under way. When women assume top leadership positions, family issues come into the conference room in ways that challenge past assumptions. When people of color enter the workforce in unprecedented numbers, the traditional assumptions of Euro-American male success models become outmoded. When portable computers and other support technologies expand the traditional concept of an office to include phone messages, faxes, and modems, the need for face-to-face meetings decreases.

These shifts in our society require managers to respond with vigor. Yet they remain responsible for planning, organizing, staffing, coordinating, hiring, rewarding, budgeting, and evaluating, even while the rules change. None of these permutations will be easy. Change breeds resistance; conflict will become more visible; there will indeed be winners and losers. Those organizations with adaptive cultures will emerge as models, while rigidity will doom others.

As members, we support the core values of the NTL Institute of Applied Behavioral Sciences, which stress the importance of different cultures, multiple approaches, and alternative designs. We at the institute value both diversity and managers' struggles as they attempt to respond effectively to these challenges.

Management often jumps on a fad and embraces short-term trends. How many of us remember ZBB (zero-based budgets)? Did Management by Objectives (MBO) make a long-term difference? What exactly was a 5,5 management style? Is just-in-time production likely to remain, or will it join the Scanlon Plan in the Management Hall of Fame? As these examples show, there is no Holy Grail. One of the salient features of the material in this volume is that it was written for this book. It is not part of any contemporary movement.

With this in mind, where should managers turn for advice, information, and options for action? This book builds on the central theme that major changes will characterize our future. Hopefully, it will serve as a useful complement to professional meetings, in-house training programs, and other literature. Managerial development is indeed a lifelong process, and *Managing in the Age of Change* offers practical advice for first-line supervisors, mid-level supervisors, upper management, and top leadership. The material applies equally to those who work in the health and human service sector and those employed in high-tech firms. Public agencies and small enterprises face different competitors, yet they do so in the same environment; this book will assist managers in these organizations as well.

The contributing authors have served as chief executive officers, managers, trainers, consultants, entrepreneurs, educators, policy makers, board members, and researchers. They work in family businesses, large bureaucratic organizations, and temporary task forces. Individually, these contributors have lived through periods of unprecedented growth, downsizing, mergers, consolidations, takeovers, and political transitions. Collectively, their decades of experience provide the best of current wisdom in one integrated volume.

USING THIS BOOK

This book presents current perspectives on major issues confronting managers. If you are looking for information on a specific topic, the extensive index will help. Each chapter has an excellent Executive Summary highlighting its major points. And each chapter seeks to answer the following questions: "How can I use this information?" "What does this mean to me?" and "What should I do next?"

The book's two parts have complementary focuses. There are important changes that are underway both in the United States and internationally. While managers face unique problems in their own jobs, there are themes and trends that affect them all. Part I focuses on the critical skills that will help managers respond to these changes now and in the future. These skills reflect the basic functions of management; whether one serves as a first-line supervisor, an associate vice-president, or the chief executive officer, there are managerial functions that vary only in their scope, magnitude, and impact. These include planning, budgeting, performance appraisal, conflict management, career development, using consultants, organizing staff, and using time effectively to meet predetermined needs. Part I contains 16 chapters, each focusing on a skill that we believe will be part of the successful manager's repertoire.

Chapter 1: Why Managers Don't Manage by Arthur Freedman identifies the reasons why some managers shy away from opportunities to make a difference. Could it be that these managers were promoted for their excellent technical skills, only to move into a different profession without realizing it? How can organizations avoid this problem? The chapter concludes with a set of helpful questions to assist managers and organizations in strengthening their managerial teams.

Based on a management classic, **Chapter 2: Situational Leadership II** by Kenneth Blanchard helps managers understand the dynamics of their jobs. Situational leadership defines the connections between the policies, skills, needs, and demands of specific situations and the managers' approach to problem solving.

Chapter 3: Managing Professionals by Patricia Williams uses an expanded definition of the term *professional*. The workforce of the future will become more differentiated between those employees with basic abilities and those who possess specialized knowledge and highly technical skills. This chapter presents strategies managers can use to respond effectively to both the organization's need for control and the professionals' desire for autonomy.

Chapter 4: Developing High-Performing Teams by Jane Moosbruker gives practical advice for managing work teams, task forces, and temporary systems. Given the dynamic environment, managers must become adept at creating teams that can promptly respond to client, customer, and competitor demands. They must also effectively manage and coordinate the activities of their department, programs, and staff. In order to meet these requirements, managers will have to understand and influence the phases of group development. When successful, high-performing teams result, increasing both the satisfaction of their members and their contribution to the organization's goals.

Robert Marshak's **Chapter 5: Managing in Chaotic Times** explains that we are in the midst of a fundamental change in the social role and function of organizations. Centuries ago, the advent of the Industrial Revolution altered society in ways that its participants could not foresee. Today, we are in a similarly momentous shift. Hints for managers who feel frustrated by this change provide both solace and alternative courses of action.

Chapter 6: Appreciating Resistances by Robert Lee begins with the premise that people and organizations resist change. In fact, policies and procedures are designed to provide consistency and predictability. When managers learn how to acknowledge and transform resistance into energy, planned changes will then be successful. The specific actions proposed in this chapter will help managers transform resistance into realistic responses to the needed change. They help put people back in control.

Brendan Reddy's **Chapter 7: Intergroup Competition and Conflict** recognizes the inevitable problems created by competition and conflict. The days of "don't rock the boat" have been replaced by an understanding that managers must respond effectively to these new dynamics. This chapter offers a framework for action.

Chapter 8; A Manager's Guide to Employee Appraisal by Robert Walters and **Chapter 9: If We Don't Know It's Broken, then How Can We Fix It?** by Larry Porter explore the difficulties in helping employees learn, grow, adapt, and improve their performance. Often the lack of skills and the shortage of role models make these tasks unpleasant. Both chapters provide advice and ideas for transforming performance appraisals and ongoing feedback into constructive interventions.

Chapter 10: The Manager's Role in Career Development by Caela Farren and Marc Young stresses the need for organizations to use their available talent fully. Supervisors are often in the best position to help their subordinates grow in planned directions. Such efforts are likely to save the organization valuable time and money; they also form the basis for sound human resource practices. We should invest in our employees. Specific strategies designed to meet this need assist managers in making a habit of this investment.

Chapter 11: A Planned Transition Process for the New Manager/Chief Executive Officer by Robert Lapidus helps organizations respond to the problems created by the inevitable departures and arrivals of new managers. The future is likely to be characterized by more turnover in executive leadership, and lifelong appointments will fade. Elements of planned transitions include helping subordinates adjust smoothly while assisting the new manager in establishing authority, support, and direction.

Roger A. Ritvo's **Chapter 12: Managing Time Effectively** offers practical advice on different approaches to using this valuable resource. All managers must balance the need to be available with the need to plan effectively. This chapter provides specific actions to gain control of your calendar and avoid time-wasting tasks.

Chapter 13: Human Dimensions of Budgeting by Srinivasan Umapathy acknowledges the fact that money affects people. Developing or implementing a budget challenges managers to maintain a proper perspective between financial responsibility and the needs of the workforce. The six steps to creating an appropriate organizational climate for budgeting will help managers overcome the battles that often cause budgets and financial planning to fail.

Chapter 14: Using Consultants Effectively by Mikki Ritvo and William LeClere helps managers use outside expertise effectively in accomplishing their jobs. Whether the consultant is from the same organization or an outside firm, the manager-as-client role has special requirements. This chapter presents rules for successfully working with consultants.

John Adams's **Chapter 15: Staying Well during—and after—Stressful Periods** helps managers understand the physical and emotional impacts of stress. Stress can be conceived of as energy. How do we manage our lives so that we remain healthy, productive, and effective? This chapter proposes easy-to-implement strategies to resolve this problem.

In **Chapter 16: Developing the Whole Person in Organizations,** Arlene Scott and Sheldon Hughes postulate that the "whole person" integrates his or her physical, emotional, mental, and spiritual dimensions. As managers work toward this end, their effectiveness increases and they serve as role models for others.

Part II: Managing Diversity Effectively explores in depth the numerous issues that confront managers in contemporary organizations. There has been a dramatic change in the demographics of the workforce; Part II's chapters present the challenges of creating and managing diversity in the workplace. As more Euro-American women join employees of Asian, Hispanic, and African heritage, those organizational leaders who know how to adapt will succeed while their counterparts search for answers. The concepts in these chapters help managers understand the complex environment in which they will work, compete, and succeed or fail.

Chapter 17: Meeting the Challenge of Managing Cultural Diversity by Octave Baker establishes the general framework for action. Managers must develop new competencies and skills if they are to respond effectively to the multicultural workforce. Additional problems are created by a lack of role models and the slow upward mobility experienced by people of color in many organizational systems.

Chapter 18: The Clonal Effect in Organizations by Natasha Josefowitz tells us why implementing organizational strategies to increase diversity often fail. At some level, we tend to value those who are "like us" over those who are not. Only by consciously changing these preferences will managers be able to achieve the diversity they espouse. Organizational rules, policies, and procedures must support actions that are successful and must challenge the subtle stereotypes that prevent change.

Sophie Hahn and Anne H. Litwin's **Chapter 19: Women and Men** acknowledges changes both in the number of women in the workforce and in the responsibilities they have assumed. This chapter explores the implications of this new reality for both men and women as they confront gender-related style differences.

Chapter 20: Issues for Women Managers by Katharine Esty should be of interest to *all* managers. There are indeed special considerations and problems facing women as they move into managerial roles: a shortage of mentors, pressures to succeed, sexist language and attitudes, balancing work and family, the "glass ceiling," and sexual harassment. This chapter challenges women (and men) to break these cycles; concrete actions are also presented.

Chapter 21: Answers to the Mommy Track by Trudi Ferguson cites examples of how nationally known women have managed their careers and family responsibilities. Organizational policies and practices must be reviewed, and these case studies illustrate how to create a positive environment. Tips from successful corporate executives and mothers help make this material easy to understand and implement.

Chapter 22: Combating Sexual Harassment in the Workplace by Anne H. Litwin and Sophie Hahn clearly defines what managers can and must do to stop these insidious practices. Managers need to know how to react when the issue emerges and are responsible for creating an environment that prevents its reoccurrence. This chapter tells managers what the appropriate actions are and how to implement them for the benefit of all concerned.

Written by Toy-Ping Taira, **Chapter 23: Sensitizing Managers to Asian-American Diversity Issues** helps managers understand the special circumstances that confront workers of Asian heritage. With sensitivity to Asian-American traditions, cultures, and values, managers will be able to help this expanding part of the labor force grow professionally and make their full contribution to organizational success.

Lee Butler's **Chapter 24: African-American Women and Men in the Workplace** gives a historical perspective on the barriers facing these workers today. The unique problems faced by African-American employees must be understood before appropriate strategies for full participation can be developed. Managers need to confront attitudinal, structural, and procedural barriers in their organizations. Guidelines for action are presented to help managers and employees respond effectively.

Chapter 25: Hispanics in the Workplace by Cresencio Torres presents a historical overview of the different Hispanic populations in our domestic workforce today. The first step in responding to these distinct cultures lies in knowing that the distinctions exist; then managers can work effectively with their Hispanic counterparts. Workers of Mexican origin have different perspectives, values, and traditions than their colleagues with Puerto Rican, South American, or Cuban roots. The strategies presented will help organizations, Euro-American managers and Hispanics overcome many barriers to creating multicultural work environments.

Chapter 26: Diversity Skills in Action by Ilene Wasserman, Frederick Miller, and Martha Johnson provides an excellent summary of the various approaches needed for this developmental process. Managers and organizations can accept the challenge by acquiring new skills, information, and abilities. The multistep process defined in this chapter begins with establishing a business case study and takes the reader through the problems and myths encountered in multicultural mentoring.

Chapter 27: People with Disabilities by Jan Nisbet and Jo-Ann Sowers defines new strategies that will help managers respond to the challenges presented by the Americans with Disabilities Act. As we expand the concept of diversity to include people with disabilities, the workforce will change. The question remains: How? The answers lie in the work of management; suggestions lie in this chapter.

A word about language and cultural heritage: Other than Native Americans, the United States is a fabric woven out of a variety of cloths. We are, by land of origin, a polyglot society in its truest sense. Who we are by subgroup, and the label by which we prefer to be called, varies as we evolve both societally and as different subcultural entities.

This is one of the issues the editors were forced to address. Should all Americans who trace their ancestry to Spain be called Hispanic American? Perhaps not; on the West Coast, some who came to the United States by way of Mexico have different feelings.

So-called African Americans have a similar concern. For example, many who hail from the Caribbean would prefer the label Caribbean American. This too is made complex when yet others, whose origins are part African, prefer to be called Hispanic or even Mexican American. Similar issues abound with respect to people of Asian descent.

We do not pretend to have the answers. We do, however, acknowledge their fundamental importance. What we do offer is some sensitivity, along with a demonstrable lack of clarity as to which course to follow—one that would free us from this semantic despair, one with which no one would have a problem.

Alas, we fear there may be no such solution. We note this at the outset and ask the reader to forgive any unintended slights. We also accept full responsibility for any errors, omissions, and misstatements.

Books require thousands of hours of labor and the collective efforts of dozens of people. We hope this book will be of interest and assistance to you, the managers who are responsible for tomorrow's successes. We are grateful to the contributors for their willingness to remain committed to their ideas and ideals while demonstrating the necessary flexibility to meet deadlines, page limits, and format constraints.

Robin Mayers at the NTL Institute's central office provided administrative and emotional support. Paula Sarette at the University of New Hampshire fulfilled the seemingly endless tasks of manuscript organization, typing, editing, and proofreading. Cindy Zigmund and Mary Conzachi at Irwin Professional Publishing provided the needed power surge to help us clear the final obstacles. And, finally, we express our gratitude to the thousands of managers we have met in our professional lives. We remember the rewards, pressures, pleasures, challenges, and opportunities that you respond to daily.

Managers of tomorrow will have to blend current skills and intuition in a dynamic world. There is no one right way to proceed; our goal is to help you make informed choices.

Good luck and success in your practice!

Roger A. Ritvo
Anne H. Litwin
Lee Butler

Contents

MANAGING IN THE AGE OF CHANGE

MANAGING EFFECTIVELY

Chapter One

Why Managers Don't Manage

Arthur M. Freedman

Executive Summary

In his piece, Arthur Freedman observes that an individual's high performance in one position does not always predict successful performance in another. This is particularly true when the movement is of a high-performing individual from a technical-specialist role to a managerial role. Freedman is particularly concerned with helping us understand that the essential aspect of the transition is the adoption and personal mastery of skills having little or no resemblance to the requirements of the prior role. Therefore, there is minimal transference of pre-existing skills.

Several other writers in this volume are concerned with the development of team skills. Hence, from Freedman's discussion, the editors stress that training and development of the new manager in functioning as a member of a team is as important as personal mastery in managing and developing subordinates. Thus, transformation must take place along two dimensions: (1) from being a "star individual player" to guiding the work of others; and (2) becoming a member of a synergistic team in which individual technical mastery has less value and fewer cultural rewards than does learning to skillfully work with peers and subordinates.

Organizations will expend more and more energy attempting to achieve synergy throughout their structures. As these organizations undergo modification in response to environmental turbulence, so too must internal structures change. At the level of the individual participant, those most adept at collaborating effectively with others in the achievement of team outcomes will benefit. Managers will be rewarded for their ability to create and build effective work teams.

This chapter is important because it makes it abundantly clear that as organizations undergo transition, success will be determined by the extent to which new managers master a full range of new role requirements. Managers who are able to do this will be prized and highly valued. Freedman implores organizations to think this process through with the utmost care and develop it as an important priority.

M any chief executive officers (CEOs) complain that some of the individuals occupying their companies' critical middle and senior management positions do not perform to expectations. These CEOs are puzzled because they carefully selected people who demonstrated dedication, loyalty, and high performance in their previous positions. Yet, in new managerial roles, many were underachievers and some were counterproductive. CEOs may seek assistance from managerial and organizational consultants to correct such problems. They may feel let down, betrayed, and angry. They also may be prepared to fire, transfer, or demote those with whom they have become disenchanted. Such acts ''get rid of the evidence'' of their poor judgment. Only the rare CEO understands that weak managers are as much an organizational issue as they are personal or professional problems. These are the CEOs who are most likely to request assistance in planning and taking actions to prevent such ''person–position fit'' problems in the future.

Underachieving managers adversely affect the productivity, profitability, innovation, and morale of their organizational work units. The issue also has serious implications for any company's managerial succession and organizational continuity processes. Such managers are financially and emotionally expensive. Before any meaningful corrective or preventive action can be planned or implemented, the causes of poor managerial performance must be identified and understood. This requires a comprehensive organizational diagnosis.

Most CEOs and executives are oriented to quick action; they are impatient and are satisfied only when they see tangible results. These characteristics of executive temperament may be functional and appropriate for those who bear the burden of corporate responsibilities in rapidly changing local and global economies. Few

CEOs are sufficiently farsighted and systemically oriented to recognize the value of diagnostic efforts, despite the costs entailed in authorizing them, supporting them, and using their results. Most want to minimize the damage, remove the evidence, and move on to other pressing issues. Their past experiences with corrective organizational actions may generally be limited to such expedient solutions as (1) changing the organization's structure; (2) modifying existing procedures; (3) refining job descriptions; or (4) transferring, demoting, or terminating the "problem" employee.

These Band-Aid solutions focus on symptoms and are rarely effective. At most, they distract attention from the underlying root causes. Band-Aids will be even less effective in the future as changing demographics, new markets, new technologies, and the global economy create increasing demands on employers and employees.

WHAT WE KNOW

Organizational consultants encounter these problems and can often help CEOs save valuable time. Taking lessons learned elsewhere, consultants can test to ensure that they apply to any situation at a given company. The resulting data can then be used for planning and for taking both corrective and preventive actions.

Most organizations have neither designed nor installed functional, formal executive and managerial succession and development systems. Those systems that do exist are often superficial and do not go beyond the rudimentary step of having each manager identify the best available replacement if a vacancy should occur. Therefore, fully qualified internal candidates for open positions may not be readily available. It is as though the need for replacements comes as a surprise to line and staff leaders.

When a position opens, these companies usually choose between two alternative tactics for filling it. One option is to "pirate" a potentially qualified candidate from a similar position in another firm. This may send unintended or undesirable signals to employees who think of themselves as potential successors. Going outside the organization may be perceived as an implicit acknowledgment of the failure of the managerial succession system. This may also be construed as an implicit criticism of the organization's leaders and the quality of their stewardship of the organization's continuity.

The second option is to screen subordinates of the previous incumbent to find someone who seems acceptable, who knows the work of the unit, and who can get along with people. This may be someone who is considered to be capable of growing into the job. This "best available candidate" strategy is often considered the least objectionable alternative and is frequently employed by companies to reward loyal and dedicated employees.

Associated with these scenarios is a convenient belief to which many managers seem to subscribe: All a new manager needs is to have worked for the previous incumbent and/or performed well in a job that was subordinate but related to the open position. When this belief is a fundamental element of a company's culture, its validity is not questioned; the myth becomes an unchallenged truth. Limitations may include the probability that the best available candidate is an outstanding technical specialist or professional in one of several functional areas reporting to the open managerial position. Such individuals would have little understanding of the functions for which they would be responsible as a manager. The successor may not know the people in the other functional areas, the nature of their work, their preferences, or their requirements. The candidate is also unlikely to understand or appreciate the vital transactions conducted between the new organization and the suppliers and customers. Therefore, the successor may make biased, partially informed decisions without adequate input or participation. This is an example of inadequately preparing promotable employees for the next step in their careers. It comes from the failure to understand the differences between high-performing technical staff and high-performing managers. Under such circumstances, low-performing managers may be less at fault than they are victims who, generally out of ignorance, collude with the system.

THE HIGH-PERFORMING MANAGER

Typically, when employees demonstrate superior technical performance, they justifiably expect recognition or reward. Companies often satisfy these expectations through promotions. Employees typically expect to move into the ranks of management as their appropriate reward. However, they may not be adequately familiar with the managerial role and may be unprepared to perform their new responsibilities. As an ancient Chinese curse notes, "Be careful what you ask for. You may get it."

Somehow highly competent, promotable employees and newly promoted managers must learn, understand, accept, and adapt to their new role. They must acquire new knowledge. They must learn to recognize which gears to shift and understand when to shift them in order to become effective managers. This type of learning is not entirely the responsibility of uninformed employees. Organizations should play a major role in mapping the unknown territory of management for their aspiring, upwardly mobile employees.

If an organization wishes to reward or recognize extremely effective individuals, it need not promote them into line managerial positions for which they are neither prepared nor equipped. There are alternatives, such as pay for skills or pay for knowledge. Another alternative is the "dual career hierarchy" through which a person may be promoted to higher levels of professional or technical responsibility, without taking on line managerial responsibilities.

If the organization chooses to promote technical specialists and professionals into managerial roles as a reward for their individual contributions, it must provide them with active assistance in understanding and coping with this major career transition.

Business Factors: Sources of Organizational Pain

Low-performing managers and underlying corporate cultural beliefs tend to be ignored or avoided during favorable economic, market, and regulatory conditions. When there is little fiscal or sociopolitical pressure, leaders appear to tolerate managerial ineptitude and ineffectiveness—especially by long-time, homegrown, loyal employees. They seem to accept underachievement as an unavoidable cost of doing business. Few leaders seem willing to rock the boat. Few challenge their companies' underlying beliefs and myths. After all, as the saying goes, "Don't fix it if it ain't broke."

Reciprocal Demands and Expectations

Effective managers anticipate and effectively respond to many simultaneous demands. They are expected to perform diverse tasks, activities, and functions—all at the same time. Managers are accountable to numerous individuals and groups—their stakeholders—both inside and outside the organization. Some accountabilities are formal and explicit; others are informal, not part of the performance evaluation. No person or work unit exists in isolation. Although it may not be recognized, all parts of the organization are interdependent; that is, each person and each work unit depends upon others for its success. If the entities do not receive what they need in a timely manner from their internal and external suppliers, they cannot adequately perform their work. If they do not satisfy the requirements and preferences of their internal and external customers, they prevent those customers from becoming successful. Therefore, everyone has a stake in everyone else's business.

This systemic view of organizational dynamics overrides another cherished organizational belief: To do the management job properly, one need only be competent in the technical functions for which one is responsible and to communicate primarily up (to one's boss) and down (to one's direct subordinates), as required.

THE MANAGER'S RESPONSIBILITIES: CHOICES AND CONSEQUENCES

It is unrealistic to expect managers to fully satisfy all of their stakeholders' demands all of the time. Yet to disregard any of them could result in professional suicide, corporate disaster, or both. Managers may neglect some responsibilities that their stakeholders may consider critical. When their preferences and legitimate requirements are not satisfied, disappointed stakeholders usually create negative consequences. Regardless of the individual managers' formal job descriptions, it is incumbent upon them to create and define their own roles. Managers invariably decide which stakeholders to satisfy and which they will risk disappointing—usually without thinking about possible adverse consequences.

The result is as tangible as it is paradoxical. Every manager is expected, by some stakeholder or another, to perform at least some of a long list of responsibilities.

As a self-assessment exercise, consider the following: Which responsibilities would you specify for yourself? Which stakeholders would be satisfied and, consequently, would support you? Which stakeholders would be disappointed and, consequently, would withhold their support from you? The following is a composite list of responsibilities that many new managers in a variety of industries have cited over the past several years. These have proved to be critical to their success.

1. Assess and define the requirements and preferences of your internal or external customers.
2. Actively seek feedback from your customers about their needs and preferences as well as their degrees of satisfaction with the quality, delivery time, and attentiveness associated with your products and services.
3. Define your work unit's preferences and requirements (people, money, raw materials, information, regulations, and equipment) and communicate them to your internal and external suppliers.
4. Establish goals for your unit and provide direction.
5. Convey senior management's philosophy, perspectives, concerns, and priorities to your subordinates.
6. Convey the perspectives and concerns of your subordinates to senior management.
7. Plan workflow, processes, and procedures.
8. Within your work unit, specify the nature, frequency, and quality of relationships and transactions.
9. Screen, select, place, and train new staff.
10. Allocate and deploy staff.
11. Ensure that your staff develops appropriate performance objectives and work standards.
12. Develop your team.
13. Ensure that the unit's work culture (i.e., its philosophy or values, norms, and practices) is compatible with corporate culture.

14. Provide reinforcing feedback and corrective counseling to enhance the performance of your subordinates.
15. Redesign (enlarge or reduce) jobs to meet changing needs.
16. Incorporate new technologies and innovations into unit operations.
17. Perform required administrative functions such as budgets, periodic reports, and records.
18. Constantly seek ways to encourage your team to reduce or contain costs.

Addictive Managerial Habit Patterns

Poor managers adapt slowly or inappropriately to changing conditions. They may repeat ineffective and counterproductive behaviors. They frequently build up internal tension and pressure. Frustrated managers often (1) display increased irritability and impatience with themselves and others; (2) reach premature, inaccurate conclusions; (3) make snap decisions; (4) are unwilling to accept corrective feedback or to admit errors; (5) misunderstand what others say; and (6) attribute malicious intent to others when things do not work out as planned.

When we confront managers who are behaving in this fashion, we often hear them make quite remarkable rationalizations to justify their own inflexibility and failure to adapt to new or changing job conditions. Popular rationalizations include:

"I have to act this way. I have no choice. My people wouldn't respect me if I acted differently."

"It's not me; it's my people. They're lazy and untrustworthy. They know the schedules. They should know what to do and how to do it. But I don't get results unless I beat them up. Even then I wind up doing most of their work for them."

"They don't mind. They're used to this style. That's the way things are done in this business."

When we look at what's behind these justifications, we get a different message: These managers are anxious and often unaware of alternative approaches. They usually do not consider the options that they do know about because they may not be able to use them proficiently. They convince themselves that their fears reflect realistic, unchangeable constraints. Are these rationalizations a function of the manager's inadequacies and deficiencies? Or do they result from the organization's failure to adequately prepare managers to tolerate ambiguity, take risks, learn from mistakes, cope with confusion, and learn to adapt to constantly changing conditions? Or are both theories correct?

Anxiety and aggressive managerial styles complicate these issues. A new manager's fears often start with the paradoxical methods by which companies reward technical staff for high performance. The technical role could be that of a research chemist, quality control test specialist, physician, nurse, therapist, design or field engineer, nuclear physicist, auditor, tax accountant, news analyst or broadcaster, systems analyst, computer programmer, mechanic, or salesperson. Specifically, companies tend to reward employees for observable contributions toward achieving short-term, bottom-line results—the so-called 90-day perspective. Employees tend to do tasks that are rewarded and to neglect those responsibilities that are not. And they avoid whatever they think may be punished.

LESSONS CONFIRMED

It is clear that high performance in one position is not an adequate predictor of high performance in another. Experience confirms that preparation, training, developmental assignments, on-site consultation, and coaching are essential. New managers need training or developmental experiences to acquire the following concepts, techniques, and skills:

- Risk taking and assertiveness
- Counseling underperforming subordinates
- Designing professional development experiences for subordinates
- Learning leadership functions, philosophies, and styles
- Identification and specification of operational problems

- Managing conflict constructively
- Managing resistance to planned organizational change
- Role negotiation
- Controlling one's own anxieties and self-doubt
- Increasing tolerance for ambiguity and uncertainty
- Curbing one's impatience
- Creating motivating work environments
- Exerting positive political influence with peers and other stakeholders
- Time management
- Task delegation
- Building high-performing, self-directed teams
- Scanning the internal organization and external market for early indicators of changing conditions

An ideal process for new or prospective managers to acquire these required competencies includes:

1. Understanding the existing competencies and developmental needs of candidates for promotion
2. Reviewing and discussing opportunities with these candidates
3. Working on professional development plans with the candidates' immediate superiors
4. Matching human resource development opportunities with candidates' needs
5. Developing appropriate training and project assignments
6. Identifying external seminars, courses, workshops, and educational opportunities that meet the candidates' developmental needs
7. Incorporating project assignments in a proposed career development plan for each candidate
8. Creating a realistic provisional schedule for implementing the proposed career development plan
9. Submitting the proposed career development plan and provisional schedule to each candidate's current (and potentially future) immediate superior for review, approval, or modification

10. Assuring that future superiors allow the candidate appropriate opportunities to use these newly acquired competencies
11. Allowing for a comprehensive review and revision of this plan *when* conditions change (and they will!)

Arthur M. Freedman

Arthur M. Freedman, PhD, has been an organizational development (OD) consultant and human resource development specialist and trainer since 1961. Among his current clients are the Russian Ministry of Atomic Energy and Industry (planning for privatization; retraining psychologists as OD consultants), the Higher Humanitarian College of the Russian Ministry of Defense (repatriation and demobilization; management of ethnic diversity within the armed forces), EC Scandinavia (training OD consultants), R. R. Donnelley & Sons (transformational organizational change), the Illinois Education Association (collaborative labor–management efforts to improve public education), and APV Crepaco (strategic planning; integrating total quality management with high-performance teamwork; designing and installing a gain-sharing system). He received his BS (1960) and MBA (1963) degrees from Boston University and his PhD (1971) from the psychology department at the University of Chicago. He is a member of the American Psychological Association, NTL Institute, Society of Psychologists in Management, World Future Society, and OD Network. He is a Registered Psychologist in Illinois.

Chapter Two

Situational Leadership II

Kenneth H. Blanchard

Executive Summary

Beginning with Douglas McGregor's publication of the famous *Human Side of Enterprise* at the beginning of the 1950s, management literature has been replete with various theories of management styles. Among them were Tannenbaum and Schmidt's "How to Choose a Leadership Pattern," published in the *Harvard Business Review* in 1957, and *The Managerial Grid* (1964), written by Robert Blake and Jane S. Mouton.

As Kenneth Blanchard observes, all of the discussions of management style prior to his introduction of situational leadership assumed the existence of one best leadership style, one that was democratic and allowed subordinate freedom and participation in decision-making processes. Hence, in McGregor's work there is a definitive bias in favor of Theory Y; in Tannenbaum and Schmidt there is a bias toward "Join"; and in the Blake and Mouton grid there is an arguable bias toward the "balanced" leadership style.

The most lively debate has occurred between the proponents of the Blake–Mouton managerial grid school and the Blanchard school. Sometimes approaching an acerbic tone, this chapter, an update of one prepared by Blanchard for *The NTL Managers' Handbook* (NTL Institute), places great stress on the appropriateness of a given leadership style to the specific situation with which the leader is confronted. The essential element in the situation is the level of skill and confidence possessed by the subordinate. From this standpoint, there is no such thing as one best management style.

Though this model has been an important part of the management style lexicon for close to 25 years, its relevance has not diminished. Indeed, as environmental complexity has increased and words like *chaos* and *white water* have entered the language to describe it, the relevance of situationally-based leadership has increased. Managers

in the decades to come will benefit greatly from a thorough understanding of the ideas presented in this chapter, augmented by consum-
mate skill in their application.

T he acceptance of the Situational Leadership model as a practical, easy-to-understand approach to managing and motivating people has been widespread over the last decade and a half.
Paul Hersey and I first described Situational Leadership as the
"life-cycle theory of leadership" in 1969.[1] Until now, the most
extensive presentation of the concept has been our text, *Management of Organizational Behavior: Utilizing Human Resources*, now in
its fourth edition.[2]

For those of you familiar with Situational Leadership, you'll see
as you read this article that I've made a number of changes to the
original model. These changes reflect conversations with my colleagues at Blanchard Training and Development, Inc.—particularly
my wife, colleague, and friend, Margie Blanchard; Don Carew;
Eunice Parisi-Carew; Fred Finch; Laurie Hawkins; Drea Zigarmi; and
Pat Zigarmi[3]—my own experiences, and the ideas managers all over
the world have shared with me. This article and the book *Leadership
and the One Minute Manager*, coauthored with Pat Zigarmi and Drea
Zigarmi, mark for all of us at Blanchard Training and Development,
Inc., a new generation of Situational Leadership thinking, which is
why we now call the model Situational Leadership II.[4]

LEADERSHIP AND LEADERSHIP STYLE

Any time you try to influence the behavior of another person, you
are engaging in an act of leadership. Therefore, *leadership* is an
influence process. If you are interested in developing your staff
and building motivational climates that result in high levels of
productivity, as well as human satisfaction in the short *and* long
run, then you need to think about your leadership style. *Leadership
style* is the pattern of behaviors you use when you are trying to
influence the behavior of others, as perceived by them. While your
perceptions of your own behavior and its impact on others is interesting and important, it tells you only how you *intend* to act. Unless

it matches the perceptions of those you are trying to influence, it is not very helpful. For example, if you think you are an empathetic, people-oriented manager, but your people think you are a hard-nosed, task-oriented person, whose perception of reality will they act on—yours or their own? Obviously, their own.

For years, when people talked about leadership style, they identified two extremes—an autocratic (directive) leadership style and a democratic (supportive) leadership style. *Autocratic* leaders used position power and authority to get results, while *democratic* leaders used personal power and involved others in participative problem-solving and decision-making processes. Tannenbaum and Schmidt, in their classic *Harvard Business Review* article, "How to Choose a Leadership Pattern," argued that these two leadership styles—autocratic and democratic—were "either/or" styles of leadership.[5] They described a continuum with very authoritarian leader behavior at one end and very democratic leader behavior at the other end.

SITUATIONAL LEADERSHIP II

Further research, however, showed that leadership styles tend to vary considerably from situation to situation, and that it is not helpful to think of leadership style as an either/or continuum.[6] While the behavior of some leaders is characterized mainly as directing their followers' activities in terms of task accomplishment (directive behavior), other leaders concentrate on providing socio-emotional support and on building personal relationships between themselves and their followers (supportive behavior). In other situations, various combinations of directive and supportive behavior are evident. Thus, it was determined that directive and supportive leader behaviors are not either/or leadership styles. Instead, these patterns of leader behavior can be plotted on two separate and distinct axes, as shown in Figure 2–1.

Each of the four leadership styles depicted in Figure 2–1 represents a different combination of directive and supportive leadership behaviors.[7] These combinations differ on three dimensions: (1) the amount of direction the leader provides; (2) the amount

FIGURE 2–1
The Four Basic Leadership Styles

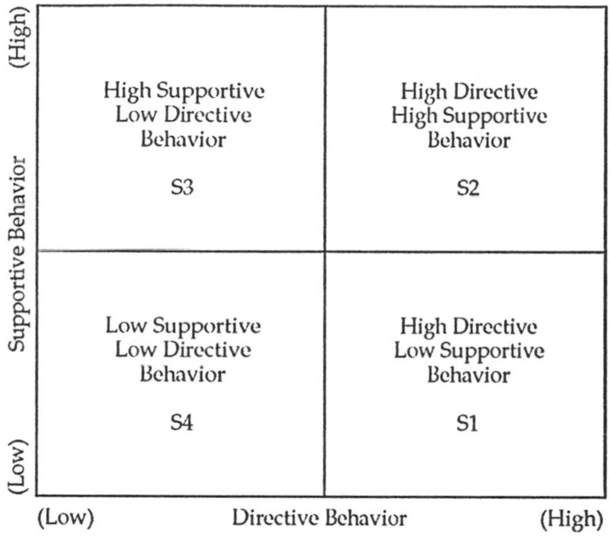

of support and encouragement the leader provides; and (3) the amount of follower involvement in decision making.

Directive and Supportive Leader Behaviors

Directive behavior is defined as:

> The extent to which a leader engages in one-way communication; spells out the followers' roles, and tells the followers what to do, where to do it, when to do it, and how to do it; and then closely supervises performance. Three words can be used to define directive behavior: structure, control, and supervise.

Supportive behavior is defined as:

> The extent to which a leader engages in two-way communication; listens, provides support and encouragement, facilitates interaction, and involves the followers in decision making. Three words can be used to define supportive behavior: praise, listen, and facilitate.

In style 1 (see S1 in Figure 2–1), a leader is high on direction, low on support. He or she defines roles and goals, provides specific instruction to the followers, and closely supervises task accomplishment. When using style 2, the leader is high on both direction and support. He or she explains decisions and solicits suggestions from the followers but continues to direct task accomplishment. Style 3 leader behavior is characterized by high supportive and low directive behavior. The leader and followers make decisions together and then the leader supports the followers' efforts toward task accomplishment. In style 4, a leader provides low support and direction. He or she turns over decisions and responsibility for implementation to the followers.

Leadership Behavior as Problem-Solving and Decision-Making Styles

As defined earlier, leadership style is the pattern of behaviors you use when you are trying to influence the behaviors of others, *as perceived by them*. Since the basic behaviors that subordinates respond to in assessing your leadership style are related to the types of problem-solving and decision-making processes that you use with them, each of the four leadership styles can be identified with a different approach to problem solving and decision making, as illustrated in Figure 2–2.[8]

High directive/low supportive leader behavior (S1) is referred to as *directing*. The leader defines the roles of followers and tells them what tasks to do and how, when, and where to do them. Problem solving and decision making are initiated solely by the manager. Solutions and decisions are announced; communication is largely one-way, and implementation is closely supervised by the leader.

High directive/high supportive behavior (S2) is referred to as *coaching*. In this style the leader still provides a great deal of direction and leads with his or her ideas, but the leader also attempts to hear the followers' feelings about decisions as well as their ideas and suggestions. While two-way communication and support are increased, control over decision making remains with the leader.

High supportive/low directive leader behavior (S3) is called sup-

FIGURE 2–2
The Four Basic Leadership Styles as Types of Problem-solving and Decision-making Processes

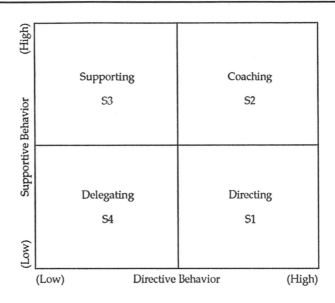

porting. In style 3 the focus of control for day-to-day decision making and problem solving shifts from leader to followers. The leader's role is to provide recognition and to actively listen and facilitate problem solving and decision making on the part of the followers. This is appropriate since the followers have the ability and knowledge to do the task whenever the use of style 3 is warranted.

Low supportive/low directive leader behavior (S4) is labeled *delegating.* In style 4 the leader discusses the problems with subordinates until joint agreement is achieved on problem definition, and then the decision making process is delegated totally to the followers. Now it is the subordinates who have significant control for deciding *how* tasks are to be accomplished. Followers are allowed to "run their own show" because they have both the competence and the confidence to take responsibility for directing their own behavior.

No "One Best" Leadership Style

Once it was generally agreed that there were four basic leadership styles characterized by varying degrees of directive and supportive behavior, some writers argued that there was "one best" style—one that maximized productivity and satisfaction, growth, and development in all situations.[9] However, research in the last several decades has clearly supported the contention that there is no best leadership style; instead, *successful leaders are able to adapt their style to fit the requirements of the situation.*[10]

While the need for a situational approach to leadership might make sense, it is not very helpful to practicing managers, who have to make leadership decisions every day. If "it all depends on the situation," they want to know *when* to use *which style.*

A number of situational variables influence which leadership style will be appropriate in which situations. These variables include time lines, job and task demands, organizational climate, and superiors', associates/peers', and subordinates' skills and expectations. While all these factors and undoubtedly others impact the effectiveness of a particular style, if practicing managers had to examine all the situational variables suggested by theorists before deciding which style to use, they would become immobilized. That is why Hersey and Blanchard based their Situational Leadership approach on the key factor that they found to have the greatest impact on the choice of leadership style—the followers. In particular, it was found that the amount of direction or support that a leader should provide depends on the *development level* that the followers exhibit on a specific task, function, or objective that the leader is attempting to accomplish.[11]

Development Level

In Situational Leadership II, *development level* is defined as the competence and commitment of your followers to perform a particular task without supervision.[12] We use the word *competence* rather than *ability* because people often equate "ability" with "potential." They talk about natural ability to describe the skills a person is born with. Competence, on the other hand, can be developed with appropriate direction and support. It is a function of knowledge or skills that can be gained from education, training, and/or experience. It is not something you either have or don't have.

Commitment is a combination of confidence and motivation. Confidence is a measure of a person's self-assuredness—a feeling of being able to do a task well without much supervision, whereas motivation gauges a person's interest and enthusiasm in doing a task.

Situational Leadership II identifies four development levels: low (D1), low to moderate (D2), moderate to high (D3), and high (D4). Each of these development levels represents a different combination of competence and commitment as illustrated below:

High Competence • High Commitment	High Competence • Variable Commitment	Some Competence • Low Commitment	Low Competence • High Commitment
D4	D3	D2	D1

Developed ◄-- Developing

According to Situational Leadership, as the development level of individuals increases from D1 to D4, their competence and commitment fluctuates. When first beginning a new task in which they have little if any prior knowledge or experience, most individuals are enthusiastic and ready to learn (D1). Then when they begin to get into the task, individuals often find it is either more difficult to learn or less interesting than they thought it was going to be. This disillusionment decreases their commitment (D2).[13] If they overcome this state and learn to perform the task with help from their boss, most individuals then go through a self-doubt stage which they question whether they can perform the task well *on their own*. Their boss says they're competent but they're not so sure. These alternating feelings of competence and self-doubt cause the variable commitment associated with D3—commitment that fluctuates from excitement to insecurity. With proper support, individuals can eventually become peak performers who demonstrate a high level of competence, motivation, and confidence. In other words, given the appropriate amounts of direction and support, individuals move from one level of development to another, from being an *enthusiastic beginner* to a *disillusioned learner* to a *reluctant contributor* to a *peak performer.*

It is important when thinking about someone's development level to remember that people are not "fully developed" or "underdeveloped." In other words, *development level is not a global concept; it is a task-specific concept.* That is, people tend to be at different levels of development depending on the specific task, function, or objective that they are assigned.

For example, let's say that an engineer might be highly developed (competent and committed) to handle the technical aspects of a job, but has not demonstrated the same degree of development when it comes to working with the budget. As a result, it may be quite appropriate for the engineer's manager to provide little direction or support (S4, delegating) on a technical problem, but a great deal of direction or close supervision (S1, directing or S2, coaching) over the engineer's budget making. Thus, Situational Leadership focuses on the appropriateness or effectiveness of leadership styles according to the task-relevant development level of the followers. This relationship is illustrated in Figure 2–3.

Matching Leadership Style to Development Level

To determine the appropriate leadership style to use with each of the four development levels, draw a vertical line up from a diagnosed development level to the leadership style curve running through the four-quadrant model in Figure 2–3. The appropriate leadership style is the quadrant where the vertical line intersects the curved line. As a result, development level D1 would get a *directing* S1 leadership style. Development level D2 would get a high directive and supportive *coaching* S2 leadership style.

In determining style to use with development level, just remember that *leaders need to provide their people with what they lack at the moment.* Since a D1 has commitment but lacks competence, the leaders need to provide direction (S1 directing); since a D2 lacks both competence and commitment, leaders need to provide both

FIGURE 2–3
Situational Leadership

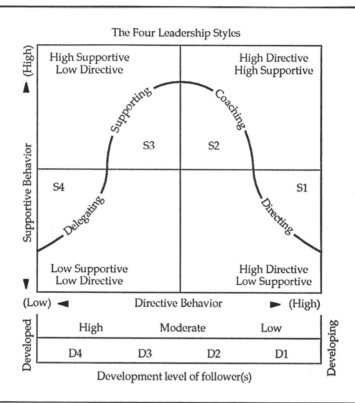

The Four Leadership Styles

Development level of follower(s)

direction and support (S2, coaching); since a D3 has competence but variable commitment, leaders have to provide support (S3, supporting); and since D4 has both competence and commitment, leaders do not need to provide either direction or support (S4, delegating).

Directing is for the low development level. People who are high on commitment but low on competence (D1) are enthusiastic beginners. They are excited to get started and learn. Thus, a directing style (S1) that provides clear, specific direction and close supervision has the highest probability of being effective. Since commitment is high, support is not needed from the leader.

Again, this style is called *directing* because it's characterized by the leader defining roles and telling people what, how, when, and where to do various tasks.

Coaching is for a low to moderate development level. People who have some competence but lack commitment (D2), need both direction and support. Thus, a coaching style (S2), that provides directive behavior (because of their lack of competence) but also supportive behavior to build confidence and enthusiasm is most appropriate with individuals at this development level. This style is called *coaching* because most people know that coaches both direct and support their people. This style, which encourages two-way communication, helps build confidence and motivation on the part of the follower, while keeping responsibility for and control over decision making with the leader.

Supporting is for a moderate to high development level. People of this development level are competent but have variable commitment (D3) toward the assigned task. This is often a function of a lack of confidence. However, if they are confident but uncommitted, their reluctance to perform is more of a motivational problem than a confidence problem. In either case, the leader needs to open up communications through two-way communication and active listening and to support the followers' efforts to use the skills they already have. Thus, a supporting style (S3) has the highest probability of being effective with individuals at this development level. This style is called *supporting*, because the leader and follower share in decision making, with the key roles of the leader being listening and facilitating.

Delegating is for persons at a high development level on a particular task. People at this development level are both competent and motivated (D4) to take responsibility. Thus, a low-profile delegating style (S4) that provides little direction and support has the highest probability of being effective with individuals at this development level. Even though the leader may still identify the problem, the responsibility for carrying out plans is given to these experienced followers. They are permitted to "run the show" and decide on how, when, and where the task is to be accomplished. Since they are psychologically mature, they do not need above-average amounts of two-way communication or supportive behavior.

INCREASING PERFORMANCE POTENTIAL

Situational Leadership, as described to this point, is helpful for a practicing manager trying to determine which leadership style to use with followers in a particular situation and on a particular task. Yet suppose you are using a directive style (S1) with an inexperienced person, with good results—the job is getting done—but style 1 is too time consuming to use all the time. Therefore, your goal should be to help your followers increase their competence and commitment to independently accomplish the tasks assigned to them, so that gradually you can begin to use less time-consuming styles (S3 and S4) and still get high-quality results.

As managers, we have two choices with the people who work for us. First, we can hire a "winner"—that is, a person who has the competence and confidence to perform at a desired level with little supervision (D4). Winners are easy to supervise; all they need to know is what the goals, objectives, and time lines are, and then they can be left on their own to do the job.

Since winners are hard to find and cost money, most managers are left with the second alternative—hire "potential winners" and then train them to be winners. In fact, unless managers realize and accept the training function in their jobs, they will be continually frustrated and confused about why their subordinates are not performing well. This frustration often forces managers into the most widely used leadership style, which we refer to as "leave alone—zap." They hire someone to assume certain responsibilities, tell that person what to do (S1), and then "leave them alone" (an ineffective S4) and assume good performance will follow. Unless the person delegated to is a peak performer (D4), that assumption would prove false. When unacceptable performance occurs, or the person does something wrong or does not live up to the manager's expectations, the frustrated manager moves quickly to a punitive S1 style and demands to know why things are not getting done—

the "zap." This change in leadership styles can leave managers frustrated and followers confused and often angry.

To avoid the ill effects of the leave alone—zap leadership style and to ensure productive and satisfied employees, managers need to learn how to increase the performance capacities of their subordinates. There are five steps to training high performers:

1. *Tell them what you want them to do.* You can't manage unless your followers understand what they are being asked to do—what their responsibilities or areas of accountability are.

2. *Show them what you want them to do.* Once people know what their responsibilities are, they need to know what good performance looks like. What are their performance standards? *Show* and *tell* are both directive behaviors. Thus, training a potential winner (D1 and D2) usually starts with a directing (S1) leadership style. Since the employees do not know how to perform the desired task without direction and supervision, decision making and problem solving are controlled by the leader.

3. *Let them try.* Once people know what to do and know the expected level of performance, the manager must take a risk and let them try to perform on their own. When you do that, you are essentially cutting back on directive behavior, since you are turning over responsibility for doing the task to the follower. The risk here is that the follower might fail, so you don't want to turn over too much responsibility too soon. Make the risk reasonable. Let the person cut his or her teeth on something.

4. *Observe performance.* When you let a follower try to do something, do not go to an "abdicating" style (S4) by leaving them alone. That sets up the leave alone—zap leadership style. Since we know that that style is not helpful in terms of productivity or satisfaction, try to avoid it. Therefore, after you let them try to do what you want them to do, stick around and observe performance. A basic component of a directing (S1) style is close supervision—which means frequently monitoring performance.

5. *Manage the consequences.* The main reason for closely supervising or monitoring performance is to manage the conse-

quences. A *consequence* is anything that follows behavior. There are three basic types of consequences:

a. A *positive* consequence, or reinforcer. Anything that follows performance that tends to increase the probability of that behavior occurring again, e.g., a praising or promotion.

b. A *negative* consequence, or punisher. Anything that follows performance that tends to decrease the probability of that behavior occurring again, e.g., a reprimand or demotion.

c. A *neutral* consequence, or no response. Unless a person is doing something that is intrinsically valuable (they would do it regardless of feedback from others), no response to good performance will gradually decrease the frequency of the good behavior.

As you can see, the only consequence that tends to increase the probability of a behavior occurring again is a positive consequence. Thus, we feel that *the key to developing people is to "catch them doing something right."*[14] Most managers seem to be best at catching their people doing something wrong. You also need to remember that in the beginning, with people you are training to be winners, you should try to catch them doing something *approximately right, not exactly right.* Exactly right is made up of a whole series of approximately right behaviors, as the little steps in Figure 2–4 indicate.

As Figure 2–4 suggests, when you let a person try to do something after the "show and tell" stage, you are cutting back on directive behavior. And then, when you observe that person doing something right (or, in the beginning, approximately right), you should recognize the accomplishment by praising progress and increasing your supportive behavior. The little steps moving up the bell-shaped curve suggest that this gradual reduction in directive behavior and increase in supportive behavior should continue until the individual or group reaches a moderate level of development (D2). If this steplike process is done well, a leader can help an individual pass through the *disillusioned learner* stage without much difficulty. As the person begins to move to higher levels of development (D3 and D4), it becomes appropriate for you to decrease not only directive behavior but supportive behavior as well. Now the

FIGURE 2–4
Increasing Performance Potential

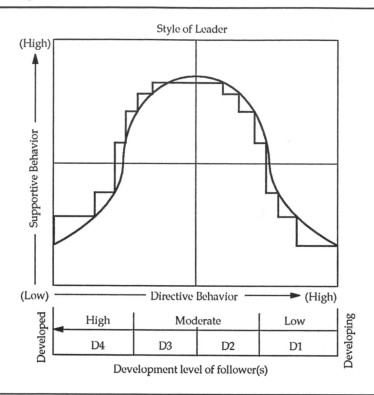

Development level of follower(s)

person not only is developed in terms of competence but is also able to provide his or her own reinforcement. This does not mean that the individual's work will have less direction but that the direction will now be internally imposed by the person rather than externally imposed by the manager. At this stage, individuals are positively reinforced for their own accomplishments when they are given increased responsibility and left more and more on their own. It is not that there is less mutual trust and respect (in fact, there is more), but it takes less and less effort on the manager's part to prove it with a fully developed person.[15]

More than praisings and other supportive behaviors, involvement in problem solving and decision making communicates to employees that you see them as confident, capable, responsible, trustworthy, and reliable individuals. These are messages that people like to hear; this type of positive feedback builds confidence and motivation.

On the other hand, if you continue to direct and closely supervise people for long periods of time, you are sending your subordinates a different message. You probably don't see them as confident, capable, responsible, trustworthy, or reliable. These underlying messages, in turn, affect performance. Thus, the developmental aspect of Situational Leadership and the need to gradually shift from external direction, control, and support to internal control is crucial for developing and increasing the performance capabilities of people.

In developing high performers, the factor that triggers a change in leadership style is *performance.* Improvements in performance motivate forward shifts in leadership style along the bell-shaped curve from directing to delegating (S1 to S2, S2 to S3, and S3 to S4). In thinking about the importance of performance, you must remember one thing: High levels of performance can be obtained when any of the four leadership styles are used appropriately. That is, an inexperienced person can perform at as high a level as an experienced person if directed and closely supervised by a manager. The question is, at what cost? The cost is time and energy for the manager—both important management resources. Therefore, we feel that the highest performance level is achieved when followers can perform at a desired level with little or no supervision.

STOPPING REGRESSION

Just as improvements in performance motivate forward shifts in style along the curve, decreases in performance require a shift backward in leadership style along the bell-shaped curve, from delegating to directing (S4 to S3, S3 to S2, and S2 to S1). In other words, whenever a follower begins to perform at a lower level, for whatever reason (e.g., crisis at home, change in work, or new technology), it becomes appropriate and necessary for a manager to adjust his or her behavior to respond to the current development level of the person. For example, take a subordinate who is presently working well on his or her own. Suppose that suddenly a family crisis begins to affect this person's performance on the job. In this situation, it might be very appropriate for the manager to moderately increase both support and even direction until the subordinate regains his or her composure.

Take another example of a person in an individual contributor position who is highly motivated and competent (D4) and therefore can be left on his or her own. Suppose this person is promoted to a supervisory position. While it may have been appropriate to leave the person alone (S4) as an individual contributor, now that he/she is a supervisor, a task for which he/she has little experience, it is certainly appropriate for the manager to change styles by initially providing more support and then increasing the amount of direction and supervision provided (S4 to S3 to S2). This high-directive, high-supportive style should continue until the person is able to grasp all of his/her new responsibilities. At that time, movement from style 2 to style 3 and eventually to style 4 would be appropriate if performance continues to improve. Using the same leadership style that was successful with this person as an individual contributor may prove devastating now because it is inappropriate for the situation.

SUMMARY

In summary, effective managers know their staff members well enough to flexibly manage everchanging demands on their organizations. As responsibilities and tasks are assigned to individuals or groups, the developmental level must be assessed. The manager should then vary his/her leadership style in response to the individual's need for external direction and/or support. It should be remembered that over time, subordinates and subordinate groups develop their own patterns of behavior and ways of operating; that is, their own norms, customs, traditions, and mores. While a manager may use a specific style for the work group as a group, that manager may quite often have to behave differently with individual subordinates because each is at a different level of development. Whether working with a group or an individual, changes in management style forward from S1 to S2, S3, and S4, and backward from S4 to S3, S2 and S1, must be gradual. It is this shifting forward and backward in style that makes Situational Leadership a truly developmental model for both managers and subordinates.

ENDNOTES

1. Paul Hersey and Kenneth H Blanchard, "Life Cycle Theory of Leadership," *Training and Development Journal* (May 1969).
2. Hersey and Blanchard, *Management of Organizational Behavior: Utilizing Human Resources*, 4th ed. (Englewood Cliffs, NJ: Prentice-Hall, Inc., 1982).
3. Additional Blanchard Training and Development (BTD) associates and colleagues who have been involved with me from time to time in helpful theoretical discussions are Irene Carew, Sylvia Carter, Calla Crafts, John Ferris, Ken Huff, Ralph Jenkins, Bob Lorber, and Kelsey Tyson.
4. Ken Blanchard, Patricia Zigarmi, and Drea Zigarmi, *Leadership and the One Minute Manager* (New York: William Morrow and Co., 1985).
5. Robert Tannenbaum and Warren H Schmidt, "How to Choose a Leadership Pattern," *Harvard Business Review* (March–April 1957).
6. Roger M Stogdill and Alvin E Coons, eds., *Leader Behavior: Its Description and Measurement*, Bureau of Business Research Monograph no. 83 (Columbus, OH: Ohio State University, 1957).
7. In *Management of Organizational Behavior*, Paul Hersey and I used the terms *task behavior* and *relationship behavior* to describe the two basic leadership style dimensions. We at BTD now use the terms *directive behavior* and *supportive behavior* because we have found them more descriptive and easier for practitioners to identify with.
8. The four leadership styles described in *Management of Organizational Behavior* were called *telling* (S1), *selling* (S2), *participating* (S3), and *delegating* (S4). The first three names were changed to *directing* (S1), *coaching* (S2), and *supporting* (S3) at the urging of Ted Thelander and other practitioners. They felt that the new names better described the styles and eliminated the need to learn a second set of labels for the styles once they understood what was meant by "directive" and "supportive" behavior.
9. Examples often cited of the "one best" theory are Robert R Blake and Jane S Mouton, *The Managerial Grid* (Houston, TX: Gulf Publishing, 1964) and Douglas McGregor, *The Human Side of Enterprise* (New York: McGraw-Hill Book Co., 1960).

10. Examples of the "no one best" approach are Fred E Fielder, *A Theory of Leadership Effectiveness* (New York: McGraw-Hill Book Co., 1967); A K Korman, " 'Consideration,' 'Initiating Structure,' and Organizational Criteria—a Review," *Personnel Psychology: A Journal of Applied Research* XIX (Winter 1966); and William J Reddin, *Managerial Effectiveness* (New York: McGraw-Hill Book Co., 1970).

11. The term *development level* is now being used instead of *maturity level*, for two reasons. First, the word *maturity* has negative connotations for most people. Second, it was felt that Situational Leadership's real contribution is as a dynamic developmental model that helps managers understand not only how to manage people effectively today but how to "grow them up" so they can eventually manage themselves. Paul Hersey is not using the term *readiness level* in his work with the Situational Leadership model.

12. The names of these two factors used in *Management of Organizational Behavior* have since been changed. "Ability" was changed to "competence" to avoid confusion with an unlearned "natural ability," and "willingness" was changed to "commitment" to suggest a concept broader than motivation.

13. The commitment aspect of both D1 and D2 has been changed significantly from the original M1 and M2 in *Management of Organizational Behavior*. M1 was considered "unable and unwilling," while M2 was thought of as "unable but willing." We now consider a D1 to have high commitment and a D2 to have low commitment. This change was urged by Don Carew and Eunice Parisi-Carew, based on research on stages of group development done by R B Lacoursiere in *The Life Cycle of Groups: Group Development Stage Theory* (New York: Human Services Press, 1980). See Don Carew, Eunice Parisi-Carew, and Ken Blanchard, *Group Development and Situational Leadership: A Model for Managing Groups* (San Diego, CA: Blanchard Training and Development, Inc., 1984).

14. "Catching people doing things right" is a major theme of Spencer Johnson and my best-selling book, *The One Minute Manager* (New York: William Morrow and Co., 1982).

15. The gradual developmental process of (1) providing direction, (2) reducing the amount of direction and supervision, and (3) increasing support for adequate performance is known as "positively reinforcing successive approximations." B F Skinner has been most closely identified with this concept over the years; for his classic work in this area, see B F Skinner, *Science and Human Behavior* (New York: The MacMillan Co., 1953).

Kenneth Blanchard

Kenneth Blanchard, PhD, is an internationally known management consultant and coauthor of the widely read textbook *Management of Organizational Behavior: Utilizing Human Resources.* He received his master's degree from Colgate University and his bachelor's degree and PhD from Cornell. He later became a professor of management at the University of Massachusetts and a member of the NTL Institute.

His advice has been sought by such distinguished organizations as Xerox, Chevron, Holiday Inn, the Young Presidents Organization, all the armed services, and UNESCO.

Chapter Three

Managing Professionals

Patricia Williams

Executive Summary

Patricia Williams' chapter outlines a full range of challenges in managing professionals in today's increasingly specialized workforce. Two antithetical trends confront management. First, today's labor force is characterized by a new layer of professionals who operate out of an "expert" model brought about by extensive training and mastery of the theoretical underpinnings of their fields. This fact carries with it a high degree of commitment to one's own particular discipline and a tendency to be inattentive to the points of intersection between it and other discipline orientations.

Second, the Lone Ranger mentality presents a challenge to managers because they must choreograph effective cross-discipline strategies that allow for collaborative efforts. Williams skillfully identifies a full range of helpful behaviors for managers confronted by a requirement to perform in this context. Managers, she says, must develop approaches that make the most of the professionals' expertise while channeling it for the good of the whole.

The new work of management is to create conditions in which this new class of professional employees can thrive. There are many important tasks confronting today's manager. They include establishing credibility, learning the language of the professionals, understanding certain aspects of the work, allowing appropriate levels of autonomy, assisting individual and group goal setting, and the like.

This chapter complements the work of others in this volume. Reddy's chapter on intergroup conflict and competition is especially noteworthy. Williams' work establishes the fact that new dimensions of intergroup conflict are emerging as we move toward the turn of the century. This fact evokes new challenges for managers in that they have a twofold task: They must understand intergroup conflict and the dynamics associated with it, and they must manage these factors creatively and well. They also need to manage intragroup dynamics borne of the continued emergence of new fields of knowledge and skill specialization.

A s American corporations become increasingly specialized and technologically complex, the need for better educated, more knowledgeable, and more skilled employees rises.[1] As a result, managers are being challenged by how to best manage employees who are highly skilled, motivated, and knowledgeable professionals. *The* next major issue for our nation's leaders may be: how to manage the semiautonomous professional.

The term *professional* can be used in both a narrow and a broader sense. In the narrow sense, fields such as medicine, law, engineering and architecture have traditionally been referred to as professions: They require specialized knowledge, long academic preparation, and licensing by a professional body. However, the term *professional* increasingly refers to people who have skills or expertise in a particular field or activity outside the traditional professions, from marketing to data processing to heavy equipment operation. Such widespread use reflects the increasing educational and skill levels of the American workforce.

Members of the traditional professions have always played key roles in organizations. However, due to changes occurring throughout American business and industry, professionals who previously functioned quite *in*dependently are now being placed in roles that require them to work more *inter*dependently with others. For example, many physicians are now employed by health care organizations rather than working as independent staff associates. Plus, the increasing sophistication of other health care workers, coupled with changes in health care financing, mean that physicians' practices are subject to review by committee. Similarly, in manufacturing firms researchers who in the past were separated geographically and functionally from marketing and other departments now participate on product development teams that cut across functional lines. How does one manage highly skilled employees whose primary identification is with their profession rather than with the organization? How does one facilitate teamwork among highly competent employees whose reputations are based on personal accountability for every detail of their individual work?

THE TRADITIONAL PROFESSIONAL

Traditional professional culture is based on the "expert" model, meaning that competence is defined by technical expertise in a highly specialized field. The length and nature of professional education become the cornerstones of a socialization process that reinforces the expert model. The training itself usually emphasizes mastery of a large body of knowledge, including the theories of experts in the field. The implication is that experts have the right answers and the aspiring professional's job is to become an expert. Professional competence is defined as the ability to make independent decisions correctly based on one's knowledge of the facts. Therefore, great value is placed on autonomy and independent functioning—leading to what may be called a Lone Ranger mentality. The length of the training, the complexity of the technical body of knowledge, and the specialized language of most professions create sharp distinctions between those who have trained in the profession and those who have not.

IMPLICATIONS FOR MANAGERS

Although employees who have recently joined the ranks of general professionals may not have had academic training as lengthy as traditional professionals, their professional identity is also based on the expert model. What, then, are the implications of the expert model for the manager of the professional employed in an organization?

First, most professional employees respect competence unconstrained by functional and hierarchical boundaries. They are skeptical of authority based on factors other than expertise and they often have little patience for bureaucratic procedures or pronouncements. These employees want to be treated as the highly trained, highly competent professionals they are. They want to know *what* results are expected without being told *how* to reach them. Detailed directives reduce the satisfaction of applying skills and expertise to complex problems and may be perceived as demeaning. Professional employees often want the freedom to order their own supplies, determine their own hours, and make independent decisions in order to achieve results as effectively as possible. At the same time, they expect first-rate, dependable assistance for clerical and other support tasks.

Because of the highly specialized nature of their respective fields, professional employees value input from those who have firsthand knowledge of the field and may discount input from outsiders ("They really don't understand what we are dealing with"). Strong professional affiliations often result in a camaraderie that excludes outsiders, even when they are employees of the same organization. A professional group may focus on its own goals and show little interest in knowing or understanding the goals of other groups or of the organization as a whole. In the extreme, this internal cohesiveness can lead to an antagonistic "we–they" attitude that undermines the achievement of overall organizational goals.

The Lone Ranger mentality operates in several ways. Most professional employees are motivated by a strong desire to achieve and take personal responsibility for every detail of their work. At the same time, they may have difficulty depending on others. For example, professionals may avoid delegating tasks because of their own sense of personal accountability. They may be reluctant to ask for or offer assistance even within their ranks, since a dependence on others may be viewed as a sign of incompetence. And they often lack training or experience in group skills in general and in joint problem solving in particular.

The Lone Ranger mentality may also lead to difficulties accepting intrusions on individual autonomy. Professionals trained to function independently may be relatively unaware of how their individual decisions and actions affect others in the organization. They may also be unwilling to alter their professional behaviors on the basis of organizational needs, particularly if there is a conflict between their professional judgment and the organization's mandates and needs.

Finally, professional employees may encounter certain difficulties in accepting changes in their own field, in the organization, and in their professional environment. Some may hesitate to question accepted theories in their fields. Others may be reluctant to obtain training updates, since to do so would be to admit relative incompetence in the face of a rapid growth of knowledge in their fields. And some may canonize the ''good ol' days'' as a time when they could do their work with less interference from outside influences. This denies the importance of shrinking resources, new management directives, and the demands of regulators, other professional groups, and accreditors.

SUGGESTIONS FOR MANAGING PROFESSIONAL EMPLOYEES

Several steps can be taken to assure a mutually productive relationship between a manager and professional employees:

1. *Establish credibility on the basis of authentic knowledge, skills, and experience.* Most professional employees respect expertise even in a field outside their own. In order to establish your credibility, share your background, training, and qualifications. Let professional employees know the extent of your knowledge about their disciplines. If you have actual work experience similar to theirs, tell them. If, on the other hand, your background is in a different field, be honest about the limits of your expertise. It is far better to emphasize your competence in your own field (including the field of management) than to exaggerate your knowledge of theirs. We all have only disdain for those who feign technical know-how—and we can spot it miles away!

2. *Use the language of the professionals' field and avoid management jargon.* Every professional group tends to develop highly specialized words, phrases, abbreviations, and usages particular to the field. Learn the language of your professionals. Common language facilitates communication: You will be better able to understand your employees' ideas and they yours. If you are unsure about correct terms and usages, ask. By doing so you demonstrate that you want to understand their discipline. Using the lan-

guage incorrectly, on the other hand, highlights your status as an outsider and will decrease your effectiveness.

3. *Learn about those technical aspects of the field that the professional identifies as relevant to your management.* There is nothing more frustrating for professional employees than to feel that management does not understand the nature of their work. They may be reluctant to seek assistance in problem solving from those within their field, let alone from managers unfamiliar with the problem. When employees are having difficulty making the transition to a new technology, for example, they generally will not request a manager's help unless the manager understands how both the old and the new systems work.

4. *Clarify goals, then allow for a high degree of autonomy in pursuing those goals.* One of the functions of a manager is to clarify organizational goals and expectations for the employee. Note the word *clarify.* Ask for the employee's input on the goals rather than handing them down as established facts. Are the goals unrealistic? Are they too modest? Are they compatible with the employee's own professional goals? Are they off the track in any way? By asking, you take advantage of the employee's expertise, and you also build commitment. Once you have agreed-upon goals, clarify your expectations in terms of timing and implementation. Then allow the professional to determine how those goals can best be achieved.

    Similar principles apply when managing a team of professionals. Because teams are likely to be composed of highly independent individuals, an important function of the manager is to clarify team goals. This can be accomplished by facilitating the group in goal setting, communicating mutual expectations, and granting leeway in how individual members complete specific tasks. The manager's task is to assure appropriate interdependence to achieve predetermined goals.

5. *Foster the acquisition of skills needed for working collaboratively.* As noted earlier, most professionals are trained to function in a highly independent manner, yet organizations increasingly require collaboration among various individuals and groups in order to solve complex problems. Managers can foster improvement in communication, group problem

solving and decision making, managing differences, and other interpersonal skills.

- Clarify that it is important for professional employees to be able to work collaboratively at times.
- Continually improve your own interpersonal skills and let your employees know about your efforts.
- Provide resources (time, money, and opportunities) that will allow professional employees to receive training in interpersonal skills.

6. *Accept a reasonable level of risk taking.* In professions such as research and development, innovation rarely occurs without a significant number of sidetracks and blind alleys along the way. Such tangents may result in new approaches or significant breakthroughs. The same principle applies to unleashing the creative energy of all professional employees. There are at least two ways in which you as a manager can foster an environment that values creative risk taking: first, by viewing the creative exploration of alternatives as productive even when there is no apparent direct benefit to the organization; and second, by accepting occasional clear-cut failures— to meet a deadline, to solve a problem, to show results. Accepting occasional failures enables you to allow competent, dedicated employees to challenge themselves with higher aspirations.

7. *Create sufficient job challenges.* Like most employees, professionals enjoy confronting and overcoming challenges but may be less likely than other employees to find work within an organization sufficiently challenging. Professionals want the opportunity to apply their professional skills. A common reason professionals give for choosing to leave an organization is, ''I want to use my talents more fully.'' One job of the manager, therefore, is to ensure that the organization makes full use of the professional's skills and expertise.

8. *Link the professional's work to the goals of the organization.* There are two important ways in which the manager can link the professional employee and the organization. First, the manager can provide a larger context for the employee's work by relating it to overall organizational objectives. By communicating a vision of the organization's

goals, managers help professional employees focus their efforts in productive ways.

A second important way to make this link is by managing the environment around the professional in ways that best support the work. The manager can ensure adequate resources, current information, and a minimum of unnecessary control.

9. *Call attention to the limitations of the expert model when necessary.* Managing professional employees has less to do with being in charge of them than with helping them develop their full potential as contributing members of the organization. At times this means pointing out the ways in which their socialization as a professional may be getting in the way of their effectiveness. For example, there may be times when you see employees discounting information simply because the source is an individual or group outside their circle. You may need to point out that people trained in the expert model often have difficulty with uncertainty or ambiguity and may fix upon an answer— even the wrong one—just to have one. Or you may note that the Lone Ranger mentality tends to foster high levels of individual achievement that can interfere with working effectively with others.

SUMMARY

The challenge of managing professionals has great relevance for managers today. As the organizational roles of traditional professionals change, managers must develop approaches that make the most of the professionals' expertise while channeling that expertise for the good of the whole. Similarly, in any organization that employs individuals who increasingly see themselves as professionals, the new work of management is to create conditions in which they can thrive. Important tasks for the manager include establishing credibility, learning the language of the professionals, understanding certain aspects of the work, allowing appropriate levels of autonomy, assisting individual and group goal setting, encouraging the acquisition of collaborative skills, ensuring sufficient challenges on the job, and providing the organizational context for the professional's work. Finally, the manager can help professionals move beyond traditional notions of professional expertise in accordance with the changing needs of today.

ENDNOTE

1. William B Johnston, *Workforce 2000* (Washington, DC: US Government Printing Office, 1987).

Patricia Williams

Patricia Williams, MD, consults with businesses and other groups that seek to improve quality, productivity, and organizational effectiveness through human and organizational development. Her clients include organizations in health care, education, financial and other services, and the public sector. Specific areas of expertise include organizational diagnosis and problem solving, strategic planning, team building, diversity management, leadership training, and managing change. Prior to training at the NTL Institute, Dr. Williams practiced and taught family medicine in a variety of settings. She is on the faculty of Jefferson Medical College and has published articles on leadership training for health care professionals.

Chapter Four

Developing High-Performing Teams

Jane Moosbruker

Executive Summary

In this chapter, Jane Moosbruker discusses her stage model for team development. She observes that contemporary organizations utilize three different types of teams: (1) management teams that have ongoing responsibility for the activity of an organization, or an internal component of one; (2) task forces designed to achieve a particular goal, after which they disband; and (3) work teams that retain ongoing responsibility for the accomplishment of a set of tasks, such as managing a product line in a factory or delivering a human service.

Her discussion of stage theory follows the patterns established by others who have written about group or team development. Now more than ever it is increasingly important that managers understand the stages that intact work groups pass through as they move toward becoming high-performing teams. Without a full appreciation of the dynamics Moosbruker discusses in this chapter, the individual manager is likely to misread the dynamics, and indeed reach erroneous conclusions about what is occurring.

It is precisely for these reasons that the underlying importance of understanding team development stages is emphasized. The dust has set on the individual performer operating autonomously vis-à-vis others in the work group and receiving only personal recognition for his or her achievements. That person must now learn to become a synergistic contributor to team outcomes. Great stock will be placed on managers who have knowledge and skill for developing high-performing work teams. Understanding Moosbruker's stages is an important element in this overall process.

I n order to cope with the demands of a constantly changing environment and increasing organizational complexity, many organizations are shifting from an individual to a team focus. Globalization, technological advances, new regulations, deregulation, consumer demands, economic fluctuations, and lifestyle changes require organizational responses. A team approach brings together many minds with different knowledge bases and skills to work on these complex problems. This chapter addresses the process of developing high-performing teams. A general model will be presented, based on the discernable stages of team development. The application of this stage theory model will be explored in depth for work teams.

Teams must go through developmental stages in order to reach a high level of performance. The same developmental issues exist for management teams, task forces, and work teams, but their resolutions differ, depending on both the type of team and the specific individuals involved. Teams must attend to their development if they are to reach their potential.

Contemporary organizations utilize three different types of teams:

1. *Management teams* have an ongoing responsibility for the activity of an organization or an internal component of one. These teams are generally composed of managers with different roles, ranging from the organization's line of work to human resources, finance, and marketing.

2. *Task forces* are designed to achieve a particular goal, after which they disband. They may be charged with identifying and (possibly) solving problems. These teams are usually composed of people from different components of the organization who may never have worked together before. Task forces are of relatively short duration however, particularly in relation to management teams and work teams.

3. *Work teams* retain an ongoing responsibility for the accomplishment of a set of tasks, such as managing a production line in a factory or delivering a human service. Team members may all do similar work, or they may include people with a variety of skills and roles.

The concept of interdependence is crucial in understanding teamwork. If the team members can succeed on their own and do not need each other to accomplish their tasks, then there is no basis for a team. Often, however, potential team members underestimate their true *inter*dependence, preferring to believe that they are *indepen*-dent. An important first discussion for any team is whether or not they do need to work as a team to accomplish their goals.

What Is a Team?

A team is a group of interdependent individuals, often with different roles and functions, whose combined efforts toward a mutually shared goal are required for the successful completion of a task.

What Is a High-Performing Team?

A high-performing team is a group of individuals whose coordinated competence and personal commitment to overall goals and to each others' success results in the outstanding performance of team tasks.

Table 4–1 provides a model of team development that helps members recognize where the group is located along the way to becoming a high-performing team. Virtually all group development theories postulate the existence of stages that all groups must go through before reaching a desired stage of high performance. Stage theory implies that stage 4 can only be reached by going through stages 1, 2, and 3. There is nothing that says teams *must* fully develop; in fact, many get stuck at earlier stages. Actually, teams can also regress in response to changes in their membership, boundaries, environment, or mandate.

HOW DO YOU BUILD A HIGH-PERFORMING TEAM?

What managers, team leaders, and team members need to know is how to move the team through the five stages. The successful management of this process builds high-performing teams; failure

TABLE 4–1
*Recognizing Your Stage of Development
on the Way to Becoming a High Performing Team*

Stage	Member Behaviors	Concerns
1. Orientation to group and task	Almost all comments directed to the leader Seeking direction and clarification Discussion is superficial and full of ambiguity Status accorded to members based on roles outside the group	What is the purpose of this group? Who is the leader? What is he/she like? Is the leader competent? What role will I play in this group? What are other members of this group like?
2. Conflict among members and with leader	Not listening leads to non sequiturs Attempts at influence Subgroups and coalitions form Conflict between subgroups and between individuals Testing and challenging of the leader (may be covert) Members judge and evaluate one another Confusion about the task and/or task avoidance	How much influence will I have? What is it we really have to accomplish? Will I be capable of doing the tasks? Are these tasks worth accomplishing? Who do I like and who likes me? Which members see things my way?
3. Group formation and solidarity	The group laughs together; members have fun Attention is paid to group norms Members can disagree openly with the leader Conflict between members becomes suppressed Some jokes are made at the leader's expense The group feels superior to other groups in organization Productivity is marginally acceptable Members support each other	How close should I be with group members? What is my relationship to the leader? Can we accomplish our tasks successfully? How do we compare with other groups?

TABLE 4–1 *(concluded)*

Stage	Member Behaviors	Concerns
4. Differentiation and productivity	Roles are clear and each person's contribution is distinctive Open discussion and acceptance of differences in background and operating mode Members take initiative and accept each other's initiative Challenging each other leads to creative problem solving Members seek feedback from each other and the leader to improve their performance Productivity is very high	Will we be successful? Do we have enough challenging work to do? Can we all stay healthy and keep having fun? How can I help others in the team? What will my/our next assignment be?
5. Ending the group	Review of past experiences Emotional expressiveness	How well did we accomplish our purpose? How was our task output valued by the organization? What have we learned that we can use next time we're on this kind of team? How can we say good-bye?

in this task means failure to use all resources most effectively and efficiently.

The Leadership Role

The team leader is clearly one of the mechanisms for transitioning the team. Table 4–2 provides a list of behaviors to help team leaders transform the group into a high-performing team. It is important to be aware that leadership functions can be shared by group members.

TABLE 4-2
Leader Behaviors Required to Transition
to a High-Performing Team

Stage	Leader Behaviors
1. Orientation to group and task	Provide structure by holding regular meetings and assisting in task and role clarification. Encourage participation by all, domination by none. Share all relevant information. Encourage questions to you and to each other. Facilitate learning about each other's areas of expertise and preferred working modes.
2. Conflict among members and with leader	Establish a norm supporting the expression of different viewpoints. Engage in joint problem solving. Encourage members to state how they feel as well as what they think when they obviously have feelings about an issue. Discuss the group's decision-making process and share decision-making responsibility appropriately. Provide needed resources to the extent possible; when it is not possible, explain why.
3. Group formation and solidarity	Talk openly about your own issues and concerns. Request and give both positive and constructive negative feedack in the group. Rotate the management of agenda items, using both a content and a process leader. Make consensus decisions on challenging problems. Delegate as much as possible.
4. Differentiation and productivity	Jointly set challenging goals. Look for new opportunities to increase the group's scope and stretch people's talents. Appreciate each other's contributions. Develop members to their fullest potential through task assignment and feedback. Help members avoid stagnation and burnout. Question assumptions and traditional ways of behaving. Develop mechanisms for ongoing self-assessment.
5. Ending the group	Facilitate a discussion of closing issues when the team has finished its work, even if members are reluctant. Provide an opportunity to say good-bye.

The Membership Role

Constructive team members make contributions at each stage. For example, at stage 1 members should talk about their capabilities, share past experiences, develop a common understanding of the work at hand, and ask questions rather than make assumptions. Table 4–3 provides a list of desirable member behaviors by stage.

APPLICATION OF THE MODEL TO WORK TEAMS

The innovation of using a team rather than individuals to accomplish the work of the organization has been studied since the early 1950s. Yet it remains the "wave of the future," according to recent surveys. Fewer than 10 percent of work areas are currently organized into teams, while it is anticipated that over 50 percent will be organized into teams within five years.

Work teams are often expected to be self-managing, self-regulating, or self-directed. The degree to which they are, and how these qualities are developed, is a critical issue in the changing work environment. Self-directed applies to the *whole* team, including the leader. It does not mean a leaderless team, but is interpreted this way in some organizations. Facilitative leadership is required, however, rather than the traditional top-down approach. This requires a change from older models of supervisory leadership.

Understanding the stages teams are likely to go through on their way to high performance can help speed the process and avoid major errors. The model can be applied to work teams because they generally have a long life and a real task to accomplish, and members must depend on each other in order to be successful.

Stage 1: Orientation

Stage 1 should provide the right amount and the right kind of structure for the team to accomplish its tasks. How to structure the group so that it will clearly understand its task, its membership, and its authority in carrying out its task are crucial aspects at this point.

TABLE 4–3
Member Behaviors in the Transition
to a High-Performance Team

Stage	Member Behaviors
1. Orientation to group and task	Ask questions in the interest of clarification. Help clarify team membership. Help clarify the team's task. Help clarify the team's resources. Share your task-relevant knowledge and experiences.
2. Conflict among members and with leader	Help the team develop and clarify goals. Help the team develop and clarify roles. Disagree, when necessary, without being disagreeable. Help reveal underlying assumptions. Speak for yourself, not for others.
3. Group formation and solidarity	Propose constructive group norms. Try to articulate implicit group norms. Ask for feedback on your task performance. Ask for feedback on your team membership behavior. Accept feedback that's offered; you don't have to act on it.
4. Differentiation and productivity	Offer help to other team members who seem to need it. Offer suggestions for improving task performance and teamwork. Be aware of team members' state of health. Look for ways to expand the work challenge when warranted.
5. Ending the group	Help clarify accomplishments. Stress individual and organizational learnings. Find appropriate mechanisms to say good-bye. Celebrate successes.

New work teams need clarity about their boundaries; for instance, who is in the group and who is not. There is usually a core team that does some ongoing work; others interact with this core team on a regular basis. For purposes of clarity, the concept of an "extended team" is useful. Sometimes the entire extended team needs to meet; at other times the core team meets with certain members of the extended team. The frequency and duration of meetings and who should attend is part of the structure that needs to be created.

Clarity about roles takes time. Many organizations expect immediate productivity improvement, but the transition to teams usually constitutes a major organizational change, requiring careful planning, two-way communication, resources, training, and time to learn new roles.

Employees' feelings about change in general must also be acknowledged. The degree of trust between workers and management needs to be assessed; it will almost always be a determining factor in how long the transition to high-performance teams will take.

The implementation of work teams usually begins with a formal training program, which is often focused on role clarification and negotiation, and problem-solving, decision-making, and communication skills. It is important to integrate the training with task work and to continue regular meetings after the work schedule is fully operational.

Selecting the leaders of work teams presents its own unique challenges. Often these teams are low in the organizational hierarchy. They need to be concerned about both internal and external (to the team) leadership. To the extent that all of the external leaders are consistent about providing the team with (1) a clear task and direction, (2) clear boundaries, (3) needed resources, and (4) rewards for good performance, the chances of success are enhanced.

It is also possible to overstructure a team, to the extent that motivation is lacking in team members. For example, strict rules about how the task will be accomplished or how the group members can interact would be too much structure for most teams.

The issues of how much and what kind of structure to provide at the earliest stage of a group's life poses a dilemma for managers, because individuals differ in how much structure they need and want. The resolution is usually a judgment call on the leader's part, based on both management style and approach; at stage 1, most groups are not yet mature enough to make decisions through a consensus process. Clear structures provided by an authority are most helpful early in a group's life. After a team has developed a sense of its own identity and autonomy, an introduction of structure from above will usually be resisted.

TABLE 4–4
Stage-Related Dilemmas in Developing a High-Performance Team

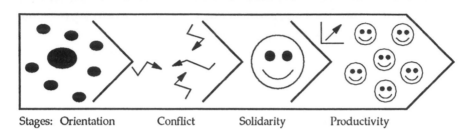

Stages: Orientation   Conflict   Solidarity   Productivity

| | Stages | | | |
	Orientation	Conflict	Solidarity	Productivity
Leadership				
Behavior	Support and guide	Encourage and involve	Self-disclosure and feedback	Opportunities and appreciation
Dilemma	How much and what kind of structure to provide	How to utilize the conflict or differences	When to facilitate vs when to join	When to challenge and when to support
Membership				
Concern	Identity	Influence	Cohesiveness	Task accomplishment
Behavior	Uncoordinated	Fighting	Togetherness— us vs them	Constructive, creative

Stage 2: Conflict

Each stage poses a dilemma for the team leader and the group. The stage 2 dilemma is about how much conflict is useful in task accomplishment and how that conflict is best utilized. A broader interpretation of this stage is that it concerns differences of opinion, approach, and background. A certain amount of differences of opinion about what to do and how to do it is absolutely essential in most complex organizational environments today. In fact, it is one important reason for using a team.

However, members who disagree may be more interested in personal influence than in creating the best product, without even knowing it; or they may be bringing old conflicts and biases to the group from other settings.

In the second stage of development, the content of the work has an impact on the degree to which exploring differences is perceived to be important. For example, a team running an assembly line might operate like a relay team, with only one person really "on" at a time. It might be easy for team members to ignore discrepancies in their ways of working "together," though even small differences are best discussed in the interest of continuous improvement of the process.

An operating room (OR) team, on the other hand, works in a very interactive manner utilizing high technology, and likely encounters a high degree of emotionality. Coping mechanisms such as joking or sarcasm are often employed. A debriefing session following an operation would allow differences in expectations and approaches to be discussed; this could greatly improve the chances of effective teamwork in the future.

The conflict stage is very difficult. Most people perceive a lot of risk in raising sensitive issues. In fact, many teams get stuck here, either unable to talk about their differences or unable to resolve them. The leader's role becomes particularly important at stage 2, first in setting a norm that makes different viewpoints not only acceptable but desirable in reaching a creative outcome. Then the leader can facilitate a discussion of the different ideas, making sure that each person listens and is heard. The leader's role also includes helping the team reach a consensus solution, if that is possible, or making the decision for the team if it is not. The stage 2 conflict can also be with the leader rather than among the members; this would make consensus much more difficult and may indicate the need for a consultant.

The content of the conflict is often about team goals, task definitions, and individual responsibilities. Through such discussions, the team can clarify goals and roles, two important characteristics of high-performing teams.

Stage 3: Solidarity

The stage 3 dilemma concerns how the team will work together internally and how its members will relate to the rest of the organization. How much mutual support and living within group norms is necessary? Is it a betrayal of the team for one member to criticize another? How does the leader's role differ from that of a member?

When teams effectively manage their internal conflicts, to the point of achieving some unity, they are ready to strengthen relationships with other organizational components. An alternative is for them to turn inward and close their boundaries to the larger organization. This latter approach will not lead to a high-performing team, but rather to suboptimization, and will limit the potential of the team and the organization as a whole.

Unfortunately, without proper training, teams may reach solidarity by finding an enemy to coalesce against, using an us-versus-them approach. Resolution of this dilemma might be achieved by rotating team membership, team leadership, or both. Cross-training is another potential solution. Policies and models for team rotation are needed, since individual workers who like their jobs may not want to move. This resistance becomes another form of suboptimization.

Organizational team building involving many levels and functions can also be very effective. Discussions could include what kinds of information should be shared with the rest of the organization and what should be kept confidential, and how much competition among teams is appropriate and when it became harmful.

Stage 4: Productivity

Highly productive teams have evolved to the point where they can work effectively within the context provided by the larger organization. Self-management is possible and desirable at this stage, but not before this stage.

The stage 4 dilemma is about how productive the team should be, and in whose interests. Success provides energy, and stage 4 teams are very successful. In fact, they are in danger of reaching too far, pushing too hard, and burning out. This can happen collectively or individually.

Team members need to discuss what challenges they should take on and when they need to rest, play, and appreciate and help each other. They also need to pay attention to the costs and benefits of their efforts. Stage 4 teams have a strong need to be recognized for their achievements. They want to be held up as models of success.

Even in stages 3 and 4, work teams need training and guidance in the process of teamwork and in the place of different types of teams in the larger organizational context. Such training can also enable team members to move up the organizational hierarchy. Without it, the best-laid plans for a truly democratic workplace can go awry.

Stage 5: Ending the Group

If a team is to end, steps must be taken to ensure a comfortable closure. There are new concerns at stage 5, and the leader must become active to a greater extent than was necessary in stage 4. The task is not just to stop, but to conclude.

One of the concerns is about evaluation: How well did the team accomplish its stated purpose? How was its output valued by the organization? Another dynamic centers on the impending loss. To the extent that the team members valued each other and their work, these elements will be missed. Finally, there is unfinished business. In any team there are things members feel they should have done, but did not. Stating these regrets can relieve tension and facilitate letting go. If done carefully, the process may provide additional opportunities for individual and organizational learning.

Active leadership is needed, because this is not easy work to do. Many of us would rather ignore endings and avoid the pain of loss. The leader can suggest ways of evaluating group performance and guide the group through the process. Encouraging members to deal with unfinished business provides a model for closure. Then the path is clear for a celebration of the team's accomplishments, which helps to provide closure.

Successful new beginnings in all aspects of life require clear and definitive endings. In order to embrace the new, one must let go of the old.

What we call the beginning is often the end
And to make an end is to make a beginning.
The end is where we start from.

T S Eliot

CHECKLIST

- Be sure the group you are calling a *team* is truly interdependent, such that members cannot succeed on their own.
- Be certain about who is a team member and who is not.
- Be sure the team has a clear task and sufficient resources to accomplish it.
- Provide sufficient time for the group to have face-to-face discussions to work out their own versions of their goals and roles.
- Help the team deal openly with differences of opinion.
- Provide adequate training in interpersonal skills as well as on task content.
- Promote discussion of team norms, including the decision-making process to be used.
- Discourage unnecessary competition with, or an us-versus-them approach to, other teams.
- Encourage the giving and receiving of task-related feedback.
- Provide an appropriate amount of challenge and support to all team members.
- If the team is to end, provide a clear and structured closure process.
- Plan appropriate celebrations of success.

Jane Moosbruker

Jane Moosbruker, PhD, is an independent consultant with over 20 years of experience in applied behavioral science. She earned a PhD in social psychology from Harvard University, taught in the psychology department at Boston College, and was a lecturer at the Harvard School of Dental Medicine for many years. She is a member of the NTL Institute.

She has consulted on the design and implementation of changes in management style, organizational design (OD), decentralization, and components of organizational culture. Other content areas include cross-organizational coordination and teamwork, team development, process reengineering, strategic planning, conflict utilization, and leadership development.

Dr. Moosbruker has published many articles in professional books and journals, including case studies of organizational change efforts in a hospital, a community mental health center, and a data processing organization. She has published articles on developing high-productivity teams and on roles for OD practitioners in the environmental arena.

Chapter Five

Managing in Chaotic Times

Robert J. Marshak

Executive Summary

Robert Marshak's chapter provides strong insights into the global unrest pervading virtually all aspects of contemporary life. His most riveting observation is that we are in the midst of a shift in eras. The changes that we see about us are of historical magnitude, the kind that comes along every 500 years or so. It is the dusk of an old age and the dawn of a new. It is not just the introduction of new technologies or new markets or new competitors, nor even the collapse of communism in Eastern Europe and the former Soviet Union that signals this shift. Rather, an epochal change is occurring, simultaneously and globally, at the deepest social, political, economic, technological, religious, and philosophical levels.

Marshak argues that we are in a transition stage between two eras, the Modern Age and a yet-to-be-named postmodern age. Much like transition stages at the group or organizational level, we are caught in midair between the now-outdated principles and practices of industrial organization and management, and the embryonic postindustrial principles and practices. Consequently, argues Marshak, "we live in a time of chaos, the paradoxical state that is entered through collapse and exited through creation." He observes that this chaotic period challenges us to "create the new paradigms, principles, and practices that will define postmodern organization and management. Its curse that we have few or no established models or certainties to turn to."

Because of the tumultuous nature of change and the unpredictability of emergent forms, it is also a time when snake oil salespeople become most active. His listing of things to expect is therefore of great assistance. For example, we should expect to be in this passageway for another 15–25 years, to feel behind the curve, and to find that many of the methods and skills that have worked for us will no longer do so. These and other cautions should be firmly entrenched in the minds of contemporary managers as they strive to make sense of the white water through which we are attempting to navigate. In this context he urges managers to strip down their organizations to their bare essentials, taking pains to avoid being top-heavy or lopsided.

The importance of Marshak's chapter is clear. It serves as a highly thought-provoking piece, capturing and providing an understandable context for the nature of the phenomena currently spinning around us. Managers must have a clear grasp of this as they attempt the most difficult job of all: managing others in a time of massive instability. Managers need to read and understand the ideas presented in this chapter if they are to be successful in the unchartered years ahead.

T hings aren't what they used to be. Sound familiar? In every age, of course, people say the same thing as they face the continual processes of change. New ideas and new technologies replace established ones. There is initial resistance, but if the new really is superior to the old, then, eventually the old is swept away in the path of the new. Yet something, somehow, *does* seem different about the changes managers and leaders around the world are facing today. What's different?

What's different today is not the *process* of change, but its *depth* and *breadth*. All available signs point to the conclusion that we are in the midst of a change in *eras*, a change of historical magnitude, the kind that comes along every 500 years or so. We are living through and witnessing the dusk of one age and the dawn of another. That's why today's change *is* different from yesterday's— and tomorrow's. Today's change stems not just from the introduction of new technologies, new markets, or new competitors, or even from the collapse of communism in Eastern Europe and the former Soviet Union. Rather, it is an epochal change at the deepest social, political, economic, technological, religious, and philosophical levels, occurring simultaneously and globally.

Unlike the transition from horse and buggy to the automobile, the current shift is more akin to the depth of changes in all institutions and beliefs that demarcated the Middle Ages (500–1500 AD) from the Modern Age. Table 5–1 shows eight great inventions: four that helped usher in the Renaissance and thus the Modern

TABLE 5–1
Era-Changing Inventions

Era Shift	Middle Ages to Modern Age	Modern Age to Postmodern Age
Inventions	Gunpowder Printing press Magnetic compass Mechanical clock	Atomic bomb Television Space satellites Computer
Cumulative Impacts	Contributed to the rise of nation-states and secular over religious authority. Expanded communication of ideas linked distant and disparate people. Global explorations led to discovery of "new worlds." Human-made machines replaced reliance on nature. Belief in the unlimited potential of individual human reason.	Threat of global destruction increased awareness of global interdependence. Instantaneous verbal and visual communication with anyone, anywhere, anytime created global village. Galactic explorations led to new theories of humanity and the universe. Human-made computers replaced reliance on human reason. Belief in the unlimited potential of harmony, partnership, and cooperation.

Age, and their four contemporary counterparts. What ultimately changed, then, was not only what people did, but how they thought about what they did across the full spectrum of social experience. Consequently, it seems safe to assert that we are now living in the transition period between the Modern Age (1500–1950 AD) and a yet-to-be-named postmodern age. More specifically, we seem to be caught in midair between the outdated principles and practices of industrial organization and management and the embryonic postindustrial principles and practices.

A TIME OF CHAOS

The result of this change is a growing sense of disorder, confusion, and loss of control as established ways of thinking and acting collapse almost overnight. Interestingly, this is also a period of great

TABLE 5–2
The End of Industrial Organization and Management

Aspect	Principles	
	Collapsing	*Emerging*
Markets	National	Global
Structures	Mechanistic	Adaptive/organic
Processes and technologies	Sequential	Simultaneous
Focus	Segments	Wholes
Coordination method	Rules/plans/orders	Values/visions/interactions
Relationships	Independent	Interdependent
Success criteria	Certainty	Flexibility
Dominant metaphor	Machine	Computer

innovation and creativity as the collapse of old orthodoxies clears the way for the creation of new insights, ideas, and innovations that were previously unthinkable.

Consequently, we live in a time of chaos, the paradoxical state that is entered through collapse and exited through creation. Trends and directions become clearer each year, even as the specifics of what to do remain elusive (see Tables 5–2 and 5–3). It is the blessing of this in-between period that we can create the new paradigms, principles, and practices that will define post-modern organization and management. Its curse is that we have few established models or certainties to turn to.

History will record that the defining characteristic of organizations and management at the dawn of the 21st century was handling the decline and fall of the old established ways of working and, out of that disorder the simultaneous creation and rise of new ways of working. For that reason, navigating through the chaotic abyss will be the quintessential skill needed by leaders and managers in all institutions.

WHAT TO EXPECT

During our journey through the tumultuous passageway between the old and the new order, we should not be surprised to encounter any or all of the following:

TABLE 5–3
Organization and Management Success Characteristics

Collapsing	Emerging
Steady responses	Fast(er) responses
Stable operations	Flexible operations
Broad/multiple directions	Focused directions
Hindsight analysis	Foresight and intuition
Tall hierarchies	Flat(ter) networks
Structured channels	Fluid flows
Fat, frills, and fads	Fundamentals
Actions lists	Follow-through on actions
Command and control	Freedom and dignity
Impersonal relationships	Friendly relationships
Smooth over issues	Face issues
Risk averse	Forgiving (enough for innovation)

1. Expect to be in the passageway for another 10–20 years before clear concepts and conditions upon which to build a postmodern organization begin to appear. Confusion and constant change will be your traveling companions.

2. Expect to feel constantly behind the curve as the cumulative and interactive effects of the new era compound until they reach the critical mass that will begin to clearly define the new organizational and managerial system(s).

3. Expect to find that many of the methods and skills you have used until now won't work well anymore. Don't expect anyone to be able to tell you exactly what to do.

4. Expect things that previously seemed impossible or unimaginable to happen, to make sense, and to pave the way for even more dreamlike realities.

5. Expect the answers to come from newcomers or outsiders, not from established managers or consultants. Beware of people who say they've seen it all before or that this is just a passing fad.

6. Expect strong emotions from everyone, due to confusion, disorientation, fear, and feelings of impending loss.

7. Expect people to be immobilized sometimes as they wish for a heroic figure who will provide direction, restore order, and help them move forward, all in a matter of weeks.

8. Expect to be tempted to play the part of the heroic figure. Don't.

9. Expect excitement, creativity, and a burst of energy when people discover new ways to solve problems.

10. Don't expect an easy, quick trip.

WHAT TO DO

To successfully manage oneself and others through these chaotic times, any or all of the following would be helpful:

1. Confront the strong emotions associated with fear and impending loss with even stronger emotions related to faith, hope, and inspiration. Be positive and engaging. This is not a time to confront negative emotions with cool, calculating reason.

2. Provide people with:
   - *Visions* of the new ways of working, to give them a destination.
   - *Vectors* to move along, to give them a sense of direction.
   - *Values* to inform their actions, to give them inner guidance and a source of strength and comfort.
   - *Valences* to the journey, to give them hope, capacity, and enough interest in the outcome to work together to achieve it.

3. Seek successes and innovators wherever you can. Develop and move them throughout your system. The magnitude of the changes is too great to happen through one grand plan or person. It's hard to know now what will be most central, or where. Movement in the right direction is what counts.

4. Be a stabilizing force as well as a change agent. You won't need to create change so much as you will need to channel and direct its forces while providing enough stability

to keep your people and operations afloat. Your imperatives are paradoxes: destroy and create, change and stabi-
lize. To help provide enough stability for people to stay
functional without getting frozen in fear or resistance, consider the following:

- Prepare for a chaotic journey. Tell people what to expect, train them in survival skills, and clarify what's important and what's not. Tell them the truth. This is not
  the time to treat others like frightened children, even if
  they behave that way and/or it makes you feel stronger
  and more powerful.

- Provide balance. Don't overdo, overstress, or over-
  whelm anything or anyone. Lead, but don't get so far
  ahead of people that they feel lost or abandoned. In
  short, navigate so that neither you nor they go
  "overboard."

- Preserve the core of the future, whatever it may be. On
  a long, rocky, winding journey you don't want to be
  overloaded, nor do you want to confuse people with
  too many nonessential things. Remember: Focus everyone on the core of the future, not the past or present.
  Everything but the core can be lost or forgotten. The
  core can provide a source of stability and strength.

- Periodically find a lull and linger long enough to regroup, reenergize, and refocus; then move on. People
  really are capable of doing amazing things under impossible conditions for long periods of time—but not forever. Even a short breather helps; this is a marathon,
  not a sprint. If necessary, create an "eye of the hurri-
  cane" retreat. Instead of planning what and how to
  change, devise ways to support each other, work together, and stay focused.

- Plan to zigzag and to travel rarely in a straight line. A
  straight line may be the shortest route between two
  points, but things will move so fast you won't have
  time to think and react. If you zigzag, you'll buy yourself extra reaction time, better visibility of what's ahead,
  and better maneuverability. Just don't lose sight of your
  destination; otherwise you may zag when you should
  have zigged.

5. Because you and your organization are in for a period of "permanent white water" in the economic river, manage as though you are shooting the rapids. That means:

   • Strip down your organization to its bare essentials. Avoid being top-heavy or lopsided; balance the load.

   • Increase the handling ease and maneuverability of your organization and management team. Redesign and/or adapt as you go.

   • Work to achieve faster response and reaction times. Don't slow your communication and decision-making systems with "nice-to-know" information. Only the minimum essential information is needed.

   • Stay alert. Everyone needs to look out and watch out. Send scouts ahead. Otherwise, constantly anticipate.

   • Learn as you go. Don't make the same mistake twice. Experiment to discover better ways of handling difficult situations. Adapt, adjust, and innovate.

   • Don't overplan; steer. You won't be able to stop to plan, nor plan to stop. Definitely set a course and prepare for the journey, then steer and navigate.

   • Maintain everyone's balance, sense of direction, and anticipation. Minimize boat rocking and instability. Lead by example.

   • Develop ways to recover people and things that fall overboard. Also, develop ways to put people safely ashore who need to get off. Jettison any *thing* that is not needed or gets in the way.

   • Inspire, challenge, and encourage everyone to pull their weight. You can't afford hangers-on.

   • Always remember: Your job is to get your organization and its people through the rapids; not to attempt to escape the rapids by going ashore.

   • Finally, build trust in yourself, your people, your organization. Make courage, faith, hope, and inspiration your watchwords. And, oh yes, look out for rocks!

As the leader/manager, you also have some special responsibilities. You will need to:

- Prepare by getting your own act together.
- Let go. Start out. Keep moving.
- Be bold. Take calculated risks.
- Focus on outcomes, not problems.
- Be visible. Communicate constantly. Inspire.

These are the best of times and the worst of times. Great challenges lie ahead. New worlds are being created; old ways are passing. Fear, hope, malaise, and excitement are in the air. It's time to get up, let go, and move out. Good luck!

Robert J. Marshak

Robert J. Marshak, PhD, is president of Marshak Associates. He has been an organizational consultant for over 20 years, with a national and international practice focusing primarily on strategic change, managing conflict and differences, and the development of executives and change agents. In addition to his work with corporations and public agencies, Dr. Marshak has taught graduate and executive seminars at American, Georgetown, and Johns Hopkins universities. He is the author of numerous publications, a frequent presenter at professional conferences, and the cocreator of the Covert Processes Model™ for understanding the hidden dimensions of groups and organizations. He has served on the board of directors of the NTL Institute and of the Training and Development Consulting Institute in Seoul, Korea.

Chapter Six

Appreciating Resistances

Robert J. Lee

Executive Summary

This chapter may be seen as a companion piece to Chapter 5, Managing in Chaotic Times. There, Marshak's perspective is a macro one, in which he looks at the epochal change now occurring at every level. Robert Lee, on the other hand, looks at the ways in which change, on either a macro or micro scale, impacts individuals. Those in organizations who are responsible for implementing change projects often view as problems others who are unpersuaded of the efficacy of the change. They are resistors! They want things to remain in the status quo state! These are not uncommon assertions about those who resist change.

However, Lee argues that change managers must learn to appreciate resistance. Its full appreciation is evidenced when managers of change are able to recognize that uncertainty abounds systemically as an organization moves from one state to another. Knowing this, a manager must spend major amounts of time communicating all aspects of what she or he knows, and clarify those areas in which there is uncertainty. Boundary management within the components of an organization or between the components and the outside world must be managed in an active way to cope with planned change.

As organizations are impacted by the chaos Marshak describes, they will function in less predictable, faster changing, more diverse, or more interdependent environments. Because of this, Lee observes that organizations must therefore have a less-specialized division of labor, greater flexibility, more interaction among people, more concern for how well the whole organization is doing, more communication, and fewer policies.

A system or person going through an important change becomes *underbounded*. People within the system become nervous, unsettled, and resistant. Change managers must publicly acknowledge the legitimacy of these feelings and the actions that might flow from them. Lee says, ''Whatever people feel is being taken away—in fact or in fantasy—should be dealt with as if it were important.'' And indeed it *is* important at the level of the individual.

Lee ends his chapter with nine specific actions and responses that managers can select to maintain control and maximize positive outcomes during a major change process. This chapter's importance lies in its timeliness and its straightforward way of discussing and recontextualizing a pervasive, often misunderstood organizational phenomenon. His observations speak to the very heart of much of the dynamics occurring in most parts of organizational life today. From this vantage point, his piece is of great significance for managers across a broad spectrum of organizational types.

P eople react to change. And they resist it. Certainly, they rarely ignore it. Change could be caused by being part of an organization that is undergoing planned (or not so planned) shifts or transitions. Or it could be happening in your immediate work group, in your family, or in your own management style. Change can be very exciting, though not always in a purely positive way. People generally will not change something important until circumstances virtually compel them to make that change. When people see change being imposed on them (if they feel they don't fully ''own'' the change), suspicion and anxiety are common, even when the changes are beneficial, logical, and perhaps inevitable.

To understand this paradox, it is necessary to go beyond the pros and cons of any particular change and look at how change affects people. Here are some common responses:

1. Personal and organizational change can mean losing some control, living with confusion, ingesting an extra dose of pure risk, trusting people you'd rather not trust, and generally having a lousy time going through the transition.
2. Something of value may have to be given up—something familiar, useful, comfortable, meaningful, or safe. Endings often aren't fun. Losses almost never are.
3. There is no guarantee that what you'll end up with will be better than what you have now. Conflicts usually exist; trade-offs and compromises are common. What you care about may be sacrificed.

4. It takes energy and time to go through a change, whether it is a diet, a new way of dealing with clients, new computer software, or the restructuring of international product lines. And typically there is not much relief from the usual workload or expectations.

"STABLE" APPEARS MORE NATURAL

For the most part, people and organizations resist change. They try to continue doing what they have been doing. Most organizations, and most peoples' lives, are designed for efficient, predictable repetition rather than for change, adaptation, spontaneity, variety, surprise or innovation. So if you're feeling some resistance to the changes happening to you, welcome to the club! You're in good company!

Of course, if people and organizations do not adapt, they risk becoming obsolete, less effective, and less competitive. It happens all the time. Even when obsolescence is a risk, many people and even the leaders of healthy organizations feel that if they change too much, too fast, or too often, they run the risk of killing something essential about "the way we are." Finding a balance between continuity and change is the key to surviving effectively.

Resistance is a healthy, useful function of living organizations, not just something to be overcome. When the resistance is personal, it is a little easier (though not automatic) to appreciate it as valuable. When it occurs in other people, however, a new perspective may be required to appreciate its value. For example, the planners of a large corporate change project should take into account the employees' need to maintain a longtime tradition that gives them a sense of pride.

THE IMPORTANCE OF BOUNDARIES

All social systems have boundaries *within* themselves so their various components can function effectively. They also have boundaries *between* themselves and the outside world. These internal and external boundaries need to be managed in an active way as we cope with planned change. Boundary-management questions constantly arise: membership questions (Who belongs to which team?), resource questions (Where will we get the money, materials, and other resources?), authority questions (Who can make which decisions?). Across boundaries, there are various mechanisms for getting the work done and for managing the work flow, among them planning, negotiating, conflict management, and departmental structures.

Boundaries can be visualized in many ways. There are no simple rules for how tight or loose boundaries should be; it depends on what work needs to be done now and in the near future. It depends on the culture, personalities, and skills of the people involved. Organizations and employees in relatively stable environments can be more tightly bounded, or "structured." People in those settings want very stable habits and predictable, comfortable, long-term relationships. Companies in stable settings can have highly specialized units, a lot of autonomy between the units, localized measures of successful performance, limited channels of communication, and many "rigid" policies and procedures. These arrangements lead to operating efficiencies; they reinforce the ability to buffer small changes from the outside world.

On the other hand, organizations functioning in less predictable, faster changing, more diverse, or more interdependent environments often need to lean in the other direction: a less-specialized division of labor, greater flexibility, more interaction between people, more concern for how well the whole organization is doing, more communication, and fewer policies.

Organizational boundaries are clarified and changed over time through the managerial process. New boundaries reflect the variety of tasks, the working relationships, and the physical or geographic arrangements involved; the rhythms and cycles of the company; and the formal and informal teams that emerge over time. The boundaries that exist now are the result of solid experience, negotiating and horse trading, organizational and personal histories, expectations for the future, and power politics. They represent the organization's culture or the individual's personality—"the way things are done."

When an organization is properly bounded, communication flows, decisions get made, and problems get solved. The system works efficiently and effectively. When individuals have the proper boundaries and are managing them well, they too communicate well, make decisions, and solve problems. But neither people nor organizations change their boundaries without much thought and serious consideration. Simply put, there is resistance to changing a boundary. The more important the boundary, the more resistance to the change.

WHAT HAPPENS DURING AN IMPORTANT CHANGE?

A system (or person) going through an important change becomes underbounded. There's just no other way for change to happen. People become nervous, unsettled, resistant. Comfortable dependencies are upset. People may become angry, stressed-out, and ill. Altruism and loyalty may diminish. Boundaries have become shaky or ineffective. There is risk to the established identities, rewards, and roles of the individual(s) in the system.

High ambiguity. Fuzzy goals. Loose energy. More stress. More intergroup conflict. Less information. More rumors. Performance results at risk. Less control. These are not very happy circumstances. Something needs to happen to get back into control, and to allow both the transition and the usual work or living to continue.

THE IMMEDIATE, NATURAL RESPONSE

When something tries to change an important boundary (e.g., habits, relationships, schedules, or resource flows), systems call on self-healing methods—analogous to human antibodies, warrior bees, or tree sap—to "fix the break" in the system. This may be done by attacking the foreign element, sealing off the break, replacing a missing part, or whatever else needs to be done to recreate the old stability.

An outside observer would see some positive things happening: people volunteering, gathering in groups, working harder, asking questions, sharing their resources, and developing new information. The observer also may see some negative behaviors:

gossiping, rumoring, intolerance of diversity, hoarding, with-drawal, aggressiveness, and other indicators of increased tension.

If you are trying to make the change happen more smoothly, it can be helpful to publicly acknowledge the legitimacy of these feelings and actions. Whatever people feel is being taken away—in fact, in possibility, or in fantasy—should be dealt with as if it were important. It really may be. Making the feelings legitimate is also important because people can then deal with the emotional level of the resistance, which is always lurking, just beneath the rational explanations.

PUTTING PEOPLE BACK IN CONTROL

There are specific actions and responses that managers can select to maintain control and maximize positive outcomes.

1. *Accept that people are the core part of almost every change process, not obstacles to an otherwise perfect plan.* Let them know you care. Listen to them. Include them. Let them know you recognize that there are important elements being discussed, threatened, compromised, or lost. People who are left out at such times have a way of reminding us that they really are important.

2. *Pay attention to resistances.* When you sense a resistance, ask about it. Get it on the table. Treat it with respect. It may be the clue to an important part of the culture or organizational functioning that needs to be honored, thus allowing the whole change effort to happen smoothly.

3. *Be flexible.* You may decide that part of the change is an error or not necessary at this time. Adapt accordingly.

4. *Understand organizational strengths.* This is the apple cart problem: how to change some things without spoiling a lot of other things.

5. *Overcommunicate.* Underbounded systems (and people) don't hear well. Set up new and better ways to communicate. Find people to talk to. Spell out all the details. Be honest and quick in sharing what you know, acknowledging that there are some things you don't yet know.

6. *Develop a clear vision of what will be.* Translate the vision into action with implementation plans and timetables. Know where you fit in. Let people see where they fit in. Most of us fear the unknown, but enjoy being a part of a design process for the future.

7. *Revisit boundary issues.* Who will be on my team? Who's my boss? Who works for or with me? Where do I work? Who's my client? What's my territory? Where are my friends? Will I know how to do the new tasks? What's changing, and what isn't? Each person will want answers on a very personal level.

8. *Create a method for mourning* to the extent that there is real loss, so that it can be made a part of an honored history. The predictable "grief curve" will take its course (disbelief, denial, depression, letting go, reality checking, making sense of things, and becoming a part of a new world) if you give it time and a little help.

Robert J. Lee

Robert J. Lee, PhD, is co-chairman of Lee Hecht Harrison, a nationwide outplacement and career services organization based in New York City. He works with executives and professionals going through career transitions and with organizations that are restructuring and downsizing. He earned a PhD in industrial/organizational psychology from Case Western Reserve University and is a member of the NTL Institute.

Chapter Seven

Intergroup Competition and Conflict

W. Brendan Reddy

Executive Summary

In this chapter, Brendan Reddy reviews a host of familiar themes in the area of intergroup competition. The importance of this chapter rests in the realization that many managers, when queried, will deny the existence of conflict between their department and others. Somehow, many of us operate with two competing mental scripts, one saying that we must cooperate and help others, the other that we should win, and not lose. Somehow, acknowledging our intense, culture-borne competitive tendencies borders on the antidemocratic. Because of this, denial is often in the offing in response to inquiries into our competitive natures.

Reddy allows that winners in competition become self-congratulatory and encounter great difficulties when examining their own behavior. The dynamics that occur within the winning group serve to build higher, less-permeable barriers between it and other groups. Self-examination of one's own behavior and that of others is the only real path in learning and developing alternative ways of handling potentially disruptive conflict.

As Reddy correctly points out, we should also recognize that conflict is a naturally occurring phenomenon in organizational life. While it may be disruptive, it can also serve as a basis for learning. Herein lies the importance of this chapter for managers. The message is that the manager should not seek to stamp out conflict, which could be counterproductive. Instead, the effective manager can use conflict as a productive resource for continued growth and change by examining his or her own motives and those of others, bringing them to the surface, and openly discussing them.

O nly when competition and conflict are denied, badly managed, or seen as inherently bad do they become negative. This chapter will acquaint (or reacquaint) the manager with the dynamics and behaviors of intergroup conflict and competition. If you understand intergroup conflict and competition, you can use that skill to your advantage. Moreover, by examining your own assumptions, feelings, and behaviors in the intergroup situation, you can learn to understand your role, contribution, and collusion. You are then in a better position to change your behavior. The organizational setting is replete with conflicts. Interdepartmental and interpersonal situations require knowledge of intergroup competition and conflict dynamics. For the purposes of this chapter, *conflict* is defined as one party not obtaining what it needs or wants and actively seeking a goal in competition with another party.

FROM INNOCENCE TO INTENSITY

Conflict can begin in either formal or informal competition. Informal competition is often generated whenever participants belong to different groups. In an organization, for instance, employees may identify with their department, and they might hear comments and humor about another department. Invidious comparisons and good-natured kidding take place between members of each department. Publicly, employees tend to defend the actions and behaviors of their manager. Privately, however, they may have grave doubts about their manager's competence, and the other department can appear more advanced and technically astute. Worst of all, the other employees always seem to have more fun! Resentment builds toward the other department.

Then comes the formal competition, built into the organization, over scarce resources, turf, or ambiguous jurisdictions. Disparaging remarks become commonplace. Humor takes on a more aggressive and hostile tone. Winning the competition may become an obsession. Interpersonal and communication skills go by the wayside. Members do not consider collaboration to be an alternative strategy. Under pressure, behaviors and insights are, at least temporarily, swept aside by more primitive impulses. Quick decisions, conformity, stereotypical thinking, and tunnel vision become the norms. Win/lose is the new form, rarely win/win. Power and manipulation are now in vogue.

Even if formal competition ends, informal competition often continues. Members stay in competition and resist examining the precipitating dynamics. The manager may become fair game for disgruntled employees who believe their department is losing. Generally, members of the successful group have the greatest difficulty examining their behaviors. Success often precludes understanding the dynamics. "We won; we must have done something right!"

Members who ordinarily are timid, quiet, rational, and seemingly self-aware become, in the heat of group competition, intense, competitive, and aggressive, and they resist looking at their behavior. Those who are willing to examine their behaviors, listen to feedback, and learn what they have contributed to the situation take a giant step toward altering their behaviors.

Is it happening in your department? Probably! If you see the described behaviors and hear the comments, intergroup competition and conflict are operating. As stated, we typically hear it in the humor and disparaging remarks members of one group make about another. The manager will find it helpful to explore members' negative comments. Try to discover what is behind the remarks and the perceptions. Competition may be a smoke screen for other feelings.

SYMBOLS, SYMPTOMS, AND NORMS

Other clues about intergroup competition come from the use of symbols. For example, groups sometimes adopt aggressive, macho, warlike, or military names. Emblems, insignias, graffiti, caricatures, and signs identify the group and its members. Members refer to "our room," and "our leader," and use other possessive descriptions. In large group meetings, group members sit together, sometimes with their backs to others. Competitive groups frequently create negative "pet" names for other groups, members, and leaders.

FUEL FOR THE FIRE

How are these dynamics fueled? A number of conditions feed the fires of intergroup competition. First, let us look at some antecedents to competition and conflict.

Given that the American culture is aggressive and sports-oriented, chances are good that feelings of competition and subsequent conflict will surface readily. Our achievement- and production-focused business climate increases that probability. Within many group members, the pilot flame is already lit. Now add some combustible elements commonly found in organizations:

Performance expectations. Some departments believe they must meet certain standards of behavior. If an activity is designed to create one winner, the expectation for quality performance is increased.

Task or goal ambiguity. When the path to a particular task or goal is ambiguous or the decision making involves a high degree of uncertainty, two or more departments dealing with the same task will increase their competition. They then strive to gain information that will give them a competitive edge.

Resource availability. If a prize (e.g., money) or public recognition is awarded for accomplishment, the levels of competitive intensity and conflict increase.

Time constraints. Given these three elements, the shorter the time available for a given task, the greater the intensity of the competition.

EFFECTS OF INTERGROUP CONFLICT

Members of each group perceive the other group as bad and themselves as good. It is us versus them. They see the negative stereotypes in the other group and the positive stereotypes in themselves. Moreover, if the group members interact, they tend not to use the communication skills they have learned earlier. People suppress basic skills such as listening and paraphrasing. Conflict and hostility accelerate. Humor becomes more aggressive and disparaging.

Members begin to hurl epithets, particularly about the "unfair" practices of the other group or department.

Within each group, meanwhile, cohesion and loyalty become obvious. Conformity is demanded of group members. Deviance, such as the suggestion of collaboration, is not tolerated. The task becomes all-important; individual needs secondary. Autocratic leadership is tolerated, if not encouraged, and each group becomes more organized. Members want to present a strong and united public face. At this juncture, consultants and managers find it difficult to get group members to examine their own behavior or group dynamics. The tyranny and power of the group is paramount.

WINNERS AND LOSERS

Schein[1] has graphically described winners and losers after competition. The winning team retains and intensifies its cohesion. Concern for work and task drops off and intragroup cooperation increases. Tension is released in the form of play and kidding. The urge to fight is reduced; complacency sets in. It is difficult for winning teams to examine their dynamics; they prefer to confirm their positive stereotypes of themselves and the negative stereotypes of the losing teams. Winning minimizes learning about the conflict, intergroup dynamics, or oneself.

Conversely, losing teams regroup and work harder "for the next time." While members may find it difficult to examine their dynamics, they have broken stereotypes and can maximize their learning. However, an initial period of denial often precedes splintering, intragroup fighting, and the surfacing of unresolved conflicts among group members. Intragroup cooperation falls to its lowest level. Losing groups do reorganize, become cohesive, and are realistic about losing; in the long run, they can be more effective.

Is there a positive side to intergroup conflict? Absolutely. If managed well, competition and conflict help create achievement, comradery, loyalty, and esprit de corps. In the struggle to manage and resolve conflicts, many creative alternatives and solutions can emerge that might not have been considered earlier. Competition and conflict can produce high energy, motivation, and improved performance. Only when competition and conflict are denied, badly managed, or seen as inherently bad do they become negative. While competition and conflict can be and are frequently permitted to get out of hand in many organizations, it does not have to be that way.

HOW DOES THIS RELATE TO MY DEPARTMENT?

There are many groups in your work setting; therefore, competition and conflict exist. Think for a moment of your own department, section, division, unit, or area. Almost any interaction holds potential conflict. It is certainly in your best interests to understand the difference between appropriate and inappropriate behavior. By examining your own feelings, assumptions, and behaviors, and those of others, you will better understand these dynamics in your work setting. Struggle to understand what *you* bring to the situation. What do you contribute? How do you collude? How are your feelings of competition activated? Learn to separate what is irrational in you from the reality of the competition and conflict.

ENDNOTE

1. E H Schein, *Organizational Psychology*. (Englewood Cliffs, NJ: Prentice-Hall, 1965).

W. Brendan Reddy

W. Brendan Reddy, PhD, is professor of psychology and director of the Institute for Consultation and Training at the University of Cincinnati. He is cofounder and principal in Reddy • Phillips, an international consulting and training company. Dr. Reddy is a fellow of the American Psychological Association and a member of the NTL Institute. He is the author of numerous articles and book chapters and is the coeditor of *Team Building: Blueprints for Productivity and Satisfaction*. His latest book is *Group Process Consultation*.

Chapter Eight

A Manager's Guide to Employee Appraisal

Robert Walters

Executive Summary

This chapter serves as a companion piece with Chapter 10, which concerns the linking role that managers play in career development. While Farren and Young discuss in Chapter 10 the important role that managers play in balancing the continuous development of employees' skills and the evolving needs of the organization, Robert Walters discusses the important role of performance in that process. Walters correctly points out that the performance appraisal process is one of the most critical roles played by managers; at the same time, it is one of the most poorly practiced.

To the degree that this assertion is correct, it becomes clear why and how systems break down. There is a disquieting disconnection between where the organization's mission and vision may be moving and, almost simultaneously, where the efforts and direction of the individual participant may be moving. One predictable outcome of all this is that the organization will often inexplicably fall short in achieving its performance targets.

Walters says the appraisal process yields three crucial pieces of information: (1) it identifies the critical elements of position-specific success; (2) it documents the specific feedback given about performance; and (3) it provides a record of the agreed-upon actions that all involved in the process will undertake in the future, as well as the expected outcomes of those actions. He then goes on to point out six attributes of an effective system and the manager's role in it.

Those attributes are fairness, relevance, consistency, value congruence, integrity and ease of delivery. Clearly, the performance appraisal process, at the level of the individual performer, is the most powerful and effective mechanism available to an organization for focusing its overall goals. In its absence, organizations become rudderless. The agent through whom this all-important process must be mediated is the manager, and the key skill will be his or her ability to clarify goals in ways that infuse meaning into the individual's day-to-day performance.

M any organizations have made extraordinary strides in quality improvement, yet these companies have not put the same emphasis on excellence in the appraisal process. A recent analysis of almost 20 Baldrige Award finalists, work-team members and human resource specialists documented how little the employee appraisal process has changed, despite an emphasis on "world-class quality" and societal changes that have created a clear need for effective employee appraisal processes. Some of these societal changes include:

- An increasingly cynical workforce that feels entitled to honest feedback,
- Corporate downsizing, which has created large pools of disgruntled ex-employees who may seek legal recourse over perceived wrongful discharges,
- Greater emphasis on employee productivity and accountability,
- An increasing use of pay-for-performance or pay-for-knowledge systems,
- Heightened corporate awareness of diversity issues and systemic biases,
- An increased desire to humanize the workplace and create productive relationships.

For all these reasons, the employee appraisal process should have the following goals:

- Identify the critical elements of position-specific success
- Document the specific feedback given to employees about their performance when compared to the critical elements
- Provide a record of the agreed-upon actions that each party will undertake in the future, as well as the expected outcomes of those actions.

This chapter reviews the goals of employee appraisal systems, identifies the attributes of an effective system, and describes managerial actions that will result in these attributes being obtained.

ATTRIBUTES OF AN EFFECTIVE SYSTEM

The managerial role is shifting to include the skills of change agent, coach, boundary manager, and group coordinator. Central to the effective fulfillment of these roles in a changing society is the implementation and practice of an effective employee appraisal system. Current research indicates that an effective appraisal system has the following six attributes:

1. *Fairness.* The perception by all parties that the appraisal process represents an honest and complete review of the employee's performance. Furthermore, fairness implies that appropriate performance criteria are used, that feedback is based on actual performance, and that ratings reflect behavior and not an arbitrary ranking or statistical system.

2. *Relevance.* Assures that performance factors relate to job-specific success.

3. *Consistency.* Assures that the feedback in an appraisal review uses similar standards over multiple reviews over time. Similarly, since an employee is supervised by several managers over time, it is important that similar standards be used by the different supervisors.

4. *Value congruence.* Assures that the organization's appraisal process reflects the values that the organization espouses. Very few events have more power to reinforce or undermine these espoused values than the employee appraisal.

5. *Integrity.* The strength of a whole system caused by the effective interrelation of its component parts or subsystems. An appraisal system is just one of the many implicit and explicit ways that employees are acknowledged, coached, rewarded, and indoctrinated. For an appraisal to be effective, it must reinforce the other elements in the human resource system. Where there is a relationship between the appraisal system and these other parts, such relationships need to be explicit. Where the relationship is weak or nonexistent, a relationship should be created.

6. *Ease of delivery.* Mandatory for ensuring that the employee appraisal system will endure. If it is not easy to operate, the methodology will eventually be abandoned or misused.

ACTIONS OF MANAGERS

These six attributes are the criteria for an effective employee appraisal system. In addition, they are the main concerns of managers who desire to fulfill their role in a productive workplace. What actions can managers take that will lead to the appraisal system successfully incorporating our attributes?

These actions fall into three main categories: (1) before the interview, (2) during the interview, and (3) after the interview.

Actions before the Interview

Ninety percent of the success of the appraisal interview is contingent upon advance preparation. The most important preparatory actions include:

- **Reaching agreement about the results and actions** that are being appraised.
- **Reaching agreement on the performance standards** that apply.

These first two actions are often done during the previous appraisal or the job interview.

- **Collecting appropriate performance data** covering the entire appraisal period.
- **Comparing data from multiple sources or situations** to identify trends. This is especially important when reviewing an employee for the first time.
- **Reaching an agreement on a time and place** for the appraisal to take place. This should occur at least one week before the formal appraisal meeting.
- **Choosing a setting** where private conversations can occur without interruptions or other distractions.

- If possible, each party **receiving a copy of the other person's performance perceptions** at least one day prior to the interview. This can greatly facilitate a discussion by immediately identifying points of agreement and disagreement.

Actions during the Interview

If the critical success factor before the interview is the manager's ability to plan, the critical success factor during the interview is the ability to communicate. Actions that greatly enhance the quality of the interview itself include:

- **Being systematic** by working sequentially through the appraisal document. It is often confusing to both parties if the appraisal topics are not discussed in the same sequence as presented in the document.

- **Staying on the topic** by finishing one area of concern before working on another. Frequently, an employee who disagrees with performance feedback may bring up new, extraneous, or incomplete information, which may disrupt the flow of the discussion.

- **Admitting new and relevant information** in the process. The outcome of an appraisal interview should not be completely predetermined. Allowing new information to make a difference demonstrates flexibility and openness.

- **Empathizing** or letting the other person know that you understand how they feel, which can create a climate of collaboration. Like any human process, the appraisal interview has both emotional and intellectual components. True understanding and commitment come from acknowledging both facts and feelings.

- **Checking for understanding.** This is an excellent way to make sure that both of you share a common perception. Typical techniques are paraphrasing (saying what the other person said but in different words), asking questions, or using examples. Using examples deserves separate discussion.

- **Using examples.** This is absolutely essential for a good appraisal interview. Examples ensure that the appraisal is based on mutually understood facts and mutually understood events that occurred during the period under review. Feedback that cannot be supported by examples has no place in an appraisal process, for both legal and managerial reasons.

- **Investing appropriate time.** This is also essential to a high-quality outcome. Frequently, the employee being appraised judges the importance that you give an appraisal by how much time you spend on it before and during the process. Generally, appraisal meetings should last between one and two hours. Less time may result in an incomplete discussion; more time may result in a discussion that does not stay on the topic.

Actions after the Interview

Your actions after the interview serve to create continuity among periodic appraisal interviews. Most employees indicate a need for more frequent feedback; for this reason, we advocate short, monthly minireviews for the purpose of giving and receiving feedback.

In addition to regular performance feedback, the following actions will enhance the outcomes of both the just-completed appraisal interview and the next one:

- **Follow through** on agreements. Lack of follow-through sends a clear message of unreliability or lack of support on your part.
- **Keep records of every employee's performance** during the period between appraisals. Do not trust your memory of events that have occurred during that period. An easy way to do this is to create a file folder for each employee and drop notes into it for review at the time of the appraisal; these become your examples.
- **Maintain a balance of positive and negative information** that you collect. Every employee (yourself included) has successes and failures throughout the year. This same balance should be present in the performance appraisal as well, since it is the best motivator for improved performance. A sound approach builds on strengths while reducing weaknesses.
- **Don't rely on the appraisal to be the sole motivator and source of feedback** during the year. Differences in culture,

ethnicity, cognitive processes, expectations, and experience imply that effective strategies for motivating and coaching employees will also display variety and repetition. Most important, do not assume that whatever motivates you will motivate others. If you do not know what processes will help others do their best, ask them: "How do *you* know when you are doing a good job?" "How can I improve the way I coach you?" Generally, people will be able to give you some clues. Asking such questions clearly demonstrates your interest both in improving your performance and in developing flexibility toward the people that work with you.

FUTURE TRENDS

It seems that in the future, more organizations will adopt some, if not all, of the following methods of operation:

- Flexible compensation systems that reward team and/or corporate gains
- Self-managed or autonomous work teams
- Participatory cultures that highly value feedback and horizontal data flow
- Temporary work groups that are process-focused and product-specific
- Flatter work structures with fewer pay grades
- More coaching provided by peers
- "Work cell" or "focused flow" work systems that organize production groups to complete as many value-added steps to a product as possible before it moves across a boundary to another group.

These changes will result in alterations in performance-management processes. In the future you will be seeing a higher reliance on "360-degree" appraisal systems that formally collect information about an employees' performance from peers, customers, the employees themselves, and immediate supervisors. Technology will make it possible to manage the appraisal process in a way that reduces the administrative load.

SUMMARY

The assumption of this chapter, and indeed of this book, is that managing is a set of skills that can be measured and learned. One of the requisite skill areas is the appraisal process. Many managers have been promoted because of their technical competency. As the competitive advantage of an organization is based more and more on the effectiveness of its employees, the manager's role will evolve to one of process facilitator and away from technical expert. The appraisal process is a specific example of this evolution. We will always perform employee appraisals, but as our role evolves there will be a higher reliance on this process in assisting the simultaneous development of the organization and the individuals that make it up. They are linked as never before, and the functional manager is the main linking mechanism. By viewing the appraisal as a three-step process (before, during, and after the interview), rather than as an isolated event, its effectiveness as part of an overall management system will create human dignity, productivity, and empowerment in the workplace.

ACTION CHECKLIST

Before the Appraisal Meeting

- Create a representative group of performance examples.
- Prioritize the points of feedback that you want to communicate.
- Choose a mutually acceptable time and place for the appraisal dialogue.
- Exchange written feedback categories to be covered.

During the Appraisal Meeting

- Keep the dialogue on track.
- Treat the dialogue as a critical event in an important relationship.
- Make sure that your high-priority topics are discussed and resolved.

- Write down new information or agreements that come up during the meeting.

After the Appraisal Meeting

- Regularly review agreements and progress.
- Hold brief (15-minute) minireviews.
- Maintain notes of performance examples.

Robert Walters

Robert Walters serves as corporate director of organization development at Harley-Davidson. He has a 15-year career in the field of organizational change, specializing in total quality management and employee involvement. He founded Strategic Systems Corporation, an international consulting firm specializing in organizational renewal and cultural change. In addition to his ongoing work with the industrial sector, he recently founded the Education Group, a consulting team formed exclusively to assist schools and communities in managing complex change. He holds undergraduate and graduate degrees from the University of Wisconsin and has taught college courses in organizational behavior, operations management, and research methods.

Chapter Nine

Giving Effective Feedback: If We Don't Know It's Broken, How Can We Fix It?

Lawrence C. Porter

Executive Summary

Larry Porter postulates a direct correlation between how effectively managers communicate with workers and the degree to which they are able to encourage employees to make the best use of all of their abilities on the job. An essential element of communication in organizations, feedback, is the fundamental mechanism for continuously improving the information flow among people at all levels. Making effective use of a thermostat metaphor, Porter illuminates several absurdities that result when we reject feedback.

The complexities involved in giving and receiving feedback are many and varied. Porter points out in his prelude to listing 10 helpful hints that if we choose to give feedback for any purpose other than to be helpful, the probability is that the interaction and its outcome will not be positive. Though hard to acknowledge, most of us have at one time or other chosen to give feedback to another person for reasons other than helpfulness. Even when our motives are pristine and honorable, that does not guarantee that the receiver will be pleased with our offering.

In his listing of the criteria for giving helpful feedback, Porter includes the need to (1) describe the behavior; (2) use timely information; (3) give it directly to the person; (4) be open about our own feelings in the process; (5) ask questions for clarification; (6) spell out the consequences of the behavior, if it continues; (7) focus on behaviors that the person can change; (8) remember that it is a two-way street; (9)

recognize that the recipient will not necessarily appreciate even the most effective feedback; and (10) check for clarity.

This chapter is important because, as Porter points out in his introductory comments, "the ability to give and receive interpersonal feedback effectively is more important now than it ever was. Organizations stress becoming more creative and productive by making fuller, better use of the workforce through increased participation at all levels." Porter says that the age in which it was necessary for employees to "check their brains at the time clock" has long since passed.

M ost of us are familiar with the concept of feedback, yet we may have different ways of defining it and different reactions to it, ranging from a positive acceptance and valuing of it to anger and an avoidance of it.

Still, effective feedback is an essential element in today's organizational world, whether it has to do with working mechanisms, skill development, or interpersonal communications (the focus of this chapter). The ability of managers to give and receive interpersonal feedback effectively is more important now than ever as organizations struggle to be more creative and productive by making fuller, better use of the workforce through increased participation at all levels. To do this managers must (1) learn to appreciate and fully include within their operations an increasingly diverse workforce, and (2) empower workers to use the full range of their abilities and not—as has traditionally been the case—to "check their brains at the time clock."

The premise of this chapter is that there is a direct correlation between how effectively managers communicate with workers (and with each other) and the degree to which managers are able to encourage employees to make the best use of *all* of their abilities on the job. Feedback is an essential element of effective communication.

WHAT IS FEEDBACK?

Webster's *Third World Dictionary* defines *feedback* as: "a) a process in which the factors that produce a result are themselves modified, corrected, or strengthened, by that result; b) a response, as one that sets such a process in motion." The term was, of course, originally used in electronics and mechanics but now is commonly used in reference to interpersonal communications.

Perhaps the feedback mechanism best known to most of us is the thermostat, in which the factors producing too cold a temperature are "corrected" and cause the furnace to start delivering heat.

If a furnace is not doing its job well (i.e., keeping a room warm enough), then somebody may get rid of it and get a furnace that can do the job. But suppose the furnace wants to keep its job, wants to do a good job, but doesn't *know* it's not doing its job. Suppose that instead it's doing something as obviously self-defeating as getting angry at the thermostat for giving it feedback that the room is too cold! ("What do you mean, it's too cold?" "You're always complaining!" "Don't tell me how to do my job!" "Who are you to decide what's too cold?" "I don't want to receive any more feedback from you!") We have little difficulty understanding at the *mechanical* level how self-defeating this is; however, we sometimes do similarly self-defeating things at a *personal* level without ever being aware of it. And sometimes we pay a high price for our lack of awareness.

The value of feedback devices is that—*if they are accurate and if we choose to pay attention to them*—they help us know whether we should continue to do something, change how we do it, or stop doing it. It is the *usefulness* of the information for correcting errors, developing skills, and exchanging information that makes feedback valuable to us.

Organizations must have feedback devices in order to discover and correct errors. At the most basic level, it would be unthinkable to run most production lines without gauges and meters that give feedback on temperatures, capacities, and weights. To survive, more and more organizations are depending on customer surveys or focus groups. Feedback systems such as performance appraisals let people know how they're doing in their jobs. Almost all skills training requires a very basic set of actions: hearing and seeing how to do a task, trying to do it, *getting feedback on how we've done*, and trying it again until we've met the standard.

Finally, and this is where we most often get into difficulties, if we really are to work effectively with each other, it is essential that we provide each other with information (feedback) that will keep us informed about "how we're doing." Suggestions include:

- "What do you think of my idea?"
- "How is this meeting going?"
- "How does my style affect you?"
- "What am I doing that makes you like working with me?"
- "Why do our meetings always start so late?"
- "Do I interrupt people too much?"
- "Are we really listening to each other right now?"
- "How do I tell you it upsets me when you're so often late to meetings?"
- "Could you tell me what this conflict is all about?"
- "Why do our group decisions so often not get implemented?"

If, like the furnace, we misuse interpersonal feedback, we may spend a lot of time flying blindly, either as individuals or as a work group. A parallel error would be choosing to misuse the fuel gauge in our car: We could put tape over it so as not to be disturbed when the needle approaches E. Or we could just tell ourselves that it's inaccurate, and perhaps try to wrench the needle back toward F. Or we could compete with it and see if we couldn't make it to "just one more off-ramp." Or we could hit the gauge in frustration, either to punish it or in hopes of getting it to jiggle back toward the feedback signal we *want* it to give us! Finally, perhaps the simplest way to avoid it, we could just refuse to even *look* at the gauge.

Most of us at one time or another have tried to cover up the "negative feedback" gauge ("I don't want to talk about it!"), or to wrench the needle from E to F ("You're just upset with me; it's nowhere near as bad as you say it is"), or to compete with it ("Well, *you* do the same things!"), or to punish it by any number of direct and indirect means ("What makes you think you can get away with telling me that?"), or just to ignore it, even when it is offered ("Yes; now let's get back on topic"). Work groups are notoriously feedback-averse, often on the unstated grounds that the group needs no feedback and therefore self-assessment and feedback are a waste of time. Sometimes this resistance even rises to the level of calling such a process "touchy-feely."

Why do we get such responses? Probably for one or more of the following reasons:

1. Our personal experience with feedback has left us with negative feelings about it. Perhaps our teachers or our parents did not use it well (how many people *do?*). The kind of feedback we received as we grew up was painful, often making us feel inadequate or worse. We may also have been punished when we ourselves tried to give feedback. So it's a tough area for many people, which blocks them from being able to see any value in it.

2. Resisting, denying, or diluting feedback can be a way of not accepting responsibility for our own behaviors. If I refuse to believe that there's something I'm not doing well, then I don't have to do anything about it. If I somehow make it clear to those around me (and most of us have a number of direct and indirect ways of doing this) that I don't want to know that there's something I'm not doing well, then I can just continue to behave the way I want to in the comfortable assumption that all *is* well. If, as a work group, we confine our feedback about how the meetings are going to complaints to each other *outside* the meeting, then we won't have to face the need to improve our meeting skills.

3. Finally, for those without much formal training in giving feedback, it remains a confusing and threatening interpersonal issue. In addition, we may never have learned how to *receive* or, better yet, *solicit* feedback, nor how to help others do a better job of giving us feedback.

Therefore, receiving and giving feedback will probably continue to be uncomfortable for many of us. So let's take as a given that giving and receiving feedback—especially negative feedback—is always going to have some discomfort in it, and even some pain at times.

However, there's another given: Whatever the reasons and/or justifications that led us to have problems with feedback, moving effectively through our work lives *without* it is very difficult. And so the question remains: As managers, how can we be more effective as both givers and receivers of feedback?

First, we can reframe our way of looking at feedback. Instead of thinking of it as a negative, we might think of it as "disconfirming." (We may never want to use such jargon in our conversations, but as a way of reconceptualizing negative feedback it may be useful.)

If I do something you don't like, and you tell me about it, I may hear your feedback as negative, as saying, in essence, that I'm a bad person. On the other hand, I could instead choose (and remember, the choice is always mine to make) to hear it as your disconfirming rather than blaming me; that is, I may hear you telling me that my behavior did not have the effect I intended. This may not be easy to do, but it can improve my ability to accept feedback from others and move away from the painful feelings. Does that mean that I'll never feel uncomfortable when people tell me that I've missed the mark? No, but seeing the feedback only as "disconfirmation" will free me to deal with my *behavior*; I'll view it as an opportunity to improve my performance, and I won't get stuck with feelings of inadequacy, of being wrong, or of being a bad person. The same is true with respect to giving feedback to others. If my mental set is that I am not punishing the individual but merely providing course-correction information (i.e., disconfirmation), I may be able to deliver it in a much more usable form.

EFFECTIVE FEEDBACK

Improving feedback skills requires that we first clarify what effective feedback is, and that we utilize that knowledge in our interactions with others. The following ten guidelines will help managers upgrade their feedback skills. If this list sounds intimidating, remember that some of the guidelines are easy to make use of once you're aware of them. In addition, you probably won't need to concern yourself with all of them. You may instead find yourself focusing on a few, or perhaps a cluster of four or five, in areas you believe need some improvement. These guidelines will *not* be useful if you attempt to give feedback for any reason other than to be helpful. If you want to punish the person, to get even, to show how virtuous you are, or to inflict pain, then you are not using feedback effectively. Don't be surprised if it doesn't have the effect you want, even though you're following all the rules.

1. *Describe specific behavior.* Don't use generalizations or judgments. It is much more effective to say, "At meetings, you frequently don't let people finish their sentences"

than it is to say, "You're just not a good team member" or "You're frequently rude to people at our meetings."

2. *Give feedback as soon after the event as possible.* Sometimes it's wise to hold off until your negative feelings have gone away or lessened. Sometimes you may wait so you won't embarrass the recipient in front of others. Sometimes you may not think it helpful to "pile on" when the recipient is already dealing with a lot of feedback. But it is never helpful to hang on to it, gather more of it, and then dump it on the person all at once. By then it may be too late for the recipient to do anything with it anyway, and this can lead to frustration and anger rather than to anything useful.

3. *Give feedback directly to the person.* Don't ricochet it off others if it's really something about which *you* have some feelings: "Chris, how does it make you feel when Sandy doesn't support your ideas?" Tell Sandy how *you* feel. Take the risk of talking directly to Sandy rather than through Chris.

4. *Don't deny or distort your feelings or thoughts about what the person is doing.* Why not say, "I feel confused when you . . ."? or "It frustrates me when you . . ." If you *do* have strong feelings, then you're confusing the interaction when you say, "It doesn't really bother me when you . . . but people are talking." Take responsibility for your own feelings rather than shifting them over to a generalized "people," "policy," or "upper management."

5. *Ask questions only for information.* Don't try to intimidate or trap the other person. It's much more clear to ask, "Are there some particular things that make it impossible for you to get that report in on time?" than to ask, "How long do you think you can get away with being late with reports?" or "How do you think it makes me feel when you're late with reports?"

6. *Define the consequences of the other person's behavior.* Spell them out (but only if you really mean them!): "The next time you miss a meeting without an acceptable reason, I'm going to take you off that project" rather than, "If you think I'm unhappy *now,* just wait until you miss *another* meeting!"

7. *Focus on work-related issues.* Don't expect feedback to be helpful if it has to do with something over which the person doesn't have true control: "Things would go better for you if you laughed more at people's jokes."

8. *Remember that feedback, if it is to be helpful, is a process.* It must be seen as a two-way street; the manager should take into account that the other person may also have a position on the issue: "I'm getting frustrated by your slowness in getting ready" may possibly be responded to by, "I know, and I'm impatient with your need to rush into everything." In other words, feedback is less likely to work well if the people giving it assume that they are completely right and the other person is perfectly wrong.

9. *Don't expect the recipient to feel great about the feedback.* Most of us simply have not grown up that way. Give the feedback and allow the other person's feelings to surface—or better yet, help the person work through those feelings—rather than saying, "You're over-reacting" or "Come on, you're not as angry as you think you are" or "You're just being paranoid."

10. *Check for clarity.* Does the other person understand what you're saying? What is the issue? If you find yourself saying something like "Shut up and listen," you need to realize that you're more interested in "dumping" than in helping.

That may seem like a lot to keep track of, especially given the fact that most of us have had extensive training in how *not* to give feedback. Here are some suggestions you may find helpful:

- *Find out which ineffective behaviors you most want to get rid of.* You can do this by paying careful attention to reactions you get from those to whom you give feedback and by asking people what, if anything, you do when giving feedback that is not effective.

- *Don't expect miracles.* Disconfirming feedback almost always carries some sting, no matter how much care and skill went into it. Some people are more easily stung than others.

- *Test the waters.* If for some reason (e.g., fear of reprisal or lack of confidence in your skills) you don't want to try more effective feedback methods, then don't. But pay attention to the choice you are making, particularly any losses you may suffer because you are not willing to try. Under these circumstances, you might want to test giving feedback in small doses and see what happens.

- *Remember reciprocity.* The 10 guidelines listed earlier are useful to you as a receiver as well as giver of feedback. Try to use them as a way of managing the feedback you receive. If someone tells you you're being foolish, you may choose to feel hurt or angry, or you may choose to be curious (perhaps in addition to being hurt or angry) enough to ask for descriptive information. "What am I doing that makes you see me as foolish?" You can request greater clarity as to what the consequences will be for you (guideline 6). In short, you may be able to help someone do a better job of giving you feedback, so that the two of you are problem solving rather than attacking and defending.
- *Don't become a feedback addict.* Sometimes people get excited about, and thus overuse, new lessons. Not *every* event needs to be "worked on" with feedback. Above all, don't use others as guinea pigs for practicing your feedback skills.

By now you may be muttering to yourself, "But it's so complicated, it sounds like hard work, and it also sounds risky." Yes. But then so is flying blind!

Lawrence C. Porter

Larry Porter, EdD, has been in the human resource development (HRD) field since 1970; on the NTL Institute staff (1970–1975); with the organization development (OD) group at Lawrence Livermore Laboratory (1976–79); a senior consultant with University Associates and a freelance consultant (1979 to present).

He has specialized in the training of HRD trainers and consultants, specifically in group dynamics, group facilitation, and team building, and has served as a team-building consultant to many organizations. He has served on both the NTL Institute and Organization Development Network boards of directors (1977–1980 and 1973–1990, respectively) and was editor of the *OD Practitioner*, from 1973 to 1981. In an earlier career, for 17 years he was professor of English literature at a number of midwestern colleges.

Chapter Ten

The Manager's Role in Career Development: Linking Employee Aspirations and Organizational Aims

Caela Farren

Marc Young

Executive Summary

Conventional wisdom in organizational life has said worker commitment was a function of the link between the goals of the individual and those of the organization. Where there was congruity at this intersection, a match holding the promise of "marital compatibility" was in the offing. Caela Farren and Marc Young extend this conventional wisdom by interposing the manager between the individual and the organization, in a role called the "linking pin." The authors draw a sharp contrast between two time horizon elements: the job versus the career.

Farren and Young argue that there must be a viable integration of three levels of organizational needs—the individual, the manager, and the organization—in achieving an effective career development program. However, they posit the fundamental responsibility for career development with the employee, "since it is his (her) career at issue." However, they point out that the organization must provide resources and support for employee career planning if it wishes to derive the benefits of a career-minded workforce.

In addition to the proactive role that the employee must play in career development, organizations must provide an appropriate infrastructure that incorporates a clear sense of mission, strategies, objectives, training opportunities, coaching, and counseling resources. Managers' linking-pin role involves such things as mission communication; identification of skills, values, interests, and career fields; and connecting with appropriate resources and people. The authors point out that the "movement from passive acquiescence to a partnership with the organization in the employee's career development is often accompanied by an upsurge of innovative action on the job."

This chapter is important for at least two crucial reasons. First, in rapidly changing business environments, it is essential that all levels of employees view themselves as engaged in careers that demand continued growth and development. Viewing their roles as simply carrying out specific job functions is inconsistent with the business needs of ever-changing and evolving organizational entities. Second, the act of adopting a career development perspective, rather than a job perspective, not only provides the organization with a more solid performer, it also gives the individual a broader skill base. With it, his or her marketability is enhanced across a wider sweep of industries. In these terms, career development enables everyone to win.

WHY CAREER DEVELOPMENT IN THE 1990s?

I n the past, increasing worker productivity was likely to be a process that managers accomplished administratively by overseeing timetables and production schedules. In the future, successful organizations will depend largely upon their ability to link employee aspirations with the broader aims of the organization. The challenge for today's managers is to increase the long-range commitment of their employees by encouraging them to be *career* oriented, not just *job* oriented.

Accomplishing this requires a shift in the role of managers from merely supervisory to advisory as well. Managers must be prepared to function as mentors and coaches in the process of career development. By participating in the career planning of employees, organizations can provide a long-range perspective that will enable workers to seize control of their futures, with a resulting increase in productivity and creativity. Workers who are focused on the future can forge partnerships with their employers by aligning their career goals with the strategic aims of the organization. This largely eliminates the distraction of turnover and aimless job hopping. Managers, in turn, will have an easier task of overseeing a workforce that is self-motivated. Clearly, employees, managers, and organizations will reap dividends from active career planning. Consider the essential differences between careers and jobs shown in the box.

Job	*Career*
• Short-term time horizon	• Lifetime scope
• Immediate results	• Long-range development
• Defined by the organization	• Defined by the individual
• Set within the current organization	• Set in a profession, discipline, or industry
• Meets organizational needs	• Integrates individual values with organizational needs
• Fixed, limited resource incentive systems (usually based on money and/or advancement)	• Multiple incentives based on meaningfulness to individual (e.g., job enrichment)

CAREER DEVELOPMENT: WHOSE RESPONSIBILITY IS IT?

The needs of three parties—the individual, the manager, and the organization—must be integrated into an effective career development program. Fundamental responsibility for career development lies with employees, since it is their careers at issue. However, the organization must provide resources and support for employee career planning if it wishes to derive the benefits of a career-minded workforce. In turn, managers must help employees integrate their career goals with the strategies, constraints, and resources of the organization.

The career development roles and responsibilities of each of these three parties can be summarized as follows:[1]

Employees

- Develop proficiency in chosen career field
- Engage in self-assessment of competencies, skills, values, and interests
- Demonstrate competence in current job
- Discuss career expectations with managers
- Make use of career development opportunities, education, and training
- Establish a reputation for competence and dependability
- Research organizations, industries, and career fields to identify opportunities and future trends
- Set career goals and implement detailed action plans to achieve them

Organizations

- Set and communicate mission, strategies, and objectives so employees can align their career planning with them
- Train, support, and evaluate managers as developers of their subordinates
- Provide information to managers and employees on in-house career opportunities
- Provide coaching and counseling resources to assist employees with career planning
- Provide training, education, and development assignments for employees

Managers

- Communicate mission, strategies, and objectives of the organization
- Help employees identify skills, values, interests, and career fields
- Link employees with appropriate resources for career development
- Provide opportunities for employees to enhance their reputations
- Discuss the impact of the changing needs of business on competencies and skills

- Provide training and development opportunities consistent with organizational goals
- Continue their own career development

The relationship managers have with their employees provides a unique vantage point for helping employees with career issues. Managers observe employee performance daily; this enables them to identify strengths and areas for development. At the same time, since managers are generally more familiar with the organization's structure and policies, they can help employees align career aspirations with real organizational opportunities and needs. In this sense, managers are "linking pins," joining the futures of both the individual and the organization.

Career discussions between managers and employees link organizational and individual aspirations and serve several important functions. For organizations, career discussions are human resource management tools. They provide a forum for communicating to employees the organization's strategic direction, priorities, and structure. Without a clear linkage between organizational intent and individual career planning, employees may allow their technical skills and knowledge to become outmoded, thereby reducing their own capabilities. By helping employees better understand future trends and current resources, the organization can extend the productivity payback it receives from its investment in training and developing employees. Simply put, if people see where the organization is headed, they will set career goals consistent with that direction. This in turn will keep their skills current and support new ways to put those skills to use on the job. This increased workforce flexibility will stand both the individual and the organization in good stead when circumstances dictate rapid change.

For the individual, career discussions are a source of empowerment. One of the field's founders, Kurt Lewin, demonstrated that one of the key differences between the psychological "life space" of an adult and that of a child lies in the adult's ability to envision alternative pathways to a goal.[2] Whether by accident or design, complex organizations often attempt to simplify the environment of the individual employee, filtering out information about larger purposes and longer time scales and limiting the scope

TABLE 10–1
Career Development Model

Self-Question	Manager Role	Outcome
Who am I?	Coach	Self-statement
How am I seen?	Appraiser	Reality check
What is the organization like; what are my options?	Adviser	Goal identification
How can I achieve my goals?	Referral agent	Development plan

of available actions. This places competent adults in a dependent position. Regular career discussions help break this debilitating cycle by providing a broader understanding of the organization and its opportunities. In the career conversation, managers encourage employees to identify the nature of the contributions they want to make and the reputations they want to establish, and explain the options available to them in the organization. Armed with this information, the individual can set personal goals with realistic applications to the organizational setting and can create pathways to attain them. The movement from passive acquiescence to a partnership with the organization in the employee's career development is often accompanied by an upsurge of innovative action on the job.

In Table 10–1, common employee questions about career development are linked to the appropriate managerial role and the expected outcome for the organization.

FOUR ROLES FOR MANAGERS IN THE CAREER DEVELOPMENT PROCESS

For each stage in an employee's career development, there is a corresponding role managers can play. Four such roles are: *coach, appraiser, adviser, and referral agent.* Individual managers may find their personal styles more compatible with providing organizational advice and action than with the personal exploration and feedback required for the coaching and appraising roles. A good career developer, however, uses all four roles as appropriate and interchanges them as necessary.

Managers can *coach* employees in completing their self-assessments. Key skills for coaching include effective communication practices, especially active listening, and familiarity with career development self-assessment techniques. During career development discussions, managers coach employees to identify personal factors that should be considered part of their career planning. These personal factors could include:

- *Choice of field.* Fields are areas of specialization having a history of development over time, a reasonably stable and predictable future, widely accepted principles and standards of practice, a common body of knowledge or literature, and recognized experts. Examples include engineering, administration, finance, information systems, human resource management and marketing.

- *Competencies and skills.* Competencies are broad categories encompassing the core practices necessary for mastery of a given career field. For example, in the field of management the competencies include planning, organization, communication, resource management, staffing, and evaluation.

- *Values.* Career values make work meaningful and worthwhile to an individual. Examples include autonomy, stability, recognition, technical challenge, service to others, flexibility, financial rewards, and collegiality. Dominant career values may change over the course of one's lifetime; for example, when new family responsibilities make security a more pressing concern.

- *Interests.* Interests are the properties of work that a person finds intrinsically rewarding. The manager should help a subordinate identify those areas that motivate the employee.

Managers *appraise* employees when they provide them with a "reality check" on how others see their present performance and reputation. Key skills for appraising include the ability to relate reputation to career options, set clear performance expectations, and give constructive feedback. During career development discussions, managers help employees identify what they must do

---

Career Discussion Activity

Lifeline

Purpose: Identify relevant career factors in personal history

Give the employee a blank sheet of paper. Ask the employee to draw a line with critical incidents represented by high points and low points, with meandering spirals for periods of confusion. Be sure to specify that the Lifeline need not be restricted to work experiences, nor is it a résumé of dates and job titles. Its purpose is to identify critical growth experiences and challenges that helped define the individual. Ask the employee to write a word or two about the significance of each turn in the Lifeline as a memory aid. Discuss the completed Lifeline with the employee, listening for themes that reflect his or her chosen career field, competencies and skills, values, and interests.

---

in their current positions in order to acquire reputations for competence in their chosen career fields.

A misconception held by many employees, particularly technical specialists, is that proficient task performance is the primary basis for career advancement. Employees sometimes miss the important point that being good at what you do is only half the battle. The other half is being *known* for being good. The way in which a person is spoken about by others shapes his or her career options in the organization as much as actual performance does. Managers can best help employees by stressing the interdependence of performance and reputation, and by articulating clear, objective performance expectations that link the employee's career aspirations to the needs of the organization.

Establish a clear agreement about your performance expectations and their relationship to your role as a speaker for the employee's reputation.

Managers become *advisers* when they help employees scan the organizational environment to identify cultural norms, trends, issues, and problems having a bearing on career opportunities. The adviser offers employees information and guidance in setting real-

---

Career Discussion Activity

Expectations Exchange

Purpose: Establish a performance contract. You and the employee independently complete the following statements in writing. Then exchange and discuss your written responses to these exercises with the employee. Explore areas of congruence.

Employee	**Manager**
• My manager wants me to do more . . .	• I want you to do more . . .
• My manager wants me to do less . . .	• I want you to do less . . .
• The part of my job that matters most to my manager is . . .	• The part of your job that matters most to me is . . .
• Excellent performance in my job requires . . .	• Excellent performance in your job requires . . .
• I should prepare myself to take care of . . .	• You should prepare yourself to take care of . . .
• I think my manager would tell others that my performance is . . .	• I would tell others that your performance is . . .

---

istic career goals. Key skills for advising include the ability to provide accurate information about the larger organization, access to its resources, and assistance in formulating specific, attainable goals. During career development discussions, managers can advise employees on identifying and choosing from among the options available to them in their career fields.

Advisers can assist employees in their goal-setting process in a variety of ways, including:

- Sharing knowledge of the formal and informal organization,
- Helping employees understand other departments and job requirements,
- Pointing out trends that may have implications for competencies required in the future,

---

Career Discussion Activity

Scanning the Future

Purpose: Predict career opportunity trends

Help the employee identify resources and written sources of expert information on his or her chosen career field. Ask the employee to research/interview those sources in order to identify the 10 most important trends. Then ask the employee to speculate, briefly and in writing, what the career implications of each of these trends will be. Discuss the significance of these speculative outcomes with the employee as they apply to setting career goals.

- Helping employees understand the current opportunities and limitations in the organization,
- Identifying a variety of alternative career development pathways.

Given economic uncertainties, quantum leaps in technology, and strong competition in the global marketplace, organizational structures will be flatter. With more qualified candidates competing for fewer midlevel positions, alternative pathways for career development are especially important. Advisers can help employees consider options such as *exploratory* or temporary assignments in other departments, *lateral* movement to positions with different responsibilities, or *enrichment* of their present jobs to include more of the elements they want from their careers. This is an area in which the receptivity of the organization to creative employee suggestions can yield great dividends.

Managers move into the *referral agent* role when they focus on ways to assist employees in achieving their career goals through contacts with people and resources. Managers help employees develop detailed action plans and provide guidance or direct assistance with implementation as appropriate. Key skills when in the referral agent role include the ability to build networks of support and information throughout the organization and the ability to critique the employee's action plans.

Even an employee with specific, realistic career goals may not

Career Discussion Activity

Critique a Development Plan

Purpose: Ensure that plans are realistic. Review the employee's career development action plan. Answer the following questions together:

	Yes	No
• Is the plan based on a realistic goal with an appropriate time frame?	____	____
• Are measurable success indicators specified for each action?	____	____
• Do the goal and the time frame stimulate and motivate, or intimidate, the employee?	____	____
• Are the actions specific, related, and in an appropriate sequence?	____	____
• Does each action have its own milestone dates for initiation and completion?	____	____
• Are all necessary contacts and resources clearly identified?	____	____
• Does the plan include varied developmental activities, not just training courses?	____	____

know exactly how to go about achieving them. One task of the manager is to help employees convert their ambitious goals into a series of discrete actions, each with its own timetable and conditions for completion. A manager can serve as an informal consultant for employees as they implement their action plans, helping them build strategies for overcoming obstacles. Perhaps most important, managers can intervene directly on behalf of the employee as part of the action plan, arranging introductions to other managers, access to appropriate training, or opportunities to take on special projects and assignments. In order to fulfill this role satisfactorily, managers must maintain their own network of contacts throughout the organization. Managers who isolate themselves from the rest of their organization thwart their own careers as well as those of their subordinates.

CAREER DEVELOPMENT IN ACTION

Career management builds the organization and the individual. The reason it belongs on a manager's agenda is that it has a direct payoff for the organization. As this chapter suggests, a powerful competitive advantage accrues to systematic employee career development. People are our most valuable renewable resource. Managers are a powerful link between individual aspirations and organizational achievements.

ENDNOTES

1,2. Z Leibowitz, N Schlossberg, and C Farren, "The Manager's Role in Career Development: A Link Between Employees and the Organization," in *The NTL Managers' Handbook*, ed. R A Ritvo, and A Sargent (Washington, DC: NTL Institute, 1983).

Caela Farren

Caela Farren, PhD, is a business consultant specializing in strategic business planning, organizational design, and career and management development. She is the chief executive officer of Farren Associates, Inc., in Annandale, Virginia, and a founding partner of Career Systems, Inc., a leading publisher of career development products and services. Dr. Farren is recognized for her pioneering work in the field of career development. The book she coauthored for Jossey-Bass, *Designing Career Development Systems,* is regarded by human resource consultants in the United States, Canada, and abroad as the definitive work on the subject. Dr. Farren is a visiting professor at American University.

She holds the PhD in organization behavior from Case Western Reserve University and is a member of the OD Network, the American Society of Training and Development, and the Human Resource Planning Society.

Marc Young

Marc Young is an organization development consultant with clients in private industry and public service. He has 14 years of experience in the design and delivery of services, including executive team building, quality management, and career development systems design.

He has written on preretirement planning, career development, employee participation, and other topics of organizational concern. His clients have included health care, aerospace, financial, telecommunications, and consumer products companies. He has a strong research interest in the work of Kurt Lewin and his theories of force field analysis as applied to human systems dynamics.

He is a graduate of the American University/NTL Institute master's degree program in human resources development and is an adjunct faculty member of the American University Graduate School of Public Affairs.

Chapter Eleven

A Planned Transition Process for the New Manager/Chief Executive Officer

Robert D. Lapidus

Executive Summary

Hitting the ground running in a new managerial or leadership position is highly desirable but often difficult to achieve. Land mines are often liberally planted throughout the organizational field, some more survivable than others. In this chapter, Robert Lapidus discusses an intervention strategy that does not obliterate them completely but provides enormous intelligence about their locations, severity, and possible strategies for overcoming them. In addition, his approach enables the development of some early hypotheses about how the culture of the particular organization works.

Lapidus advocates the utilization of a transition management intervention process that engages front-end consultation with the new executive, the acquisition of valid information through interviews and surveys, the feedback and discussion of that information, and follow-up activity, including a transition workshop. In this manner, much of the early uncertainties about issues embedded in the fabric of the culture are brought out in bold relief.

The conditions that precede the entry of a new leader in an organization range from one in which the former leader may have had an outstanding reputation (making her a hard act to follow) to one in which the former leader had performed poorly and the new executive is hired to "clean the place up."

Lapidus outlines a number of key strategy-related questions on which the new leader should obtain some views from his or her key people. Extrapolations from Lapidus's practice are cited as examples of strategy-sensitive matters that may flow from a transition management intervention. These include (1) lack of clarity about the purpose of the organization, (2) responsiveness to primary users, and (3) distribution of financial assets by a comptroller to individual department directors.

This chapter is of particular importance at this white-water stage in society when many of the major institutional arrangements are undergoing massive, new paradigm-setting changes. The approach is highly advisable because it promises the accumulation of valid information, full discussion of that information, and the formation and clarification of leader expectations. All of this is achieved with a vision for the organization at the very front end of the new leader's tenure. Accordingly, its major advantage is the avoidance of an otherwise unproductive and unrewarding period of time as a new leader "sniffs out" relevant issues that require attention.

"Who are you?" said the caterpillar. "I, I hardly know, Sir, just at present," Alice replied rather shyly. "At least I knew who I was when I got up this morning, but I think I must have been changed several times since then."

Lewis Carroll, *Alice's Adventures in Wonderland*

M anagement transition and leadership turnover are major issues in organizational life. While the long-term outcomes of key management changes are often beneficial, the short-term effects are frequently counterproductive for the manager and the newly formed team. Possible consequences include a disruption in organizational continuity, a hesitancy to communicate honestly, delayed decision making, employee anxieties over the change, and rumors about possible hidden agendas (reorganization, reduction in staff, changes in working conditions). Furthermore, while great care and effort are devoted to the recruitment and selection of new managers, few organizations develop a strategy for smoothing the entry of the new boss during the first few weeks and months on the job.

This chapter offers a straightforward and productive process for maximizing organizational and managerial effectiveness during this critically important transition period. A planned transition process culminates in a transition meeting held to identify issues and the expectations of the incoming manager or chief executive officer (CEO) and the key management team. Positive feedback from managers who have experienced planned transitions earmark it as an effective intervention. The process meets the following objectives:

- To provide the new executive/manager with the information needed to establish priorities and implement changes
- To identify the major goals and priorities for the next six to nine months
- To enhance organizational effectiveness and teamwork
- To articulate the new executive's leadership style in order to provide more effective support.

THE LEADERSHIP TRANSFER

One of the formative studies about the effects of leadership transition on organizational effectiveness was conducted in 1975 by Michael Mitchell, an internal organization development consultant for Kaiser Aluminum. He found that decreases in organizational effectiveness typically occurred during the first six months following key changes in leadership. Subsequent practitioners have concurred that this decline in performance (referred to as "downtime") often occurs regardless of the competence, leadership qualities, or desires for success on the part of the incoming executive.

Table 11-1 reflects the hopes and fears underlying the boss–subordinate relationship, which are generally left untouched by most unmanaged transitions. This results in increased anxiety, accelerated stress, and reduced performance.

THE TRANSITION PROCESS

How does the leadership transition process occur? The first step explores the initial reasons why an organization undertakes a transition process. The following are a few examples:

TABLE 11-1
Hopes and Fears

New Boss	Subordinate
"I hope my staff will give me accurate, timely, and reliable information. I don't like surprises."	"Is the new manager here to clean house? Will I lose my status around here?"
"I want my staff to see me as strong, yet approachable."	"Is there going to be a reorganization or a realignment of personnel?"
"How do I compare to the previous boss? I hope they will accept me for who I am."	"I hope someone tells the boss the truth about what's going on."
"I hope the staff will be loyal to me."	"I'd better keep quiet until I get a sense of him (her)."
"I hope I can make positive changes and receive due recognition."	"I hope the manager values me and sees that I really want to do a good job."

- A leader with an outstanding reputation suddenly retires and is a "hard act to follow."
- The new manager, if selected from outside the organization's ranks, is unfamiliar with both the function and the people.
- A new executive is hired to "clean the place up."
- A manager is selected from among strong inside candidates and must deal with potential rivalries and jealousies.
- The vice-president for human resources is confronted with an expanding organization in which new managers are constantly rotating into new locations and positions.

As these examples illustrate, the transition process addresses different issues and occurs in all organizations. Therefore, while there is a general strategy for managing transitions, the specific pieces of the process must be tailored to the needs of the individual executive/manager and the organization. If there is an organizational sponsor, the process can be initiated and planned prior to the arrival of the new manager. Some organizations have institutionalized a planned transition process for new managers in concert with their leadership teams and human resource departments.

THE INCOMING MANAGER AND THE CONSULTANT

The key to successful transitions lies in the collaborative relationship between the incoming manager/CEO and the consultant. Experienced consultants can play an instrumental role in assisting with the initial development of the manager's vision, organizational priorities, and leadership style.

Although the manager retains control of the process, the consultant and the manager should also make joint decisions about who should attend the transition meeting, what areas should be covered in the data-gathering effort, and the focus of the meeting's agenda. Instrumentation on the manager's leadership style can be most helpful in providing the manager with insight that can be used to describe managerial preferences to the staff. If used properly by the manager, consultants can be valuable advisors, providing an objective perspective into both the organizational and interpersonal dynamics.

INTERVIEWS AND SURVEYS FOR THE TOP TEAM

Although employees want to tell the new boss the truth about important issues, their reluctance comes from a fear of reprisal, a lack of trust, or not wanting to appear disloyal to the previous leadership. Preparation for the transition meeting provides an excellent opportunity for the new manager as well as the members of the top team to share information and perceptions in a nonthreatening, confidential manner. Each member of the top team is typically interviewed anonymously by the consultant. This stimulates participants to think about the important issues in the organization so they are fully prepared for the meeting. Some examples are:

- What is your view of the vision and direction of the organization?
- What's important or what really counts in this organization?

- Who are the key stakeholders (e.g., customers, community leaders, outside contractors, regulators) that the new manager needs to know and understand?
- What would you like to know about the incoming manager that you don't know already?
- If you were the new manager, what would you like to start, stop, or continue doing?
- What is the most important thing that the incoming manager should know about as he or she assumes responsibilities?
- What myths, attitudes, and beliefs are helpful or unhelpful to the organization?
- What are your wishes for the new team as it begins to work together?

In addition, if the manager so desires, a short organizational assessment survey, tailored to the needs of the organization, can be used six to nine months later as a pretest and posttest evaluation of the success of the transition process. Participants are asked to select the answer, based on a five-point scale, that most accurately describes how they feel about each issue. Sample questions, which are similar to the interview questions, are shown below.

- To what extent does the organization have a clear-cut sense of purpose?
- To what extent does the organization meet the needs of its customers?
- To what extent are decisions made at the appropriate level in the organization?
- To what extent is recognition extended to those who deserve it?
- To what extent does top management work as a team?
- To what extent are you satisfied with the productivity of the organization?
- To what extent is managing diversity an important leadership priority?

The final step is the feedback of the data from both the interviews and the surveys to the incoming manager. This session familiarizes the new leader with the major organizational issues that need to be addressed, including any staff expectations of the manager's role. It may also highlight "show stoppers"; that is, those issues that must receive immediate attention. For the new manager this is often a most valuable process because the information sometimes reflects a perspective not previously heard. This is due in large part to the anonymous nature of the interview process, which often produces a candor unequaled in other situations.

THE TRANSITION MEETING

Now that the new boss and the staff are prepared to discuss key issues affecting their future organizational life, the meeting will be beneficial for the new team, its work together, and the entire organization. Due to the importance of this event in the organizational life cycle, an off-site location will facilitate group interaction and lend significance to the proceedings.

Brainstorming techniques (nonevaluative, idea-generating methods) ensure maximum sharing of ideas during the issue identification phase of the group's activities. After the issues have been incorporated into broad major themes according to the top organizational priorities, the manager receives a report from a group spokesperson. Participants may desire to articulate individual viewpoints within the context of the group report.

The discussion between the manager and the staff concerning issues of mutual concern is usually dynamic and varies from one organization to another. Here are some examples of issues that have surfaced during previous, real-world transitions:

- Executives at a large metropolitan hospital had conflicting opinions about the purpose of the organization. Was the primary emphasis on research, teaching, or patient care?

- A manufacturer's top managers were concerned about the responsiveness of the organization to its primary users. Was the organization appropriately structured to meet their needs?

- The top staff of a research and development organization was displeased with the distribution of financial assets to individual department directors. Most managers viewed the entire financial allocation process as highly secretive and against their best interests. Should the comptroller be vested with so much power and control?

Examples of questions concerning the role of the new manager that have surfaced in actual company transitions are:

- How much independence will we have in running our own areas?
- What types of communications will you employ and how frequent will they be (e.g., staff meetings, management review updates)?
- What should we do if we think you are making a mistake?
- How frequently do you want to see department or branch managers?
- What is the role of the assistant in running the staff?
- What is your success criteria for us and how do you handle performance reviews?

The major role of the new manager during the meeting is twofold: to present the overall vision and expectations for the organization and staff, and to be a good listener. The executive should also answer questions concerning management style or personal preferences on how to run the staff. The manager should probably refrain, however, from making any decisions regarding future organizational policy unless there are compelling reasons to do so.

After responding to and acknowledging the finalized list of concerns, the new executive may want to present a vision or a road map for the future. Finally, the manager delivers closing remarks that assess the progress of the meeting and the staff in reaching the desired objectives.

FOLLOW-UP

An action-planning session addressing the major issues that surfaced during the transition meeting is highly desirable. A posttransition meeting between the manager and the consultant will help determine which issues the CEO/manager can personally resolve and which should be referred to the staff for further analysis.

Depending on the nature of the issues that emerged from the transition process, a variety of activities might be needed, among them strategic planning (to address confusion over purpose and direction), role and responsibility clarification, or survey-guided development (to increase commitment from the middle and lower levels in the organization). It is important that the top staff actively review the goals and priorities generated from the transition process on a periodic basis.

CONCLUSION

The leadership transition process can be a win-win proposition for all members of an organization. Considering the potential rewards, the time expended is minimal. Perhaps the best summary was provided by an experienced CEO, whose span of control extended to 58 subordinate organizations. Addressing those final comments to the staff at the conclusion of the transition meeting, the CEO remarked: "The openness and honesty with which you in this management group were willing to share your best ideas for our future success is immensely gratifying and helpful to me. Although I was skeptical of this process when it began, I am fully satisfied now. This has been the singular, most valuable management effort I have undergone in my career."

Robert D. Lapidus

Robert D. Lapidus has worked as a consultant in organizational and human resource development for the past 20 years. As a consultant to chief executive officers and key managers, he has implemented a wide variety of interventions, including leader transition, management development, strategic planning, survey-guided development, and team building. He is a member of the NTL Institute, an adjunct professor at Johns Hopkins University, and an advisor to the American University/NTL master's program.

Chapter Twelve

Managing Time Effectively

Roger A. Ritvo

Executive Summary

On the surface it would seem anachronistic that in a culture steeped in the work ethic, space in this volume would be given to managing time effectively. Yet if an analysis were done detailing hour-by-hour the ways in which managers utilize their time, the amount of unproductive hours would stagger the imagination. More staggering yet would be the associated costs to organizations and to society of this unproductive time. In this chapter, Roger Ritvo explores the myths about time and proposes clear actions to help managers use this most valuable of resources more effectively.

Ritvo discusses internally and externally imposed time wasters. As he observes, it is easy to blame circumstances beyond our control for the existence of time wasters. But that's only half the story. After a review of time wasters that come from sources *outside* of managers, and are often beyond their control, Ritvo goes on to examine "internally developed time wasters." Unlike those for the external ones, the remedies for the internal ones lie *within* individual managers. It is in this context that endless cultural myths abound. He outlines seven broadly held myths about the use of time. Chances are, most managers will be able to see themselves in one or more parts of this discussion.

The fundamental point of this chapter is that managers need to remain clearheaded about how they are using their time. Ritvo outlines 10 ways to respond to the challenge of becoming an effective time manager. Among those discussed is the requisite need to schedule open time. This acknowledges that subordinates require access to their immediate supervisor, but rather than maintain an open door policy, wherein all of a manager's time is subject to subordinate access, he suggests that managers set aside a particular time during which it is understood that she or he is available to meet with subordinates for up to 15 minutes.

Embedded in this discussion is another issue with which managers must come to grips. The manager who takes the position that she or he must handle all of the *tough* assignments is one who is failing to meet arguably the most important managerial requirement of all. Tough assignments often serve as the best opportunities for managers to develop subordinate capabilities. In most complex organizations, this is the most highly prized role a manager will ever be asked to perform.

This chapter is important because it raises an issue that is becoming more and more pervasive in conversations among managers. How do we go about managing all of the complex requirements constantly coming at us? Clues to the most productive path through this often nightmarish thicket are contained in this chapter.

H ow much does one hour of lost time per day cost? If your company pays an employee a $50,000 salary, those 60 minutes per day are expensive—$6,250 each year. The figure is $2,500 for the employee whose salary is $20,000. Lost production time can never be recovered. It can be saved, however, if managers are willing to look at how they spend their own time. Organizational cultures support different work patterns and habits, ranging from extended coffee breaks to the open door policy, which may mean a steady stream of interruptions. Effective time-management programs increase organizational productivity and efficiency while controlling costs. The overall bottom line will be improved, even in service and nonprofit organizations. In addition, managers benefit directly through reduced stress. This chapter explores the myths about time and proposes clear actions to help managers use their time more effectively. If you have "too many fires to fight," then this chapter is written for you.

WHAT ARE TIME WASTERS?

There are numerous ways to waste time. Individually, none may seem onerous; collectively, they decrease individual and organizational effectiveness. Alone, none of them are difficult to change;

together, they form a pattern of behavior that requires a planned refocusing of work habits. Here is a list of a dozen common time wasters:

1. Lengthy socializing
2. Too many unplanned visitors
3. Waiting for upper management to approve routine decisions
4. Too many meetings
5. Extended luncheons
6. Unclear priorities
7. Can't see the top of your desk
8. Too many interruptions
9. Junk mail
10. Unrealistic deadlines
11. Trying to do too much at once
12. Competing demands

SOURCES OF TIME WASTERS

It would be easy to blame circumstances beyond our control for the existence of these time wasters. Yet that would only tell half the story. Some do indeed come from outside forces, but the other half come from within the person reflected in the mirror: the individual manager.

Externally Imposed Time Wasters

Some of the problems that managers encounter in attempting to utilize their available time effectively are externally imposed. The following should sound familiar to many first-line supervisors as well as chief executives:

- Unexpected assignments from the boss
- Lengthy telephone conversations
- Unproductive meetings

- Poor communications
- Crises
- The responsibility of solving problems created by subordinates

In each of these instances, the manager responds to meet the needs of others. The irony is that the manager is often forced to reach decisions without having complete information, knowing of other possibilities, or having time to reflect on the implications of the decision.

Effectively responding to the time pressures created by externally imposed circumstances often requires assistance from others. Support staff can help think through the desired outcomes of a meeting before it begins. Clear communication with the secretarial staff can prevent memos and letters from constantly being retyped and edited. Junk mail can be screened by staff and discarded as necessary. It may be a valuable intervention to ask subordinates to present several options along with the problem.

Internally Developed Time Wasters

Other concerns about managing time have an internal source. These come from within each of us: They may be part of our identity and our self-concept, but they certainly contribute to the problem. Examples include:

- The inability to say no
- Procrastination
- Poor listening skills
- Outside activities
- Poor planning
- Unclear priorities
- Trying to do too much for too many people

The remedies for the internal time wasters lie within the manager, who should ask the questions shown below on a regular basis. The answers go to the heart of effective time management. But more importantly, they are at the core of effective management.

- Do I have written goals for the next six months?
- What are my primary responsibilities?
- What can I delegate?
- What areas of responsibility can I get preapproved now?
- Do I delegate challenging as well as routine tasks?
- Do I know how I spend my time?
- What is my prime time? When am I at a low point?

COMMON MYTHS ABOUT TIME

Myths abound. Time is so precious in our organizational and personal lives that we have created a number of fallacies to justify the way we work. Here are a few common myths:

Myth 1: *Lots of activity brings results.* Clearly, something will get done. But there is another axiom that states, "There is never time to do it right, but always time to do it over." The key is to plan and implement the right activity. The axiom's cousin, "Don't just stand there, do something!" implies the same thing: that any action is better than none at all. Of course, improper actions consume time, deflect energy from other tasks, and require additional resources later to rectify. Lots of activity does not mean that desired results will occur.

Myth 2: *Efficient workers are effective.* Speed is valuable, but not if it leads to errors or if there is nothing to do once a job is completed. By accentuating task completion, we give more weight to the process than to the results. Efficiency focuses on the use of resources needed to complete a task. Effectiveness assures that the completed tasks are done correctly. One does not assure the other. Since the output of one employee's job often becomes the input for another's, the role of management is to assure that the work flow is smooth, predictable, and appropriately timed. Finishing too early can actually cause other problems.

Myth 3: *If I want the job done right, I have to do it myself.* The myth is that others are not able, capable, available, or willing to do the work. Thus, this can actually become a self-fulfilling prophesy. As long as a manager keeps doing the work, delegation to others is impossible. So who gets to do the job the next time? The same manager—while the halls echo with the refrain, "If I want the job done . . ." The assumption of managerial omnipotence stands firmly in the way of change. Potential consequences of this managerial approach include high stress, burnout and myopic perspectives.

Myth 4: *The harder you work, the more you will get done.* Hard work obviously has important payoffs. But, like an elastic band, if pulled too hard it will snap. And by the same logic, if pushed too hard or too long, employees will burn out. It is important to distinguish between hard work and successful engagement. A related issue lies in the collusion between supervisors and staff to always "look busy." Every successful manager knows that there are peak periods and slower times. If we perpetuate the myth that the entire system works at peak speed all the time, the culture will eventually revolt.

Myth 5: *A stitch in time saves nine.* This homily is so widely known that it warrants special attention in the Mythology Hall of Fame. Evidence supports the idea that an hour of planning can save two of misdirected work. But it has to be the right stitch, with matching thread. Often, system maintenance activities fall into this category. It is easier to delay a repair job than to schedule one now, because "we are too busy." or "that report needs to get out by the holidays." Then when the machine breaks down, the entire process comes to a halt.

Myth 6: *There is always a shortage of time.* Assume that no one has all the time needed to do all they want as perfectly as they would like. The illusion is that there is not enough time. The reality is more likely to be mismanagement of available time. We all become victims of our own choices. At some level, we want to be busy—and be seen that way by others—as a justification for our job. Often this comes out in the organizational axiom, "Never go home before the boss."

Myth 7: *An open door policy improves communication.* Perhaps the open door does say that management is accessible. But in other instances, it tells employees that their supervisor expects them to check all decisions before implementation. And when will managers have time to do their own jobs? It is important that managers who keep the door open be in the office. If supervisors are preoccupied, then the open door does not work for anyone.

MANAGING TIME EFFECTIVELY

Whether internally developed or externally imposed, time wasters are indeed a fact of work life. Even successful managers have learned to cope with them. There is no single, agreed-upon method to manage time effectively in every instance. But the following principles have a proven track record. They will help overcome Murphy's Law, a variation of which postulates that "everything takes longer than you think." It doesn't have to be that way. Here are 10 ways to respond to the challenge of becoming an effective manager of your own time.

1. *Know where your time goes.* Most of us feel tired at the end of a busy day at work, but we often think, "Gee, what did I really get done today?" This classic symptom often reflects action without planning. Self-awareness is the first step toward change; try keeping a weekly log of your activities, using the following questions as a guide:

- With whom did you meet?
- What was the purpose?
- Who called the meeting?
- What was accomplished?
- How much time were you on the telephone?
- What memos did you write?
- How much reading time was devoted to junk mail?

2. *Do important tasks first.* This sounds easier than it is in practice. Most managers know the importance of planning in order to chart a course of action for the following quarter or year. Yet this same practice does not always carry over to their own daily activities, though it should. Doing too many things at once is a characteristic result of having no priorities. Some habits are difficult to break. When managers engage in light conversation with staff for the first 30 minutes of an 8 AM workday over that bottomless cup of coffee, their message is that work functionally begins at 8:30 AM. But the psychic risks of change may preclude some managers from seeing that their rigidity means that important meetings cannot occur at 8 AM—because people want to catch up with the boss.

3. *Schedule open time.* Subordinates require access to their imme-diate supervisors. Yet these occasions do not have to be on de-mand. Try open hours. This differs from the open door policy; it is a time for walk-in conversations that can be focused or unfocused. There are corporate presidents who have such systems in place. Any employee can see the president for 15 minutes; it forces the visitor to be of clear mind on the purpose of the visit.

Another option for managers lies in alternative or creative sched-uling. Instead of the traditional 30- or 60-minute meeting, try using 20- or 45-minute time blocks instead. The shorter time period will not harm the effectiveness of the conversations; in fact, it should sharpen it. And, it frees time for other things.

4. *Use available technologies.* If you are not available, there are numerous options. In addition to the standard request to "send me a note about that," ask others to leave you a voice mail message. If E-mail is available, give out your address. Thoughtful replies can be composed at your convenience. Written memos provide excellent documentation, but consume vast amounts of time. And, unfortunately, they often cry out for a formal reply . . . thus creat-ing two memos. Perhaps a quick discussion (while standing) can solve a problem or convey the needed information.

5. *Be phone smart.* The telephone warrants special attention, of course. Even with speed dialing, this instrument is cited by most managers as the source of many problems. The cornerstone of organizational communications, it is also a primary time waster. Few managers take (or make) the time to understand how they use and misuse Alexander Graham Bell's invention. Yet imagine the paradox of expecting a secretary to accomplish assignments on time when the telephone rings constantly! Man-agers need to become comfortable saying that they only have a few minutes before another appointment; this will help the caller stay focused on the topic at hand. And many managers are sur-prised when they review their own telephone logs. "Gee, I never realized that I spent so much time on the telephone!" Was it worth the investment?

6. *Plan effectively.* Remember the axioms, "An hour of planning saves two of execution" and "If you fail to plan, you plan to fail." If they start with the notion that they will never have all the infor-mation that is available on any topic, managers can suffer from

"paralysis by analysis." Others view this as a liberating message—
that at some point a decision can be made and implemented. A
related proposition is that managers must learn to accept that some
things cannot be changed. This will allow them to put their time
and attention elsewhere.

7. *Delegate appropriately.* Managers often find themselves over-
whelmed with routine tasks; this is the classic sign of a failure to
delegate responsibility and authority to competent subordinates.
Returning from vacation provides an excellent opportunity to see
how effectively responsibilities are delegated. If it takes three days
to go through the accumulated items, that should be a clear signal
to learn to delegate more effectively. In order to be an effective
delegator, it may be necessary to share more information than in
the past. Subordinates must also be given the freedom to fail, as
long as they learn from their errors. This allows managers to make
more effective use of their own time.

8. *Focus on results.* Managers have a tendency to focus on what
needs to be done—the activities of daily work life. An alternative
way of thinking stresses the results to be achieved. In addition to
facilitating appropriate delegation, it changes the manager's role
from control agent to negotiator. Sound human resource principles
stress empowering employees to meet their potential. If accepted,
this concept encourages managers to hold subordinates accountable for *what* they accomplish, not just *how* they work. Emphasiz-
ing results provides an important solution to the time crunch. Getting stuck in operational details may contribute to this problem.
There are many issues that attract the supervisors' attention. Some
shouldn't. Thus, it is important to state goals and expectations in
clear, measurable terms that relate to outcomes, not just processes
and procedures. Otherwise, managers will spend time on low-
priority items while critical tasks mount up.

9. *Have alternatives.* When an unplanned block of "free" time
opens up, managers are relieved but have few alternatives at the
ready. Create them. Sometimes it is helpful to have something to
read in case you are held up by unforeseen events, such as having
to wait for the boss!

10. *Take your vacations.* Some managers fear long vacations because they are all but certain that things will fall apart without
them. Perhaps they will, but there is a significantly greater chance

that managers who do not take time for themselves (and their families) will eventually burn out. Job stress is real. Responding with hard work may indeed be valued by the company, but it is important to remember that managers are supposed to be there for the marathon, not the short dash.

CONCLUSION

"Time is what we want most, but alas, we use worst."

William Penn

"All my possessions for a moment of time."

Queen Elizabeth I

"Either you manage time or it manages you."

Unknown

These sayings remind us that the struggle to use time effectively has been with us for centuries, yet solutions remain elusive. This chapter defines several strategies that can help managers model effective time management skills. If only they had the time to read it!

Roger A. Ritvo

Roger A. Ritvo, PhD, is dean and professor of health management and policy at the School of Health and Human Services of the University of New Hampshire. His educational background includes a PhD in organizational behavior and development from Case Western Reserve University and an MBA in health services administration from George Washington University.

Previous academic positions include serving as visiting scholar at Sheffield University in England, visiting professor at American University, and assistant dean for 10 years at Case Western Reserve University. He was founding director of the graduate program in health administration at Cleveland State University.

Dr. Ritvo has served on numerous boards of directors, including the NTL Institute; Health and Human Services, Inc. (a Catholic multihospital system); the Cleveland Arthritis Foundation; and his temple. As a consultant, his services have been used by public and private organizations in the health, human service, and corporate sectors.

Professor Ritvo's many honors include serving as a government fellow of the American Council on Education, collaborating as a World Health Organization research fellow in Denmark, serving as senior health policy adviser to two Secretaries of the United States Department of Health and Human Services; and chairing the Health Care Advisory Task Force of the Ohio state senate. He received the Outstanding Administrator award from the student government at the University of New Hampshire in 1992.

Chapter Thirteen

Human Dimensions of Budgeting

Srinivasan Umapathy

Executive Summary

In this chapter, Srinivasan Umapathy discusses a range of behaviors common to most organizations engaged in annual budget formulation processes. In the genre of Aaron Wildavsky's *Politics of the Budgetary Process*, Umapathy observes that despite various opportunities to collaborate for the good of the whole organization, budgeting often leads to such things as departments trying to put down other departments based on a desire to increase their own share during resource allocation. Umapathy observes that budgeting is frequently perceived as a win-lose proposition in which one department's win is another department's loss. He details several behavioral causes for these maladies.

He argues that budgeting is carried out in the context of win-lose expectations. While competition among managers could motivate them to increase their effectiveness and efficiency, it may be undesirable while allocating resources among *interdependent* organizational units. This is based upon the realization that collaboration and win-win strategies are inappropriate when one department's gain is another's loss, a zero-sum game that gives rise to competition, not collaboration. Instead of encouraging openness and trust among different parts of an organization, budgeting often encourages managers to play such budget games as overestimating revenues.

Managers overestimate revenues because they receive the message, sometimes directly but more often indirectly, that penalties are qualitatively and quantitatively more intense than rewards. Managers reduce their budgeted profit goals so that the chances of failure are minimized. Taken together, these behaviors and others further embed an organizational norm of distrust. Lack of trust across functions and hierarchical levels, argues Umapathy, frequently leads to cynicism and decreased morale.

From organizational budget behaviors, the author moves to a discussion on how to create an appropriate organizational climate for budgeting. He suggests six important components: (1) recognize the need for change, (2) build trust, (3) create and maintain clear channels of communication, (4) invest in improving budgetary controls, (5) build in periodic checks in the process, and (6) remember that budgets are means and not ends.

This chapter illuminates budgeting in nontraditional ways. That is, once one moves away from the often rational or logical discussions of the process, budgeting becomes an organizational practice steeped in behavioral dynamics. As such, familiar themes from this volume assert themselves. As we move toward the 21st century, managers will find fewer and fewer rewards associated with the problematic dynamics Umapathy discusses so well. Taken together, they inevitably lead to organizational ineffectiveness.

B udgeting is one of the oldest and most widely used management tools. Practically all organizations have a budgetary process, and most of them review budget-related performance at least once every quarter. Educational programs such as finance for nonfinancial managers are in great demand in both for-profit and not-for-profit organizations. Budgeting aids, including computer programs for preparing budgets and numerous books, are readily available. Under these conditions, one would expect budgeting to be practiced as a scientific tool that has been perfected, or at least as a refined craft. However, the following quotes suggest that our learning has been rather limited.

- "I was shocked to find that budgeting, as practiced by managers, is very different from what is mentioned in budgeting texts. It is not as rational and left-brain-oriented as I thought." (A financial analyst in her first year after receiving an MBA degree)
- "I am sick and tired of the budget games played by managers in my organization. My boss is expected to and will cut at least 10 percent from the requests made by his subordinates. I must collude with my boss and the system by asking for more than I need. If I do not spend all my

money, my budget is likely to be cut next year. I cannot be honest if I want to survive the budgetary controls." (A disillusioned department head with 10 years' seniority)

- "Companies that hire me as a consultant expect me to improve their budgetary controls by a mere revision of their budget request format. They think I am money hungry if I suggest that a more comprehensive solution based on a thorough needs assessment is warranted. It is extremely difficult to demonstrate to them that they have been looking at the tip of the iceberg." (A consultant who understands both the procedural and the behavioral dimensions of budgeting)

The next section identifies specific areas in which there is a gap between the intentions of the budgetary processes and the actual practices found in organizations. The causes of these gaps are also discussed.

BUDGETING: INTENTIONS, ACTUAL PRACTICES, AND CAUSES

Budgeting is designed to be an *integrative* tool. The annual budgetary process brings together different hierarchical levels, functions, product lines or divisions, and geographic areas. Managers, both those who focus on the long-term strategic direction and those who direct day-to-day activities, have the opportunity to work together during budgeting. Different parts of an organization are supposed to give up their local language (e.g., the number of widgets manufactured by a plant) and talk the financial language of revenues, expenses, assets, and equities. Despite these opportunities to collaborate for the good of the whole organization, budgeting often leads to disruptive processes, such as one department trying to put down another with an eye toward increasing its share during resource allocation. Competing organizational units perceive budgeting to be a win-lose proposition in which one department's win is another department's loss.

Causes: Budgeting is carried out in the context of win-lose expectations. Although competition among managers could motivate them to increase their effectiveness and efficiency, it may be undesirable when allocating resources among interdependent organizational units. By creating a scenario in which one department's gain is another department's loss, the departments are encouraged to compete, not collaborate.

Instead of *encouraging openness and trust* across different parts of an organization, budgeting often encourages managers to play budget games such as overestimating revenues to obtain a higher authorized head count. Lack of trust, across both functions and hierarchical levels, frequently leads to cynicism and decreased morale.

Causes: Managers often receive the message that penalties are quantitatively and qualitatively more intense than rewards (e.g., being fired for poor performance against project goals versus receiving a 10 percent bonus for excellent performance). This scenario encourages the manager to reduce the budget goal so that the chances of failure are minimized. Only naive managers believe that it is safe to be open and trusting during the budgetary process.

Although managers recognize that budgeting offers an opportunity to *improve communication*, managers intentionally create or increase communication barriers, by using their functional or technological jargon or other means, to preserve independence.

Causes: It is frequently assumed that subordinate managers clearly understand how budget data will be used. This is usually not true. Managers have either experienced or heard about situations in which decisions were made, and only later were supporting data obtained to justify the decision. They have more bargaining power and less vulnerability if they do not share complete budget information.

Budgeting can be used to *better manage risks and improve the financial performance* of some or all parts of an organization by enabling managers to conduct what-if analyses during budgeting to assess the likely impacts of alternative decisions. In reality, very few managers effectively manage risks.

Causes: Although the organizational green light may encourage risk taking, the red light is also on. It asks managers to come up with budgets that do not lead to "problems." The ambiguity of these internal messages leads to a low level of risk taking, not the intended message of calculated risk taking.

Budgeting is intended to be a *rational, equitable, and objective process*, especially during the process of allocating discretionary resources such as for product development, capital equipment, and advertising. In practice, the "richer" and better-performing parts of an organization usually receive a greater share of the discretionary resources and achieve additional improvements in their performance, while those units with poorer results find that they cannot get sufficient resources to effect a turnaround in their performance.

Causes: In reality, managers at all levels have some biases and prefer to bet on the horse with a better track record than on the horse with a poor or no track record but with much potential for improvement. Managers also find that despite sophisticated financial information systems, budgeting is not a purely rational process and that it is de facto a political process.

Although budgeting is meant to *develop realistic goals,* both superiors and subordinates collude and attempt to influence each other by giving misleading or incorrect information on goals.

Causes: Managers try to use budgetary goals for inappropriate purposes and may sometimes use budgets for purposes they were not designed for. For example, budgetary targets for motivational uses should be challenging, slightly beyond the reach of the manager, yet achievable. However, if that same budget is used for coordination purposes, which require precise information, budgetary effectiveness will decrease.

Budgeting, if correctly practiced, should lead to *more clarity about goals and how to achieve them,* and in turn *decrease managerial stress.* In most organizations, however, achievement of budgetary goals does not reflect optimal performance, and managers experience considerable budget-related stress.

Causes: Managers know, but seldom acknowledge openly, that they do not always establish optimal budgetary goals. To justify using a suboptimal goal in performance evaluation, they try to include subjective factors in the performance review process. This creates ambiguity and stress for the subordinate, as well as considerable pressure for the superior in trying to package subjective assessments so that they look like rational and objective decisions. In addition to managerial stress, goals often lose their credibility, and the achievement of budgetary goals is frequently not equivalent to optimal performance.

Budgeting is designed to foster *creativity* and to encourage managers to think about *new strategic directions, including paradigm shifts* or new ways of defining and doing their business. However, managers direct their creative energies toward a budget that they can achieve, not the one that would be optimal for their organization.

Causes: Managers have learned to believe that there is no need to fix something that is not broken. Playing it safe and not venturing in new directions are courses preferred by most managers.

Budgeting is designed to take place in a *healthy organizational climate*, and the budgetary process is supposed to improve the health of the organization. Senior managers are often shocked to discover serious issues that confirm organizational illnesses, such as a division manager intentionally furnishing inaccurate data to the corporate managers.

Causes: The concept of preventive maintenance is often ignored. Human systems probably need more preventive maintenance than do mechanical systems, since budgeting creates a stressful period for most managers. Creating the right organizational climate must be done before a crunch period, not after. Managers must use team building and organizational climate setting approaches before they start the planning and budgeting activities. They must also schedule some review time at the end of each budget cycle to identify what was helpful as well as how they can improve the budgetary process in the future. These conscious efforts to learn should contribute to increasing the commitment of managers to use budgets for their intended purposes, and should in turn lead to improved performance.

HOW TO CREATE AN APPROPRIATE ORGANIZATIONAL CLIMATE FOR BUDGETING

In order to reap the full benefits of a good budgetary process, it is important to develop an environment of openness and trust. The following six steps are recommended to improve the quality of budgeting in any organization.

1. *Recognize the need for change.* Unless managers recognize the importance of organizational climate on budgeting, it will be difficult to improve the quality of budgeting.
2. *Build trust.* In order to improve the credibility of budgetary targets, efforts must be undertaken to improve trust among managers. Team building programs for budget participants is one way of improving trust among managers.
3. *Create and maintain clear channels of communication.* Clear communication channels are essential for permitting undistorted communication within and across organizational subunits. Obtaining a consensus for upgrading budgetary controls is a prerequisite for its success.
4. *Invest in improving the budgetary controls.* In order to improve budgetary controls, managers must invest adequate time and effort to improve the quality of information at each stage of the budgetary process.
5. *Build in periodic checks in process.* Benefits of trust and team building processes do not last forever. Adequate attention must be paid to trust level before every major change in budgetary controls. Interdependent organizational units must be given some common goals to promote teamwork and cooperation.
6. *Remember that budgets are the means, not the end.* A well-prepared budget will not be effective unless it is used properly. Managers must learn the arts of preparing and using budgets effectively. Budgets serve as the basis for comparing actual with budget figures and for initiating a discussion to better understand what was managed well and identify specific areas of improvement. Instead, if the budget is used or perceived to be used to point fingers at others, or if its data are selectively used to justify decisions that have already been made, it will lead to ineffective budgeting and will simultaneously pollute the organizational climate.

WHAT SHOULD MANAGERS DO?

Each level of management has specific responsibilities that can improve budgetary effectiveness.

- *Senior managers.* Senior managers must accept the responsibility for managing the organizational climate. They should also give middle and lower-level managers the license to take calculated risks. Senior managers should periodically monitor incentives and compensation plans to verify that they lead to goal achievement. Senior managers must also ensure that budgetary goals are not only perceived as fair, but also function as clear signals of organizational priorities and offer challenging yet achievable targets. The senior management's role is vital since it builds the foundation on which the other components of budgets rest.
- *Middle Managers.* Middle managers supervise managers with budget responsibilities; they report to senior management and implement senior management's decisions, including budgetary goals and priorities. Signals given by middle managers to their subordinates must be consistent with those sent by senior managers to middle managers. Unless middle managers keep their lines communication open, both upward and downward, they cannot implement budgets effectively. Middle managers must also ensure that the specific budgeting use selected by top management is the one they emphasize. Middle managers should also monitor the process and take corrective action to keep the budgetary process in the planned direction. Inappropriate decisions made by senior managers should be identified by middle managers, who should take them back to senior managers, preferably before implementing them. It is important that senior managers respect and trust middle managers and vice versa.
- *Operational Managers.* These managers have responsibility for specific components of operational budgets. Operational managers and middle managers are both responsible for ensuring that budgetary goals are clear and fair. Operational managers should operate in a climate in which it is considered desirable that they question and challenge inappropriate decisions made by senior managers. If operational managers feel stress, then their subordinates are likely to experience the stress, too. Operational managers play a significant role in creating and maintaining the organizational climate desired by senior managers. If operational managers know how they contribute to organizational goals, they will be better motivated and more effective.

CONCLUSION

Most organizations are not realizing the full potential of their budgetary controls. This chapter identifies specific gaps between budgetary intentions and actual practices, their causes, and suggestions for improvement. It makes clear that the human dimensions of budgeting are significantly more important than the technical dimensions (such as database parameters or spreadsheet software used). Managers must recognize that **budgeting is a self-fulfilling prophecy:** If they believe in budgets and if they invest adequate time in budgeting (including time for climate setting and review), they will find that it works well and yields rich dividends. On the other hand, if they believe that budgets constitute a waste of time and if they do not devote adequate time to budgeting, they will find that budgeting does not help them. The choice to believe in budgeting is easy and rational, but the commitment needed to implement it is not equally easy.

Srinivasan Umapathy

Srinivasan Umapathy, DBA, is the founder and president of Andover Consulting and Training Group. He worked for four years as an internal consultant with Tata Engineering and Locomotive Company Ltd. and taught for seven years at Boston University School of Management and for three years at Babson College. He holds an undergraduate degree in mechanical engineering from Indian Institute of Technology and a doctorate in business administration from Harvard Business School. He specializes in integrating organizational development approaches into planning and budgeting processes and serves as a consultant on strategy formulation and implementation for proactively managing change and diversity. He serves on the board of directors of the NTL Institute.

Chapter Fourteen

Using Consultants Effectively

Miriam M. Ritvo

William LeClere

Executive Summary

Mikki Ritvo and William LeClere capture the key elements of the client/consultant relationship in this chapter, from the perspective of the client. The basic thinking and assertions contained in this chapter will likely assume greater importance in the years ahead. The reason? Part of the paradigm shift occurring in all of the more industrialized world is embodied in the logo of our time: Doing more with less.

Where a permanent staff has traditionally been in place in organizations to address a full range of internal issues (at times with consultation assistance), the new, still emerging reality will command more and more use of consultants. Streamlined structures require effective, often short-term consultation to assist in the resolution of existing problems and to develop new problem-solving capabilities in the organization. The consultation will phase out once these objectives have been met.

Toward these ends, control and autonomy are at the core of the consultant-client interaction. Effective consultants stimulate autonomy and growth for the client rather than long-term dependency. The authors argue that the effective process of consultation moves from relatively high structure and direction to a lower and lower structure imposed by the consultant, with increasing responsibilities assumed by the client system.

The point, of course, is that a consultation that increases client dependency engenders minimal technology transfer to the organization. From this perspective, it runs counter to the wisdom embedded in the "more with less" logo. Expert consultants may thus provide enormous assistance to an organization's system and create long-term dependency on their services. From the perspective of the consultant, this may well be a significant marketing outcome. From that of the client, however, it may conflict with autonomy. The authors discuss six stages of the client-consultant relationship.

This chapter's importance lies in its focus on the client and in the helpful direction it provides in making the best use of this kind of assistance, either from within, or outside the organization. Additionally, Ritvo and LeClere's discussion of the transactional nature of consultation and its provision of strength through shared expertise is of great importance to clients.

W hile the role of the consultant has been explored and described extensively in the literature, there has been little analysis of the role, rights, and responsibilities of the manager-as-client in such helping relationships. This discussion is relevant to most models of consultant-client contracts. Some consultants are full-time internal employees. Others are external, hired for a limited time or a specific project. Occasionally there is an inside-outside team. We do not warn, "Let the buyer [client] beware"; rather, and more creatively, we urge: "Let the buyer be *informed.*" This chapter examines the business, methods, and process of consultation from the *client's* point of view. It will help managers be more effective clients when using consultants.

What qualities and qualifications can a client expect from a consultant, beyond technical competencies and reputation? It would be wise for a client to find out—by asking questions and using references and experience—whether the practitioner understands and can creatively deal with diversity in a multicultural work environment. The workplace of the 1990s is increasingly a pluralistic mosaic of varied ethnic backgrounds, cultural perspectives, and geographic and political orientations.

In most organizations, whether public or private, corporate or nonprofit, large or small, manufacturing or service, employees bring to the jobs their differences in lifestyle, age, health, values, and beliefs. Whatever organizational problems exist, the consultant will be working with the client to effect and manage change in a complex economic, social, and political environment. Clients will make more enlightened decisions if they are assured that the consultant is sensitive to the basic values and differences within the workplace. The consultant must be skilled at working with the powerful, complex forces that emerge from this heterogeneous workforce.

Issues of *control* and *autonomy* lie at the core of the consultant-client interaction. How do consultants stimulate autonomy and growth for the client? In the traditional or "expert" model, consultants provide direction, suggestions, opinions, and strategies *to* the client. Both the literature and experience suggest that such relationships often result in dependency, resistance, or counterproductive behavior on the part of the client. In this highly directive, one-way, consultant-to-client transaction, there is little room for the client or client group to develop intervention skills or to increase its problem-solving skills.

When a consultant is considered for a job, the client often states goals in organizational solutions: "I need help in solving a specific conflict." A parallel goal should be to integrate the client's own needs for professional growth in the contract; the contract would be improved if those expectations were stated explicitly: "We need to learn how to manage conflict productively."

We take the position that effective consultants strive to empower their clients. In order to accomplish this result, clients must be aware of their roles, rights, responsibilities, and boundaries. This chapter provides practical guidelines to enable clients to manage such relationships most profitably. Over time, the relationship will develop an appropriate and functional balance of dependence, interdependence, and independence.

STAGES OF THE CONSULTING RELATIONSHIP

The following stages mirror many of the models previously suggested in the literature and describing the evolution of the relationship from the consultant's perspective. If the client follows this model, the client-consultant relationship will be mutually enhanced.

Stage One: Entry

In the beginning, both the client and the consultant "scout each other out," exploring mutual interests, values, fit, and the interpersonal chemistry needed for a productive relationship. The client should seek information about both the content expertise of the consultant (the *what*) and the process approach the consultant uses (the *how*). Clients must be open to the consultant's history, ideas, values, visions, and capabilities before making a final decision to hire. This is often referred to as a "psychological contract."

At this stage, the potential consultant is interested in the client's priorities and the process of goal formation. Therefore, it is appropriate for the client to probe for information about how the consultant proposes to approach the assignment. The client asks for descriptions of how the consultant has handled similar situations in the past. The consultant asks myriad questions to engage in a "situation review"; this is part of the initial diagnosis.

Entry should be viewed by both the client and the consultant as tentative, with either party free to decline further discussion amicably. If the client believes there may be a fit, it is appropriate to ask for written documentation of the consultant's approach, either in the form of existing papers or in a brief description summarizing these early discussions. In some instances, the client may ask the consultant to submit a full, written proposal. In other situations, the client may decide not to use this practitioner and should say so as soon as possible, in the best interests of both parties.

Stage Two: Contracting

Assuming the process continues, it is important to reaffirm mutual expectations, goals, priorities, responsibilities, actions, products to be delivered, and norms for working together. These elements of the client-consultant agreement are best documented in writing, first in an informal proposal prepared by the consultant (which is discussed and modified as necessary by both parties), and then finalized in writing. Clients often need one of the following types of contractual relationships:.

1. *The expert.* Consultant provides the answers.
2. *The pair of hands.* Consultant implements specified tasks.
3. *The collaborator.* Consultant collaborates with the client on a project, with each party taking the lead as appropriate in various situations.

One right the client has is to decide to engage an expert consultant and to remain dependent on that consultant throughout the engagement. This could result in excellent diagnosis and analysis and the rendering of outstanding direction and suggestions from the consultant. However, it seems that in recent years more clients wish to engage consultants in a transactional arrangement, one that strengthens the client through shared expertise.

In complex projects, the client should prepare a set of guidelines and expected results to inform the consultant's proposals. If the client seeks competitive bidding from several consultants, written terms should be provided to all prospective bidders. Understandably, clients are often reluctant to reveal their available budget for a given project. Since they know the pressures and constraints of the system, it can be mutually beneficial for the consultants to have a sense of the financial resources prior to proposal writing. The client can indicate an acceptable daily rate or a range of high and low budget figures.[1] Clients must clearly communicate the compensation and the billing process. Expect adjustments for new, emerging situations.

To develop a contract, the following questions may be asked:

1. *Who is the client?* In many client-consultant engagements, there is more than one client in the organization. One may be responsible for the financial aspects of the project; others may be responsible for the technical aspects; still others are recipients or "users" of the consultant's services. A client may be an individual, a group, a department, or a subsystem. The person doing the initial interviewing at entry may not be the key client or may be one of several clients. These issues need to be thoroughly defined and clearly understood.

2. *What are the boundaries?* Client-consultant relationships are temporary and time-bound, and often function apart from internal systems. It is the consultant's responsibility to ask, and the client's obligation to clarify, what these boundaries are.

3. *How much flexibility do we have?* Few contracts evolve precisely as anticipated. It is important to clarify, up front, what flexibility exists with regard to scope, budget, time frame, and sometimes even the focus of the planned intervention.

4. *What are the client's rights?* In addition to agreeing on mutual responsibilities between client and consultant, clients should clar-

ify in the beginning what they reserve as their fundamental rights in the process. For example, clients have the right to reject ideas proposed by the consultant and to give feedback when they think an action is inappropriate or not going as planned, when the consultant seems to be insensitive to or misses a "happening," or when they feel any dissatisfaction with the process. In addition, it is the client's responsibility to enforce organizational boundaries and to expect the ongoing transfer of skills and knowledge from the consultant. Consulting interventions may include intellectual properties such as software, copyrighted materials, or other products. It should be made clear during the contracting stage which of these properties will be made transferable and under what conditions, and which will be retained by the consultant. "Who owns the data?" should be decided before the data are collected.

The more clearly these issues can be raised, the more productive the relationship is likely to become. Either the client or the consultant may become impatient about the time required to clarify these concerns in the contracting stage, but bypassing such questions will have negative consequences later.

Stage Three: Diagnosis

In most client-consultant assignments, there is a need to gather data to develop valid information as a basis for diagnosis. The client needs to remember the principle that the people closest to the work and action are excellent resources for information. They are the experts on what affects their activities. The client and the consultant will determine what data are needed, the domains to examine, the collection methods, how the data will be analyzed, the uses of the data, and its ownership and confidentiality. These issues are discussed further in this section.

Some clients, like some consultants, have a propensity to gather more data than are needed in a given situation. (We can err on the other side as well.) This leads to problems. It is annoying to those from whom and for whom we solicit information. It can be overwhelming and confusing when we attempt to analyze it, possibly compromising the credibility of the project. "Drowning in data" can be terminal! It is important that the client work closely with the consultant to ensure that the scope of the data gathered is functional and relevant. Even if this issue was addressed during the first two stages of the relationship, it should be re-visited and reconsidered once data collection starts.

When organizational data are being analyzed, it is preferable that the client have an active role in the analysis and interpretation. Many consultants suggest an internal task force to collaborate in this phase. This generates a sense of ownership of the data among the participants.

The client and consultant should work closely to decide on methods for gathering the data, who will gather the data, and from what sample of respondents the data will be gathered. Interviews; questionnaires; observation; and examination of policies, reports, records, minutes of meetings, or surveys are common methods used in organizational consulting. The norms about confidentiality are addressed at this stage. Both parties must share the same ground rules about sensitive information. The client can expect the practitioner to offer expertise on these issues. There are a variety of ways in which data can be collected, coded, and made available for analysis with appropriate attention paid to confidentiality issues.

The confidentiality issue can become difficult. This is particularly true if the respondents in the client organization reveal data that might be viewed as critical of top management, or that might even be potentially dangerous if made known to competitors in the marketplace. If the client worries about any possible revelation or leakage, either internally or externally, it is best addressed and dealt with at the contracting stage and at any time the concern is expressed.

Stage Four: Taking Action

Planned action can take many forms. It often includes a feedback meeting with the target client groups. These sessions, some in the form of a seminar or retreat, need to be carefully planned and designed. It must be determined who should lead or facilitate the session, who should attend, and what actions are expected as a result of the feedback. The feedback documents are loaned for client use during the meeting and collected and saved by the consultant at the end (such information might accidentally get loose in an organization). Usually the consultant will design, organize, and facilitate the feedback meeting. Out of feedback sessions may come action groups that focus on team development, strategic planning, organizational design and redesign activities, and new ways of looking at old problems.

The feedback session may be a single session or a series of events. It is desirable to have an off-site retreat for one or several days. The investment of time and personnel is central to any contemplated organizational change. We assume that the explicit goals of the engagement will include moving the organization toward a more participative system, dealing with interdisciplinary, cross-organizational issues to improve effectiveness, and moving toward enabling and empowering people.

At the end of the feedback meeting, we suggest a *reality panel* composed of a selected cross section of the larger client organization to test the feedback, tentative conclusions, and to reality-test the action plans that subgroups have designed and recommended. The panel keeps a focus on what is doable and what needs further work. This step helps test the data analysis and emerging conclusions in a small group before going public with a larger organizational audience.

Stage Five: Evaluation

This stage is an ongoing process in which the client has a major role throughout the planned change project, not just at the end. Evaluation happens informally, whether the client or the consultant wish it or not. Consultants and members of the client organization often ask those involved in the engagement, "How's it going?" The client and the consultant will formalize this assessment process to track progress, measure the impact of the change efforts, and modify or correct them as indicated. Thus, ongoing evaluation continuously monitors change efforts. It may also be valuable to initiate feedback on the client-consultant relationship itself.

The client could have some firm ideas about how the evaluation stage will be formally approached, and perhaps even a clear set of success criteria by which to evaluate the intervention. This is another area in which it is appropriate for the client to expect the consultant to have more experience, skill, and knowledge about how and when to proceed. The client may have some imperatives about which criteria must be met if the planned change is to be considered successful by the company. These criteria, and a general approach to the evaluation, should be agreed upon during the entry and contracting stages of the project and modified by emerging events.

Stage Six: Phasing Out

Another issue that the client should raise during the entry and contracting stages is how the consultant intends to separate from or phase out of the organization at the end of the contract. Criteria met during the evaluation stage will signal the time for phasing out and when separation is helpful. As the collaboration ends, explicit discussion about skill and knowledge transfer will enhance the successful completion of this stage.

CHECKLIST

1. Be sure you can explain how your organization values differences in the workforce.
2. Learn how to effectively receive expert consultant services.
3. Develop skills to be a collaborator with your consultant.
4. Use consulting relationships for your professional development.
5. Make sure the psychological contract parallels the organizational contract.
6. Be willing to share *all* necessary information with the consultant.
7. Write a detailed, explicit contract summarizing your agreements about expectations, goals, responsibilities, technology, products, norms, and payment schedules and dates.
8. Clarify your role in data collection.
9. As appropriate, help the consultant deal with confidentiality.
10. Clarify your active role in the planning and implementation of the feedback process.
11. Plan appropriate celebrations and endings.

ENDNOTES

1. At the time of this writing, representative fees for organizational development consultants may range from $1,000 to $3,000 per day. Some charge by product or task, rather than strictly on a time basis; others bill by the day. Some may vary their fees for telephone consultations and for "shadow" consulting. Practitioners who are part of a firm will include in their fees overhead costs, including office expenses, research, and development.

Miriam M. Ritvo

Mikki Ritvo is a graduate of Smith College with advanced graduate work at Boston University and Harvard Medical School. She has been a member and a director of the NTL Institute, a college dean, a director of Certified Consultants International, a university professor, Special Deputy Commissioner of Education for Massachusetts, and the Massachusetts director of management and executive development. She serves as director of several corporations and is an organizational development consultant for companies in the public and private sectors, with a special emphasis on working with family-owned businesses. Recently, Mikki Ritvo was awarded the Smith College Medal of Achievement for "outstanding contributions to the field of applied behavioral sciences."

William LeClere

William LeClere specializes in large-systems change programs, management development, organizational development, team building, strategic planning, and the training of trainers. He is executive vice president of LMA, Inc. He has been a consultant to many parts of the federal government and was a senior consultant with the Sterling Institute and a vice-president of McBer and Company of Boston, Massachusetts. He completed his undergraduate work at Lehigh University and pursued graduate work at Columbia University and the University of Michigan, and was a member of the Distinguished Practitioner faculty of the Graduate School of Public Administration at the University of Southern California.

Chapter Fifteen

Staying Well during—and after—Stressful Periods

John D. Adams

Executive Summary

This chapter presents important information for managers who must first and foremost manage themselves. The most critical dimension of self-management is the management of stress. Adams lists a set of conditions that provides managers with an indication of their present stress-related health risks.

Failure to pay close attention to the factors discussed in this chapter may not only impact the quality of one's own work performance, it may endanger one's very survival. Nothing could be more basic and essential than this. Yet the factors discussed here are the very things that many managers tend to ignore or rationalize.

The more one experiences the listed conditions, the more one can assume that stress is a personal problem and a potential risk to one's health. Knowing the red flags Adams discusses is a basic step in effective stress management. "Their presence indicates that your stress levels are getting too high and that you either need to avoid some of the stress, cope with it more effectively, or build up your health to withstand it," he observes.

The implications of this chapter are obvious: In the remaining years of this century and beyond, managing begins with charity to oneself. In this context, staying well in the midst of stressful circumstances is charity of enormous consequence and importance to the individual manager and, by simple extension, to her or his organization.

T hose experiencing high personal stress will find three pieces of information useful. First, stress clearly is a risk factor associated with most adverse health changes. The more stress you experience during a given period of time, the more likely you are to become ill during the succeeding months. Second, during periods of high stress, most people do a *poorer* job of taking care of themselves than they do during periods of low stress. Third, over 50 percent of the risks associated with the leading causes of serious illness, including stress, involve lifestyle choices. This chapter explores these three points in detail and focuses on ways to respond to increased stress.

STRESS AND ILLNESS

Most illnesses do not have a single cause. Rather, they are caused by a multitude of factors that interact with each other in complex ways. Think of any given illness as an abstract puzzle in which each piece connects to every other piece.

Stress requires the body to make internal adjustments that are commonly called the "flight or fight" response. This response evolved during our very early history to help people handle the stressors of the day, which were usually challenges to survival. The modern problem of stress arises because most of the stressors we experience today (like marriage or divorce, or being laid off or reassigned) do *not* create problems of survival. Our bodies have not kept pace with "civilization," and thus they still respond to stress as they did many centuries ago. The problem arises when we have no way of using up this fight-or-flight preparedness. Obviously, neither punching the boss nor running out of the office screaming are suitable responses to stressful work situations. Therefore, the energy (adrenalin) available for that sort of response becomes bottled up inside. This can cause considerable tension within your body, commonly referred to as "strain."

Carrying around too much strain for a period of time increases one's risk of becoming ill. The illness one contracts depends on genetic makeup, personality, past health history, lifestyle habits, the environment, and even the nature and quality of past medical care. Some people develop headaches easily, while others develop high blood pressure, ulcers, colitis, or pain in the lower back.

Why do some people seem to become ill while others, who are

apparently experiencing just as much stress in life, seem unaffected? We do not yet know all the answers. Some people *do* have stronger constitutions than others. Many people protect themselves with good health habits; these are discussed later in this chapter. We have some indication that a good network of supportive relationships can protect your health during stressful periods. Also, it appears that you can withstand more stress without adverse effects if your work (and your life in general) contains sufficient *challenge*, allows you to *control* how you do things, and includes major activities to which you feel strongly *committed*.

Given this background, how do you know if you are a candidate for developing a stress-related illness? How can you tell how much stress is "getting to you"? While we have no precise way of knowing this, the following list of conditions will give you an indication of your present stress-related health risk. If you experience several of the conditions listed below, you may assume that stress presents a risk to your health. The more items you check off, the greater the risk.

- Feeling slow, sluggish, weak
- Tiring frequently and easily
- Rapid weight gain or loss
- Changes in eating patterns or amounts eaten
- Constipation or diarrhea
- Withdrawal from sex or overuse of sex
- Difficulty in concentrating; short attention span
- Smoking or drinking more than usual
- Sleep disruption
- Headaches
- Feeling nervous, apprehensive, anxious
- Feeling depressed, listless
- Being irritable and displaying misdirected anger
- Being cynical and displaying inappropriate humor
- Withdrawal from supportive relationships

You can usually recognize some of these conditions as being particularly characteristic of you from time to time. These are your "red flags." As a basic step in effective stress management, you should become sensitive to the occurrence of your red flag conditions. Their presence indicates that your stress levels are getting too high and that you either need to avoid some of the stress, cope with it more effectively, or build up your health to withstand it.

NATURAL STRESS-RESPONSE TENDENCIES

Unfortunately, when most people experience high levels of stress, they compound their problems by giving up their best defenses against the effects of stress. The strain conditions listed above become self-reinforcing and extend themselves even further in a self-destructive way, thus increasing the amount of stress.

For example, many people withdraw from their friends during periods of high stress. When the stress is alleviated, they "resurface" and speak, often to their friends' surprise, about what a rough period *they have just completed!* It is as if they feel they have to handle it themselves and not bother others, even if they know that effective use of supportive relationships is one of the best stress management techniques.

Many people allow their best nutritional habits to lapse and eat foods high in fat, sugar, and salt (i.e., highly refined or "junk" foods). At the same time, they drink and smoke more than they usually do (perhaps seeking an instant gratification to assuage their feelings of strain). These behaviors, of course, constitute additional risk factors on top of the risks associated with the stress itself.

LIFESTYLE CHOICES

An investigation of the risks associated with the most frequent major illnesses reveals that an average of 20 percent of the risk is biological, 20 percent environmental, and 10 percent attributable to health care services (drug interactions, etc.). This leaves 50 percent of the risk factors in the category called "lifestyle choices." Put another way, you can avoid or eliminate fully half of the risks to your health by making responsible lifestyle choices. The last word in long-term stress and health management is to control that which is controllable.

The following list contains most of the controllable risk factors that constitute lifestyle choices:

- Nutritional habits (the average American diet contains far too much fat, sugar, salt, chemicals, white flour, white rice, and caffeine)
- Alcohol use
- Tobacco use
- Drug use (including prescription drugs)
- Amount of rest
- Relaxation
- Exercise (aerobic, stretching, recreational)
- Body weight (percentage of fat composition)
- Psychological outlook (optimistic vs pessimistic)
- Quality of relationships
- Driving habits (speed, seatbelt use, attitude)
- Strain as a reflection of excessive stress
- Blood pressure
- Cholesterol and triglycerides

The inclusion of few, if any, of these items should surprise you. Yet most people do not score well when they assess their own practices. A recent study in California of seven good habits (no smoking, moderate drinking, sufficient sleep, recommended weight, balanced diet, regular breakfast, and regular exercise) found that 45-year-old men who practiced six or seven of the habits could expect to live 11.5 years longer than men of the same age who practiced fewer than four of these habits. The same comparison for 45-year-old women yielded a difference in life expectancy of 7.2 years. And for everyone, at all ages, the more of these seven habits practiced, the better one's day-to-day, overall health.

Take a few moments to assess the healthfulness of your present lifestyle choices. If you are currently away from home, perhaps attending a training program, are you maintaining your habits as well as you do at home? If you are a regular traveler, do you carry your lifestyle with you on the road, or do you use travel as an excuse to stop making healthy lifestyle choices?

PERSONAL PLANNING

If the preceding sections indicated that you have room for improvement in your present stress management and/or lifestyle habits, the following questions will help you get started on a more health-protective course:

1. How well am I avoiding unnecessary stressors (e.g., do I plan my time well? Do I try to stay away from certain people who seem to be stress carriers?)?
2. How well am I coping with the unavoidable stressors in my life (e.g., do I have needed conflict, influence, assertiveness, and problem-solving skills?)?
3. How well am I protecting and building my health (e.g., do I have healthful nutritional, exercise, relaxation, and relationship habits, and do I take an hour a day for myself?)?
4. What do I need to *stop* doing?
5. What do I need to *start* doing?
6. What do I need to *continue* doing?
7. Have I let my support network know what is going on with me? Are there specific ways in which those people can support me right now?

John D. Adams

John D. Adams, PhD, is an independent consultant with an international practice in organization development, serving a variety of clients including hospitals, research and development organizations, public utilities, industry, government agencies, and school systems. He also is an adjunct Associate Professor at Bowling Green State University in Ohio. Prior to becoming a full-time consultant, Dr. Adams was Director of the Professional Development Division at the NTL Institute for Applied Behavioral Sciences and a visiting professor at the University of Leeds (England). He has written numerous books and articles on these topics, including *Transition, New Technologies In O.D., O.D. in Health Care Organizations*, and *Understanding and Managing Stress*. Dr. Adams is a member of the NTL Institute, the American Psychological Association, the Association for Humanistic Psychology, and the Organization Development Network. He has served on the Board of Directors of Certified Consultants International and the Board of Governors of the Potomac Rugby Union.

Chapter Sixteen

Developing the Whole Person in Organizations

Arlene Scott
Sheldon Hughes

Executive Summary

Consider the following proposition: What if managers were uniformly able, through their own personal training and development, to help their staff tap into the energies and excitement stored *within themselves?* Because of this gift, let's say their subordinates became empowered to take risks; act as entrepreneurs and visionaries; and develop supportive, cooperative relationships with all relevant and appropriate functional interfaces. What is the payoff of all this in organizational terms?

Such an organization would typify, in behavioral terms, what Peter Senge calls the "core disciplines of the learning organization" in his *The Fifth Discipline.* When energy of this nature begins to generate in organizational subunits, what we have is the beginnings of true transformation: an organization magnificently equipped to deal with what we have come to call "chaos."

It is an organization that has taken on the form of an organism that is constantly learning, and hence changing on a number of levels simultaneously. Scott and Hughes, under the rubric of developing the whole person in organizations, provide some specific content that will help managers get to this place with their staffs. The key to getting there is the necessary expenditure of energy along four crucial dimensions: physical, mental, emotional, and spiritual. Specific ways in which we can all utilize the whole person at work are outlined.

Over the past decade, the organizational behavior literature has urged the development of organizations. Depending on the way they behave, they are able to cope with the enormous turbulence that is occurring and will continue to occur within their environments (see

Marshak, Chapter 5). The importance of this chapter resides in how to get there. Its perspective is that of the individual organizational participant working within his or her subunit. Arguably, managers who take these perhaps deceptively simple recommendations lightly do so at their own peril, and quite possibly the peril of their organizations, in the complex, clearly transformative years ahead!

T o operate effectively in an increasingly complex, competitive, and global environment, managers and workers must use all of their energies, resources, and talents. Managers must be able to help others utilize the full range of their *physical, mental, emotional,* and *spiritual* resources. This "whole person" approach to management is accomplished by tapping and making available the energies and strengths of these four interrelated levels of being. By helping employees access and use whole person energies for work, managers create the context for transforming both the self and the organization. Effective management and leadership encourage the enthusiasm, spirit, empowerment, creativity, and innovation that occurs when people tap the energies and excitement within themselves. They become empowered to take risks, act as entrepreneurs and visionaries, and develop supportive, cooperative relationships with coworkers, customers, and clients. This chapter describes the whole person model, with examples of interventions that can help integrate the organization and the individual.

HOW WE GOT STARTED USING THE WHOLE PERSON APPROACH

In team-building meetings and management-training programs, we routinely asked participants to talk about a peak moment of performance. We were surprised that most of the responses related to situations outside the business or work environment. Participants would talk about being the coach of a soccer team, leading a nonprofit organization's fund-raising effort, or creating trust and respect at home. These are not work or organizational examples. At first, we tried to find ways to break down the separation between work and nonwork behavior. Our rationale was that participants were already experiencing peak performance someplace in their lives and that their own well-being and the performance of their organizations would be enhanced by bringing more of themselves to work.

USING THE WHOLE PERSON APPROACH IN MANAGING

What is the whole person approach? Aliveness or fitness is the essence of whole person development, on all four levels: physical, emotional, mental, and spiritual. After explaining fitness at each level, a series of activities will be described that evoke the energies of these four levels. These activities (or others like them) may be useful to managers when tapping those human energies that support organizational goals.

Although many activities that tap whole person energies overlap the levels, the model is still a very useful framework for thinking about and implementing personal and organizational development.

Physical Level

When physically fit, people feel better about themselves and bring more energy and vitality to work. Physically fit managers are less susceptible to the deleterious effects of organizational stress and therefore are more healthy. During long meetings, for example, brief physical activities reenergize the body:

- Breathing
- Stretching
- Moving
- Aerobic walking
- Upbeat classical music

These energizers are useful throughout the day as people exhibit signs of tiredness and tension.

Emotional Level

Emotional aliveness releases the energies of the heart, which results in caring, bonding, and a sense of enthusiasm and fun. Emotional aliveness is one of the bases for the formation of work spirit.

Stimulating emotional aliveness and developing emotional fitness increase the ability to express oneself appropriately and to build relationships and networks. This results in stronger teams, caring, and cooperation. These qualities permeate high-performing systems, and all involve an awareness and appropriate expression of feelings.

Self-disclosure helps tap emotional energies. Possible activities include discussions on the following topics:

- What's important to you now at work?
- Describe a turning point in your career (one that was positive or painful) and its effects.
- Describe one success and one failure in trying to influence a boss or co-worker.
- What is your purpose in life and how are you living it at work?

Clearly, disclosure activities need to be related to individual, team, and organizational objectives. Positive self-disclosure builds interpersonal and team relationships.

Music and poetry are powerful forces for opening the heart energies and creating awareness of the feeling dimension of the whole person. Listening to soft music can evoke the natural bonding and caring that is the foundation for relationships. Poetry is useful in accessing a full range of energies.

Games and skits are fun ways to build group spirit. Having fun together is a key process for building excitement and enthusiasm. Not only do people get to know each other beyond the usual work roles, but playing together can also provide a natural environment for learning and practicing team skills.

Mental Level

The mental level contains the energies of analysis, synthesis, and creative imagination. Most people in organizations already have finely tuned analytical abilities. However, the emphasis is usually on "discrepancy analysis"—what's wrong—rather than an assessment of what's right. Identifying and celebrating success—what is working well and why—builds a powerful foundation for increasing effectiveness. Learning theory and individual experience teach us that knowing what we do right and studying positive models unleash focused energy for higher performance.

Make every effort to begin with success analysis and to encourage broad-based thinking. Some examples include:

- *Leadership.* Identify experiences in which you have been a successful leader.
- *Peak performance.* Describe situations and experiences in which you have been highly effective.
- *Positive models.* Who is already doing it now? What is already working the way we would like?

The use of creative imagination is a powerful influence for overcoming "stuckness" and inspiring goal-directed activity. Knowing what you want helps you get it. In the recent literature, there is an emphasis on the importance of creating an organizational (or a departmental) vision. Before you can play a key role in influencing this vision, however, you need to begin as an individual. What is your picture of a preferred future? Create the vision and use it as a starting point for a dialogue with others, shifting from your vision to a shared vision.

Spiritual Level

The spiritual level is defined by the need to relate to a larger whole beyond the self and the capacity for inner wisdom. Ask employees to talk about their own purposes and values and share yours as manager. Talk about problem definition in terms of the larger vision (usually implicit) you have for your organization. Purpose, mission, and values can be used as the context for problem-solving and decision-making meetings. Use myth to see problems in a larger perspective.

During meetings that focus on building team effectiveness, managers can use the whole person model as a rationale for:

- Climate setting
- Self-dialogue exercises for personal insight and rapport building

- Interventions to demonstrate the power of trust and teamwork
- Developing group vision to build the group dream

When managers feel "stuck," or constrained by organizational pressures, often it takes a major shift before that individual is ready to choose a preferred future—to determine what they want. A way out of this bind is for managers to see their situation in a larger perspective. At their best, stories and myth speak to the drama and complexity of human experience in the world. As managers listen to a story, they experience themselves as part of a larger story and see their situations in perspective. When managers feel stuck, it's not enough to ask them to analyze it and develop action plans. What helps is to experience their problems in a larger context; literally, to change their perspectives.

In conclusion, this model of the whole person can be used in the following ways:

- As a rationale for specific activities (such as physical energizers or the use of music)
- As a guide in the design of the meeting and programs in order to create a climate that activates the whole person

Using the whole person model and associated activities stimulates individual and group performance. Leading and managing successfully in these turbulent times demands that we make use of all the resources and energies available to us. The whole person model points to and legitimizes the use of a set of energies and abilities that lead to a higher level of individual and organizational development.

For the Manager: 12 Ways to Bring the Whole Person to Work

Tapping Physical Energies

1. Encourage humor and playfulness to reduce tension and to create a relaxed atmosphere.
2. Encourage people to utilize progressive relaxation.
3. Take time for frequent stretches during long meetings.

Tapping Emotional Energies

1. Practice self-disclosure, making time for discussion of what's important, both personally and professionally.
2. Give positive feedback and celebrate success, and make them consistent group practices.
3. Make team building a regular part of your management practice.

Tapping Mental Energies

1. Practice success analysis.
2. Create a shared vision, starting with your own picture and then inviting others to shape it.
3. Employ systemic thinking by looking at problems from the perspectives of all stakeholders.

Tapping Spiritual Energies

1. Define or refine together your purpose, mission, and core values; make decisions and structure work within that context.
2. Use ritual and storytelling to emphasize actions and behaviors that are in accord with your purpose and values.
3. Encourage the use of intuition and other processes that access the right as well as the left brain.

Arlene Scott

Arlene Scott, PhD, is principal of Scott Management Services and has provided consulting and training services designed to improve the management of organizational and human resources. Dr. Scott received her MA and PhD degrees in administration from New York University and is a member of National Training Laboratories and the Organization Development Network.

For over 20 years, Dr. Scott has worked on several large systems projects in which the overall goal was to create an organizational culture supporting peak performance. She has also participated as lead consultant responsible for developing human resource management systems to support TQM efforts. In these large-scale projects, training programs involving hundreds of executives and managers were developed and implemented in support of project goals.

Sheldon Hughes

Sheldon Hughes is an organization and management development consultant. He is a graduate of Princeton University and holds an MBA degree in management and organization behavior from New York University. He worked as an internal organizational development specialist with Bankers Trust Company for seven years, conducting companywide programs on the Blake managerial grid, management by objective, team building, intergroup conflict, performance appraisal, and job design. Since 1975, Sheldon Hughes has been an independent consultant; since 1987, he has been a partner with Hughes-Mattison Ltd. He has conducted seminars on consulting skills, motivation, human relations, time management, assertive management, and leadership development.

MANAGING DIVERSITY EFFECTIVELY

Chapter Seventeen

Meeting the Challenge of Managing Cultural Diversity

Octave V. Baker

Executive Summary

Diversity in organizations can be plotted on a 10-point scale to reflect those still stuck in affirmative action (points 1 to 3) to those have made major strides toward managing diversity, or multiculturalism (points 8 to 10). For those at the low end of the scale, affirmative action is a state or federal requirement but has no real impact on the corporation's bottom line. Because of this orientation, those other than Euro-American men are in reality quite ancillary. They are detached in any significant sense from the strategic thrust of the "real time" business culture of the organization.

On the other hand, organizational cultures that have moved from affirmative action to managing or valuing diversity have positioned themselves to take a competitive advantage in the unfolding economics of the 21st century. It is to these corporations that Octave Baker's piece addresses itself. Those mired in the compliance-driven rhetoric of affirmative action will find Baker's assumptions to be at odds with what they hold to be prevailing truths about who has value and who does not in the workplace.

Baker argues that the challenge for managers is to maximize the advantages and minimize the potential problems associated with cultural diversity. In the process, they have to learn to view managing diversity as an important, business-driven issue. Once they arrive at this point, they will be able to develop the competencies that will enable them to manage individuals from different racial, gender, and cultural backgrounds. Baker's argument is buttressed by some now-well-known demographic projections.

This chapter is important for managers to grasp and fully understand; only through a keen appreciation of these facts will the meaningful incorporation of larger and larger numbers of women and people of color take place. Without this appreciation, the existing normative "glass ceiling" will become more deeply and onerously embedded as a standard, massively counterproductive business practice, and with it will come the undoing of any viable prospect for continued economic growth in the West.

T he American workforce is rapidly becoming more culturally diverse, which presents managers with one of their biggest challenges. Left unattended, the increasing cultural diversity in the workforce can result in conflict, tension, and low productivity. If effectively managed, cultural diversity can provide the human resources for a creative and productive work environment. The challenge for managers is to maximize the advantages and minimize the potential problems associated with cultural diversity. To benefit from diversity as an important organizational resource, managers must (1) view the management of diversity as an important business issue, (2) understand the key issues in the multicultural workforce, and (3) develop the competencies required to manage individuals from different racial and cultural backgrounds.

THE MANAGEMENT OF DIVERSITY AS A BUSINESS ISSUE

The growing number of Asian-, African-, and Hispanic-American workers has a profound impact on the composition of the workforce. Managers and supervisors will be called upon to help their companies remain competitive by building a cohesive and productive workforce from this increasingly diverse population.

Recent studies underscore the dramatic changes in the racial and ethnic compositions of the workforce. Demographic projections for the 1990s include the following:

- Over the next 20 years, people of color—Asian Americans, African Americans, and Latinos—will constitute 85 percent of the US population growth.

- By the end of the 1990s, Asian Americans, African Americans, and Latinos will constitute almost 30 percent of the workforce.
- Euro-American males will be a minority in the total workforce by the year 2000.
- Immigrants, mostly from Asia and Latin America, will represent an increasing proportion of the labor force.
- The workforce will grow at the slowest rate since the 1930s, creating a potential labor shortage.

The ability to manage a culturally diverse workforce is an increasingly significant factor in a company's competitive position. A diverse workforce can provide a company with greater knowledge of preferences and consumer habits within the domestic market, which is also becoming increasingly diverse. Diversity can also help in the global marketplace. Skilled employees who speak the languages and understand the cultures of their international trading partners provide their companies with a competitive edge.

The most competitive companies will be those that can recruit, hire, and manage a diverse workforce. These companies will be able to take advantage of cultural diversity and develop an exciting, flexible, and creative corporate environment through the synergistic blending of individuals with different backgrounds and perspectives.

Companies that fail to develop competence in managing diversity will find their competitive position impaired. As the labor pool contracts, they will find it hard to compete with other companies in recruiting and hiring new, younger workers with the needed skills. In addition, productivity may decline because of costly miscommunications, ethnic conflicts, low morale, and stress. These companies may also suffer in the increasingly diverse marketplace, where a multicultural perspective would help them understand and respond effectively to culturally diverse consumers.

KEY ISSUES IN THE MULTICULTURAL WORKPLACE

To effectively manage a multicultural workforce, managers need to develop an understanding of the key issues inherent in culturally diverse organizations. These issues include a lack of upward mobility for people of color and cultural differences that may lead to miscommunications, misinterpretations, and misevaluations.

Lack of Upward Mobility for People of Color

Perhaps the most salient and potentially explosive issue in culturally diverse organizations is the barriers that people of color face when they attempt to move up the corporate hierarchy into high-status, high-skill management and executive positions. These barriers result from (1) individual discrimination and bias on the part of the dominant Euro-American group, or (2) systemic barriers in the form of the practices and policies of the organization itself. Whatever the cause, the result is that the organization may lose the advantages of increased creativity, productivity, and innovation, while suffering such negative consequences as conflicts, low morale, high turnover, and reduced productivity.

Discrimination and bias that limit progress may take the form of negative stereotypes and assumptions about people of color or, more subtly, selection and hiring processes based on undefined concepts such as "fit" and "chemistry." Ethnic stereotypes are generalizations that one applies to all members of a particular ethnic or cultural group and that guide one's behavior toward that group. They may be harmful or helpful, depending on how they are used. They are particularly harmful when they are negative, inaccurate, unconscious, rigid, and impervious to contradictory evidence.

In culturally diverse organizations, stereotypes limit the career progress of people of color when they influence judgments that lead to differential treatment. These stereotypes usually focus on presumed deficiencies in people of color that make them less suitable for management roles. For example, Asian Americans are often victims of stereotypes depicting them as passive, reserved, cliquish, highly technical individuals who lack the "people skills" necessary for managerial success. African Americans may suffer from stereotypes and beliefs that they are hired and promoted solely to fill a quota, that they lower standards, and are otherwise unsuitable for management. These generalizations are rarely true! (See Toy-Ping Taira, "Sensitizing Managers to Asian-American Diversity Issues"; Lee Butler, "African-American Women and

Men in the Workplace: Dismantling the Glass Ceiling"; and Cresencio Torres, "Hispanics in the Workplace," in this volume.)

Another more subtle and unconscious form of discrimination is the practice of hiring and promoting employees based on vague notions of fit and chemistry. This practice seems to be more common as one moves up the organizational hierarchy, when both the nature of the work and the performance expectations become more vague, nebulous, and ambiguous. In the absence of objective and measurable criteria, decision makers tend to hire and promote on the basis of subjective factors such as liking, perceived similarities, and the candidate's attitude and ability to fit into the organizational environment and culture. Consequently, decision makers often end up hiring and promoting individuals who are similar to them in terms of attitudes, beliefs, and values. Since managers and executives tend to be Euro-American males, the end result of this process is that a disproportionate number of people of color and immigrants are denied entry and promotion to managerial and executive ranks. (See Natasha Josefowitz's chapter, "The Clonal Effect in Organizations," in this volume.)

In addition to individual bias and discrimination on the part of the dominant group, people of color may also face systemic barriers to upward mobility in the multicultural organization itself. These include widespread policies, practices, and structures that perpetuate discriminatory treatment of people of color, such as (1) problems with mentors and sponsors, (2) exclusion from informal groups, and (3) the pressures of being a "token" in managerial ranks.

Mentors and sponsors.   There is a general consensus that having a mentor or sponsor is a key to career success. People of color, however, may experience problems with mentors in a number of areas. First, they may find that it takes a long time to initiate a relationship with a mentor who is from a different race or culture. They may then find it problematic to manage such a relationship and to derive the expected benefits from it. Indeed, there is more likelihood that these cross-racial relationships will end in a less-than-friendly way and provide less support than same-race relationships do. In addition, to be effective in the organization, people of color may need a different pattern of mentoring than do their Euro-American counterparts. They may need Euro-American male mentors for advice in their own functional area but same-race/culture mentors in other areas for social and psychological support.

Informal groups. Another systemic barrier to the career advancement of people of color is their exclusion from informal groups and networks in the organization. Because of perceived similarities and a discomfort with those who are different, both people of color and European Americans may tend to socialize and cluster more often with their own groups than with other groups. Consequently, people of color may be excluded from important power relationships and information networks. As a result, they may be unable to marshal support for their initiatives or to promote themselves effectively. And by not participating in the informal channels of the organization, people of color may not be able to learn about the corporate culture or its norms, values, beliefs, and accepted ways of getting things done. As a result, they are often isolated from essential communication channels.

Tokens. Still another barrier is the unwanted pressure and burden that comes from being considered a token representing a specific racial or cultural group. When people of color are few in number, and thus highly visible, they may become overloaded because of the expectations they face that their Euro-American counterparts do not face. For example, tokens may be expected to mentor other people of color in the organization. They may be expected to represent their groups in numerous meetings, committees, and task forces. They may be asked to attend events at which management wants to show that the workforce is diverse.

An additional burden comes from the perception that their individual success or failure symbolically represents the success or failure of their entire group. For example, if an African American fails at a particular task or job, all African Americans may suffer in the eyes of management. But if a Euro-American fails, it is seen as an individual matter. As a result of these pressures, people of color may become so overloaded that they are not able to perform their regular tasks well and could be seen by management as being unproductive. The situation is made worse when management is not aware that the token has become overloaded and does not consider the additional burdens and expectations when evaluating the performance of the individual.

CULTURAL DIFFERENCES IN THE MULTICULTURAL ORGANIZATION

Managers will be challenged to recognize these vast cultural differences in their organizations and to manage these differences rather than ignore them or allow problems to fester. People from different cultures vary in terms of their values, attitudes, and beliefs. In the culturally diverse workplace, these differences affect work behavior in a variety of ways. Employees may differ in their attitudes toward authority, preferred communication patterns, ways of dealing with conflict, sources of motivation, and emphasis on individual competition versus group cooperation. Of particular interest to managers are cultural differences that affect communication, team building, and interpersonal relationships.

• *Communication.* Achieving effective communication is a challenge even when the workforce is culturally homogenous. But when the workforce is diverse, with a variety of cultural and linguistic differences, effective two-way communication becomes even more problematic. For example, supervisors and managers may encounter difficulties in giving instructions that foreign-born employees can understand and in feeling confident that the instructions are in fact being followed. They may also experience difficulties in knowing how to give negative feedback and criticism to employees from different cultural groups and in eliciting opinions and feedback from them.

• *Team building.* Building a cooperative, culturally diverse team is another area that presents challenges for managers and supervisors. Several factors may hinder managers and supervisors from building effective multicultural teams. First, team members may fail to show respect for each other, may lack adequate information about each other's backgrounds, may lack common areas of interest, may have poor cross-cultural communication skills, and may hold negative attitudes and assumptions about each other.

In addition, teamwork may be hindered by the self-grouping of individuals from the same culture during work breaks, at lunch, or at social events sponsored by the company. This self-grouping may lead to mutual isolation, suspicion, resentment, and a lack of cooperation among the cultural groups in the workplace because they do not have informal opportunities to build relationships, which are essential for effective teamwork, collaboration, and problem solving.

• *Interpersonal relationships.* Managers and supervisors also experience difficulty in building and maintaining effective relationships with culturally diverse employees. Managers may lack knowledge of the employees' backgrounds and therefore are unable to identify areas of common interest. As mentioned previously, they may be unable to communicate effectively and may be unwilling or unable to show appropriate respect. As a result, managers and supervisors could find it difficult to motivate their employees, assign tasks, provide corrective feedback, and administer effective discipline.

COMPETENCIES REQUIRED TO MANAGE THE MULTICULTURAL WORKFORCE

Given the changing nature of the workforce, it is clear that the organization of the future will have considerable diversity at all levels. Accordingly, the ability to effectively manage diversity will become a basic requirement for all managers in the culturally diverse organization of the future. Managers will be required to develop the competencies that will help minimize the problems often associated with diversity and maximize the advantages of employee diversity. In other words, they will be required to manage diversity as a vital organizational resource. To meet this challenge, managers must develop the awareness, knowledge, and skills that will enable them to:

- Increase cultural self-awareness
- Enhance understanding and respect for cultural differences
- Learn about other cultures in the workplace
- Develop specific skills for multicultural effectiveness

The first step in developing competencies required for multicultural management is for managers to increase their own cultural self-awareness. This involves developing an understanding of one's own cultural conditioning and how this conditioning influences one's opinions, attitudes, values, behavior, and management style. Many Euro-American male managers may learn, for example, that they are seen by others as aggressive, competitive, task oriented, and unwilling to show their feelings when disappointed. Such an understanding allows managers to be more effective in multicultural situations because it helps them understand (1) how cultural factors influence their interpretation and evaluation of events, (2) how they project their own cultural values on others, and (3) other forms of cultural behavior from a nonjudgmental and nonethnocentric point of view.

Managers also need to develop an understanding of how cultural differences and similarities affect relationships in the workplace. It is necessary as well for managers to understand the dynamics that occur when culturally different individuals interact, communicate, establish relationships, and work together as members of a team. And it is useful to understand how these differences in communication styles may often lead to misunderstandings caused by misperceptions, misinterpretations, and misevaluations.

These understandings need to be translated into the ability to change or more effectively manage one's behavior in a multicultural encounter. The effective multicultural manager (1) has overcome the tendency to assume that everyone is the same, and (2) is able to recognize and describe cultural differences before interpreting and evaluating them. The effective manager is also able to show respect for others and their cultures, to be nonjudgmental when faced with cultural differences, to be flexible, and to tolerate ambiguity.

Communication skills that will enable the manager to work more effectively in a multicultural environment include the following:

- Pausing more frequently so the other person can ask questions and take turns speaking
- Avoiding the use of colloquial expressions, slang, or jargon that may be unfamiliar to the other person
- Watching the other person's nonverbal behavior for signs of questioning or confusion

- Paraphrasing what the other person has said to ensure full understanding

Relationship-building skills are important for all managers because they enable them to motivate their employees, assign tasks, provide corrective feedback, solve problems, and administer effective discipline. Skills for building relationships in a multicultural setting include:

- Being patient and taking the time to get to know the other person
- Identifying common areas of interest
- Maintaining the other's "face," self-esteem, and sense of competence

Skills for building effective multicultural teams are also essential for managers of the multicultural workforce. These skills include:

- Helping team members establish and maintain relationships with each other rather than simply focus on the task
- Helping the team develop group norms based on the different cultural groups represented on the team
- Appropriately encouraging equal participation in meetings and small-group discussions

MULTICULTURAL TRAINING AND DEVELOPMENT PROGRAMS

Managers can develop these competencies by participating in multicultural training programs. Such training can increase awareness of how cultural differences and similarities affect the multicultural workplace. This training also aims to achieve a number of specific objectives that can help managers become more effective in a multicultural setting. These objectives include:

- Increasing managers' awareness of their own culture and of how it influences their management style
- Enhancing their understanding of the other cultures in the workplace, in terms of values, attitudes, behaviors, and communication styles,

- Developing specific skills for intercultural communication, for building cooperative and collaborative relationships, and for developing effective multicultural teams.

Most intercultural training for managers and supervisors uses the experiential approach, focusing on a combination of knowledge, attitudes, and skills. Trainees usually participate in role playing, small-group exercises, and the analysis of critical incidents and case studies.

At the organizational level, managers must implement organizational development initiatives to integrate the policies, practices, and procedures needed for diverse employees to work comfortably and productively together. These organizational development programs may aim to create:

- Recruitment and selection systems that more adequately reflect the multicultural labor pool
- A performance appraisal process that reflects the cultural and social diversity found in the organization
- Training programs that enhance the multicultural competence of all employees
- An organizational culture that recognizes the contributions of diverse groups in the organization and that shares power and influence.

SUMMARY

With the increasing diversity of the workforce, the ability of many organizations to remain competitive will depend on how well they manage cultural diversity. The challenge for managers is to develop the awareness, knowledge, and skills that will help them manage the new multicultural workforce. To be effective, managers need to understand how cultural differences affect the workplace. They should increase their self-awareness of their own cultural traits and develop specific skills for managing the culturally diverse workforce. In addition, managers will be challenged to help their organizations develop the policies, practices, and procedures that will enable diverse employees to work comfortably and cooperatively together. In meeting these challenges, managers will be able to contribute to the success of their organizations by building a cohesive and productive workforce from an increasingly diverse population.

Octave V. Baker

Octave Baker, PhD, is a senior partner with Communication Training Consultants in Sunnyvale, California, and a member of the engineering management faculty at Santa Clara University. He has extensive experience as a management consultant, trainer, and researcher.

As a Peace Corps volunteer in Africa, Dr. Baker was trained in cross-cultural communication. He holds certificates in intercultural communication and training from the Stanford Institute for Intercultural Communication and from the Society for Intercultural Education, Training, and Research (SIETAR).

Dr. Baker received his doctorate with honors in community and organizational psychology from the University of Michigan. In addition, Dr. Baker is a graduate of the Organization and Systems Development Program at the Gestalt Institute of Cleveland. He is listed in *Community Leaders and Noteworthy Americans* and is a member of the NTL Institute.

Chapter Eighteen

The Clonal Effect in Organizations

Natasha Josefowitz

Executive Summary

This chapter explores some of the rationale that unconsciously operates beneath the surface but may impact the extent of diversity as a result of management decision making. Natasha Josefowitz argues that "individuals, groups, and organizations tend to replicate themselves or others close to them"—in decisions to hire and to promote—the clonal effect in action. Two major criteria come into play every time someone is to be hired or promoted: (1) competence to do the job, and (2) "fit" between the individual and the rest of the staff and organization. Thinking about the fit, she argues, is often driven by unconscious mental processes, gut feelings that supply valid data. Yet these data must be examined and understood in order to make a decision to act or not to act.

To the degree possible, managers must have some concrete evidence of their unconscious behavior, because through this they will have an opportunity to control outcomes instead of being controlled by unidentified motivations. Fit has to do with the unconsciously perceived comfort levels of subordinates and assumes that they are able to relate better to someone of their own sex or race. However, while this may indeed be the case, unless such biases or preferences are made conscious and explicit and are thoroughly explored and discussed, they remain untested. Making the thinking explicit and engaging in the conversation enables what Argyris terms "double loop learning" to occur. Exposing this thinking to the light of day may either justify an imminent decision or call forth an alternative decision.

This chapter has enormous significance. As businesses of virtually all stripes become more diverse through the utilization of greater numbers of workers who are different by race and gender than Euro-American men, they must learn to monitor the factors that determine who gets hired and who gets promoted. Unless this is done, organizations will continue to clone. Perhaps distressingly, cloning will be occurring in a job market in which fewer and fewer clones are available to fit in with existing Euro-American men.

Josefowitz is not prepared to advocate diversity. Indeed, she points to circumstances in which 'sameness' along the dimensions of race and gender may constitute the best outcome. She is advocating consciousness and double loop learning as essential preconditions in the processes leading to management decisions.

Clone n: the aggregate of the asexually produced progeny of an individual

Webster's New Collegiate Dictionary

W e tend to hire people who fit in well, not realizing that those who are different can be equally enriching. Individuals, groups, and organizations tend to replicate themselves or those close to them. Unconscious though it may be, the process is an example of the "clonal effect," and the most evident form of it occurs during the hiring or promotion process.

Every time someone is to be hired or promoted, two major criteria come into play. Obviously, one is competence to do the job. The other is the "fit" between the candidate and the rest of the staff and the organization. This is where the clonal effect begins.

Fit deals with the level of comfort (comfort level) the employer feels with the person being hired or promoted, and it lies in the eyes of the beholder. But how does one measure fit except by intuition? And on what criteria is the intuition based?

I do not mean to question the legitimacy of the use of intuition—far from it. Gut feelings are valid data; they are signals from the unconscious to be examined and understood before deciding whether to act or not to act.

In other words, we can exert control over our actions only to the extent that we understand them. Much of our behavior is dictated by forces unknown to us or unrecognized by us. Only when we obtain concrete evidence of our unconscious behavior do we have an opportunity to control outcomes instead of being controlled by unidentified motivations.

LEVELS OF COMFORTABLE FIT

Recent research suggests that people are often hired according to gender—not in terms of pure discrimination against one sex or the other, but in terms of fit. Data indicate that men are hired as managers more often if there are male subordinates; women if there are female subordinates. Fit has to do with the unconsciously perceived comfort levels of subordinates and assumes that they would relate better to someone of their own sex. This is not to say that the perceived comfort level is erroneous; it is important to note, however, that females will be hired as managers less often in male-dominated organizations, and that in some instances this will be an unconscious discrimination.

If employers are hiring someone with whom they will be working, the tendency is to look for someone with whom they will have a fair chance of getting along, of communicating well, and of sharing basic values in such matters as work ethics, quality standards, imagination, precision, punctuality, dress codes, humor, politics, and leisure. The list is endless and so are the possible prejudices. Whom do we trust? Those we can understand; those most predictable to us. Who are they? Those most like ourselves.

Think of your closest friends. What is your comfort level and trust based on? You will find differences, of course, but there are also similarities, which form the basis of friendship and trust. There are other people you will never know who must remain strangers and foreign to you. These strangers will not be hired, just as you will not be hired or promoted if you do not fit the comfort level of your prospective employer.

Discrimination against women, African-American men, and others are not necessarily based on gender or color alone, but are frequently based unconsciously on "otherness" or "differentness." Statements such as, "I would not work for a woman" or "I would not hire a black" express discomfort with the unfamiliar—

persons to whom we attribute a different value system that we believe will preclude our ability to understand each other.

Consider your own team, group, or organization. What are the similarities and the differences? Who is friendly with whom? Who was the last person hired? By whom? Do you see the clonal effect operating between any two people (one of whom may be yourself)? The Madison Avenue type, the cloak-and-suiter, the sales representative, the social worker—we all know what these stereotypes mean. Stereotypes perpetuate the species, for each species will keep cloning itself until stopped by its own awareness.

Was it by chance that many of the Kennedy men went to Harvard and played touch football? Or that many of the Carter men came from Georgia and played softball? With George Bush, you had to fish or play golf; with Bill Clinton, it's jogging. Is it sheer coincidence that in some companies tennis is *the* game, while in others bowling or beer are popular after work?

Just as individuals tend to replicate themselves, groups and organizations tend to replace lost members with people having similar characteristics or to add people who will not challenge the dynamics of the usual patterns of communicating. Even in an effort to add people who have complementary skills or knowledge, a certain comfort level of predictable interactions has to be maintained.

A MATTER OF CLASS

Race, sex, and ethnic origins are often cited as bases for discrimination, but class is rarely mentioned. Yet class can be as much a factor in hiring, promotion, and selection as the more readily evident race, sex, ethnicity, or national origin. Because class is more difficult to define, the clues are more subtle. Discrimination is based on often minimal indicators of class that can be as tenuous as a manner of walking, a choice of words, a piece of clothing, a look, or a joke. The way a person enters the cafeteria, orders a meal, eats, relates with the staff, and pays the check often indicates his or her class. Of course, this prejudice lies not in the acknowledgment of the difference but in the preference of one way over the other; discrimination occurs when we act on this preference. Here again, we are seeking comfort by associating with the person who comes from a background similar to our own. We tend to place more trust in persons from our own social class. Thus, class becomes a factor in the clonal effect of hiring and promotion.

INTOLERANCE FOR AGE

Similarities in age also provide a certain comfort in our relationships, but age creates a cloning need as pervasive as the factors previously mentioned. Perhaps that is because when we are young, we often feel threatened by impending age, and those who are older look at younger colleagues with some mistrust. We attach a stigma to age. Youth suggests high energy and potential; it may also suggest recklessness and lack of judgment. Although age brings maturity and wisdom, it may also mean a slowing down and a more conservative attitude. Age differences can be as potentially upsetting as differences in race, sex, ethnic origin, or class. The generation gap can be a painful reality; we often feel little in common with different generations. Age discrimination is due as much to negative stereotyping of the old and the young as it is to cloning.

ARE THERE BENEFITS IN CLONING?

Although cloning tends to reduce diversity and therefore creativity resources, there are times when conscious cloning might be appropriate. This occurs when:

1. Lines of communication are poor and people are expected to understand each other with little or no interface.
2. Language is a difficulty.
3. The culture of the organization or the country in which it is located is very different from one's own.
4. There is a great deal of uncertainty.
5. The margin of error for decision making is small.
6. There is little time available for decision making.
7. Interdependence is substantial.
8. There is little interest in creativity.

For many of these reasons, multinational companies often provide examples of cloning at the national level. Where not prohibited by law, top management of subsidiary companies located abroad is often of the same nationality as those of the parent firm; even when circumstances change, the effect continues. In recent years, many companies have moved toward installing local nationals in chief executive and other key positions when such expertise is available. Such appointments give the overseas firm a much-needed local identity.

WHAT CAN A MANAGER DO?

Since the clonal effect originates mostly in the unconscious, it is only through awareness that we can begin to exert a measure of control over the process of endlessly replicating ourselves.

With the coming European Community (EC) influencing much of our future endeavors, it is critical that managers become aware of the clonal effect at work. An article in the *London Financial Times* (October 28, 1991) mentioned the dismissal of Compaq Computer Company president and chief executive officer, Rod Canion, whose style was described as "consensus management." He opposed layoffs. His replacement, Eckhard Pfeiffer, was described as a "directive manager" who was used to autonomy and who planned to "trim management fat." We could predict what type of person would be fired and what type would be hired. It thus becomes urgent for managers to ask themselves the following questions and take the following actions:

1. What type of people do I tend to be most comfortable and most uncomfortable with?
2. What personality traits are related to the work that needs to be done and to the organization as a whole?
3. What advantages and disadvantages would diversity bring to my department?
4. When a different type of person is hired, what can I do to ensure the new employee's integration into the group?
   a. Prepare the group for the newcomer's arrival by discussing the tendency to reject the unfamiliar.

    b. Assign a "buddy" to the new person to answer questions and to assist and introduce the individual.

    c. Prepare a list of the norms (unwritten rules of how things are done, the unwritten expectations) operating in your workplace and explain them to the new employee.

5. Hold a meeting one month after the new hire to listen to the employee's perceptions of the work group. Encourage both fitting into group norms and retaining the unique talents and perspectives that a person of a different background can bring.

6. Do the same with the work group, helping employees accept the diversity as an addition to the input and not as a distraction from harmony. Since people naturally prefer sameness, managers must point out the benefits of having different perspectives in the workplace.

We need to consciously and actively look for the discomfort of diversity, the challenge of the different, the potential for disagreement. Only then will women; African Americans, Hispanics, or Asian Americans; the too young or too old; the handicapped; the oddly dressed; and others of different ethnic origins, religions, and accents have a chance to "be" and a chance to "do"; only then will all of us be able to contribute our differences and be mutually enriched by them.

Natasha Josefowitz

Natasha Josefowitz is an adjunct professor at San Diego State University and writes a weekly column on management issues for three daily newspapers. She is the best-selling author of three management books and an award-winning writer of eight books of humorous verse and a book for children. Her books have been translated in over a dozen languages. She is a well-known, international keynote speaker and a frequent guest on talk shows. She is a member of the NTL Institute.

    Dr. Josefowitz has been named Woman of the Year five times by various national and international organizations.

Chapter Nineteen

Women and Men: Understanding and Respecting Gender Differences in the Workplace

Sophie Hahn
Anne Litwin

Executive Summary

Most everyone would agree with the assertion that boys and girls are socialized differently in America, as they are in most postindustrial or "third wave" societies. Girls and boys, during their formative years, are sent endless socialization messages about how they ought to behave in order to have successful outcomes. The messages differ as functions of the gender of the particular child.

One simple example with which most of us have some familiarity is crying in response to frustration by girls and "acting out" behavior in response to frustration by boys. This chapter is a discussion of the manifold ways in which the early socialization of boys and girls is played out in the workplace, at a later stage of development, between men and women.

Managers, both men and women, must stay constantly attuned to these gender differences if they are to effectively manage across the gender divide. Anne Litwin and Sophie Hahn suggest that without this sensitivity, women's success will be impeded, and both men and women will experience unnecessary frustrations.

However, given male dominance in many organizations, the woman manager who is not fully aware of how differences based on gender get played out is more likely to suffer than a male manager who is similarly unattuned. While the woman manager may be seen as unprepared, male managers who lack skill in managing this form of diversity may find upper management in supportive collusion with them.

This chapter is important because it reveals many of the often reflexive ways that gender differences, and the behaviors associated with them, are enacted in the world of work. Many of the issues discussed in this chapter are below the surface and spontaneous, and reflect who we are by virtue of the ways in which our early socialization took place.

On this basis, frequent reference to Hahn and Litwin's piece is worthwhile counsel. Otherwise, the behaviors will be ascribed to what is considered "normal," and calling attention to them may be seen as "nitpicking"—a most unfair and unfortunate outcome not only for impacted women, but for men as well. Men who fail to "get it" will continue to manage in uninformed ways, leading to continuous turnover of highly talented women in their managerial purview, an unfortunate outcome at the organizational level.

B e it nature or nurture, by the time most women and men make it to the workplace, their life experiences and expectations have been different in certain gender-based ways. Of course, as human beings, women and men share many of the same experiences and expectations. And as individuals, they are each entirely unique. In each person, all of these experiences and expectations function simultaneously: the group-based differences, the universal human similarities, and the individual attributes and quirks. This makes for a fascinating—and sometimes confusing—human landscape.

Whenever women and men interact, gender-based group differences can come into play, at times creating avoidable misunderstandings. These are the innocent communication-, style-, expectation-, and experience-based misunderstandings that arise among women and men interacting in normal, friendly, cordial, and helpful ways, with no ill will intended. Managers need to be especially aware of the potential for such misunderstandings in the work environment, both in their own actions and reactions as well as those of their colleagues and staff toward each other.

Without diminishing the importance of the sameness, the

uniqueness, or the other group identities of human beings, this chapter focuses on how gender-based differences manifest themselves in the workplace. Throughout the chapter, certain behaviors are labeled "feminine" or "masculine" or are attributed to women or men. These labels and attributions are a shorthand way of describing characteristics more likely to be found among members of one gender or the other, and should not be read as a negation of individual differences.

WOMEN AND MEN IN THE WORKPLACE

Women and men, as groups, tend to have different communication and work styles. This has been observed and documented by sociologists, psychologists, and other social observers, despite continued debate about why such differences exist (nature or nurture) and why typically masculine behavior tends to be assigned a higher value in the workplace.

Deborah Tannen's 1990 best-seller, *You Just Don't Understand: Women and Men in Conversation,*[1] explores the different conversational styles of women and men at length. Based on her research, Tannen concludes that boys' and girls' early social lives are so different that they grow up "in what are essentially different cultures." Thus, talk between women and men is in fact cross-cultural communication, fraught with as many potential misunderstandings as communication between individuals from different countries, ethnic backgrounds, languages, or religious groups.

As a matter of basic world view, Tannen establishes that men see themselves as engaged in a hierarchical social order in which they are either "one up or one down" in relation to others. Their communication styles and reactions to others' communications often stress the need to "preserve independence and avoid failure." Women, on the other hand, tend to see the world as a "network of connections," and their communications and interpretations of others' communications seek to "preserve intimacy and avoid isolation."

Tannen's conclusions echo an earlier well-known book on this subject, *In a Different Voice*[2] by Carol Gilligan. Gilligan cites research by a number of psychologists and other experts that has found marked differences in the basic operational modes of women and men, starting from the time they are very young children. For example, in observing girls and boys at play, Piaget and Lever (in separate studies) found that as boys grow they become "increasingly fascinated with the legal elaboration of rules and the development of fair procedures for adjudicating conflicts," while girls "have a more 'pragmatic' attitude toward rules." Girls are "more willing to make exceptions and more easily reconciled to innovations." Boys' play is observed as more competitive, while girls' play "is more cooperative."

Given these basic differences in world view and behavior, it is not surprising to find that the workplace expectations, work styles, and characteristics of women and men, as groups, also tend to differ.

Table 19-1 depicts the two extremes of a spectrum of workplace styles and expectations shared by women and men, but considered more typically feminine or masculine. Many women probably will see themselves, or be seen by colleagues, as possessing certain attributes described as "masculine," and some men probably will see themselves, or be seen by colleagues, as possessing certain attributes described in the table as "feminine."

All of the views and styles described as constituting the more typically feminine or masculine ends of the spectrum are equally valid and useful in a productive workplace. Increased worldwide competition and changing workforce demographics highlight this fact. Many organizations have begun to recognize the need to move away from primarily masculine structures and norms toward a more flexible definition of appropriate workplace behavior. An emphasis on teamwork and positive employee development requires that both typically feminine and typically masculine styles and expectations be valued and reinforced. This creates new opportunities for women and men to utilize and value the different strengths each brings to the workplace.

A COMMON WORKPLACE SCENARIO: THE MIXED-GENDER MEETING

Despite an increased valuing of the attributes of both genders, misunderstandings among women and men in the workplace continue. Each gender tends to expect that the other operates with

TABLE 19–1
Gender Based Perceptions in the Workplace

	Feminine	*Masculine*
Organizational structure	**participative** (see colleagues as complementary)	**hierarchical** (see colleagues as potential competition)
Focus of interpersonal attention	**process** (care about how people treat each other in carrying out work)	**outcome** (care about "where they stand" in relation to others)
Operating style	**interactional** (interact to connect, arrive at understandings)	**transactional** (interact to pass information and give directions)
Problem-solving style	**intuitive** (trust instincts; will provide proof/explanation as necessary)	**linear** (based on methodical thinking; will not trust intuition until proof is presented)
Individual work style	**collaborative** (see work as part of a whole; discuss and review with colleagues)	**independent** (see work as a separate piece; complete work without the "help" of others)
Management style	**supportive** (seek to aid, support, facilitate, and provide comfort, meaning, and rewards)	**directive** (seek to test, direct, organize, and provide challenges, goals, and incentives)
View of work-related conflict	**disruptive** (seek to create harmony; view negative comments as unproductive)	**normal** (accept a level of conflict as inevitable; view negative comments as normal part of work)

the same set of views and behavioral expectations. The following scenario illustrates an innocent gender-based misunderstanding in which a sensitivity to the different feminine and masculine styles and expectations would have facilitated more fruitful outcomes.

Case 1. A male manager is holding a meeting with his staff, which includes both women and men, to find a solution to a departmental problem. A woman speaks first, very soon after he has presented the problem; she offers a solution. The manager is annoyed. Because she did not begin her statement with a progressive analysis of all factors and because she spoke so soon, he assumes she has not thought out her position and therefore dismisses her solution without bothering to explore its possibilities.

One of her male colleagues speaks second. He starts with a lengthy analysis and ultimately summarizes with a virtually identical solution. This time, the manager hears the solution and accepts it. The male manager has reacted favorably not to the actual solution but to his male staff member's *linear* approach to solving the problem.

Case 2. In the converse situation, a female manager is holding an identical meeting. A man speaks first, and begins with what seems to her to be a lengthy, overly detailed, and somewhat pompous justification for the point he is about to make but never seems to get to. She asks that he cede the floor so that others can participate, effectively cutting him off before he has finished.

A woman speaks second. She simply states the first solution that came to her mind, based on the manager's description of the problem. The manager happily accepts the solution—it sounds right—and continues the meeting by asking if anyone sees any reason why this is not the best solution. This female manager has also favored a certain approach to problem solving—the *intuitive* approach.

In case 1, with a male manager, the woman staff member will leave the meeting frustrated, and the manager will not recognize her contribution. This is a gender-based misunderstanding. His negative view of her may be exacerbated because the workplace tends to favor masculine work styles and characteristics. To the extent that women as a group do not conform to the male model, they may be considered less-valuable employees. From the female staff member's perspective, the experience may add to a feeling that women in the office aren't listened to or aren't respected. After all, she did provide the correct solution! If she complains, this will probably also hurt her: People will tend to perceive her as weak or oversensitive.

In the second case, with the female manager, there has also been a gender-based misunderstanding, and it is the male staff member who will leave the meeting with a sense of frustration. In this instance, however, the negative interaction can be directly harmful to the female manager as well as to the male employee. The male staff member will certainly suffer from being misunderstood by his manager. He will feel that he has been treated unfairly and may receive a poor evaluation. He may also complain to others around the office. Even though he is the subordinate, his "bad-mouthing" can feed preexisting biases in the male-defined workplace. The manager may be seen as the one with the problem and her management style considered impatient or lacking in judgment. In this example, the misunderstanding can harm both the male staff member and his female manager.

These misunderstandings, if viewed alone, may seem petty or harmless. But in most instances, they form part of a continuum of misunderstandings, acted out on a playing field that itself is not level—a playing field usually disfavoring feminine characteristics, and thus women. Bit by bit, these can lead to destructive and time-consuming animosities, a factionalized workplace, demoralized employees, and, eventually, to the loss of promising members of the staff. These types of misunderstandings are often the source of the disproportionate loss of female employees who, given their backgrounds, skills, and experience, should have thrived in their jobs.

WHAT CAN MANAGERS DO?

Ultimately, managers are responsible for making sure that workplace tasks are accomplished in an optimal fashion. They must create a productive work environment that brings out the best in each member of their staff, whatever her or his universal, group, or individual characteristics may be. The foundation of productive work environments is mutual respect and understanding.

Managers influence their work environments in three ways:

- How they act, which sets a powerful example
- How they treat members of their staff
- How they manage relations among staff members

Whatever managers do to derive the benefits of or to minimize the problems arising from gender-based differences in the workplace, they must address all three levels of influence.

The following six-step program is a manager's guide for learning more about and effectively handling gender-based misunderstandings in the workplace.

1. *Educate.* The first step for managers is to continually educate themselves about gender issues in the workplace through reading and participation in classes or workshops. Most people have a tendency to assume that all people are just like themselves. In today's world and today's workplace, this is rarely true. Learning more about gender issues can trigger a series of surprising observations, leading a manager to new understandings. The sources of certain frustrating workplace misunderstandings become obvious and more easily managed and changed.

2. *Assess.* The next step for a manager, armed with new information, is to assess the ways in which the structure, norms, expectations, standards, evaluation methods, and other attributes of the workplace may carry a bias. These elements must be taken into account in all efforts to achieve meaningful gender fairness.

For example, upon examination, a manager may note the existence of an unwritten norm discouraging crying. Since crying is a normal way in which many women express strong feelings or react to stress, the norm against crying would tend to disfavor women. If women who cry at work are considered less-valuable employees, while men experience no negative repercussions when they express strong feelings or react to stress in other ways, the manager will have identified an important workplace bias.

Although managers may be able to identify some of the potentially gender-biased elements in their workplaces, it is often advisable to engage an outside expert to guide or conduct the assessment for the manager. As members of the workplace culture, managers may have difficulty identifying biases that are fully ingrained in the environment—and thus most likely in the managers themselves.

3. *Ask questions.* Having observed the environment, a manager should next ask questions of each staff member on an individual basis. To gain relevant information, the manager should ask each employee to describe:

- The strengths they bring to the workplace
- The characteristics they value in a supervisor
- The aspects of the work they consider important

Focusing on the issue of gender-based differences, a manager should ask:

- What special, added value the employee feels her or his gender brings to the workplace?
- How the employee can benefit from the different gender-based attributes of co-workers?

Once these positive aspects have been explored and identified, it is useful to ask employees about:

- Frustrations they may have encountered in working with members of the opposite gender
- Behaviors that would show respect for the style differences between them

All of the information obtained through private interviews should be kept confidential between the manager and the particular employee.

4. *Discuss.* As a next step, mixed-gender groups should be brought together for a guided discussion and review of the same questions that were asked in the individual sessions. A good way to conclude a group discussion of gender issues is to have participants articulate explicit agreements about ways they can show respect for and benefit from both gender-based styles. This process of sharing information about gender issues can be continually refreshed and reinforced by taking the time, upon completion of major projects or at the end of important meetings, to discuss how well members of each gender feel they have worked together and to solicit suggestions for improving group interaction in the future.

5. *Listen.* For the manager, listening is especially important for three reasons. First, the individual's comments made during group discussions provide crucial management information, which employees will not provide if they do not trust that they will be listened to and taken seriously. Second, managers must try very honestly to hear the ways in which their own actions and treatment of staff members, and the staff's interaction with each other, perpetuate destructive—and thus unproductive—gender biases.

The third, and ultimately most edifying, reason to listen carefully is to discover the unique gifts each individual brings to the workplace. If the male manager from the first scenario had been listening differently, he might have heard his female staff member's correct solution. He would have been impressed by her ability to grasp complex problems quickly and see straight to the right solution. Conversely, if the female manager had listened differently to what her male staff member was saying, she would have appreciated his ability to present a well-reasoned exposition of the foundations for his conclusions.

6. *Initiate change.* Having learned, assessed, asked questions, discussed, and listened, managers will probably need to make changes at all three levels of influence—how they act, how they treat members of their staffs, and how they manage relations among staff members. Depending on the situation, each manager's strategy may be different. Some managers may find that by changing their own behaviors, the entire department or unit will change, having learned by experience and example. Others may wish to bring the issues up explicitly with staff by holding meetings, announcing new policies, or even inviting special consultants from the outside to work with them and their staffs.

Many useful books, tapes, videos, seminars, classes, and training programs can help managers create a strategy for managing change in gender-based patterns, expectations, and attitudes. These resources may be obtained through bookstores, libraries, professional associations, women's organizations, city or state human rights commissions, unions, and the company's human resources department.

CONCLUSION

Whatever the strategy and actions taken, there is no doubt that managers will confront gender-based issues in the workplace; most already do, without knowing it. They spend precious time managing situations arising from or exacerbated by gender-based misunderstandings—including their own! Both women and men with useful potential leave the organization—or end up being asked to leave. Organizations lose women disproportionately because definitions of what is right and good in the workplace are almost always based on a masculine model. Women eventually feel unappreciated and undervalued, and then they don't stick around. Being aware of and confronting gender issues frees managers to take control and turn things around, to the benefit of their staffs, their organizations, and ultimately society.

ENDNOTES

1. Tannen, Deborah. *You Just Don't Understand: Women and Men in Conversation.* New York: Ballantine Books, 1990.
2. Gilligan, Carol. *In a Different Voice: Psychological Theory and Women's Development.* Cambridge, MA: Harvard University Press, 1982.
3. Loden, Marilyn. *Feminine Leadership, or How to Succeed in Business Without Being One of the Boys.* New York: Times Books, 1985.

Sophie Hahn

Sophie Hahn, Esq., is studying for a PhD in industrial relations and human resources at the Rutgers University Institute of Management and Labor Relations. Her work has ranged from practicing law at a major New York firm to acting as organizational strategist for a large international organization. Focusing on issues of personnel management and development, diversity, gender, and culture in the workplace, Sophie Hahn has co-taught and participated in the resolution of sexual harassment and other workplace grievances. Her current research interests include abuse, equity, and healing at work.

Anne Litwin

Anne Litwin is president of Anne H. Litwin Associates, based in Boston and New York City. She has been an organizational development consultant for 18 years, serving a wide variety of organizations in the private, public, and not-for-profit sectors and specializing in diversity issues in the workplace. She is the creator of a workshop for the NTL Institute entitled "Women and Men Working Together." Anne Litwin is a member of the NTL Institute and an adjunct professor at Long Island University in the Schools of Business and Public Administration. She was also the chief executive officer of a retail business for several years.

Chapter Twenty

Issues for Women Managers

Katharine Esty

Executive Summary

Unless they understand systems phenomena, Euro-American women and, as Lee Butler observed (Chapter 24), people of color share a common tendency to blame themselves for their failures to advance to the top level in organizations. Internalizing the reasons for stalled careers shows up in a variety of ways. Both groups are victimized by the pervasiveness, across organizational types, of the glass ceiling, the barely permeable membrane that exists between upper and middle management. Katharine Esty implores women to begin to understand organizations as cultures and to become more astute students of how systems phenomena actually work.

With the depth of understanding that would grow from a systems perspective, women will have a more effective way to track and contextualize their ongoing experiences in the culture of organizations. The collusion of silence that is present regarding the failure of women and people of color to advance upwardly is the necessary and essential superstructure for embedding the "isms" as acceptable ways of operating. Esty says that women who speak out against unfair treatment make themselves vulnerable. Outspokenness on the part of women almost always guarantees that they will be called militant—a career-stalling outcome. Women are therefore damned if they do and damned if they don't; the classic double bind.

In this chapter, Esty discusses seven issues, "each of which affects the woman manager to some degree differently than managers who are men," she says. Although her focus may be essentially Euro-American women, in truth, Esty's issues impact people who are not Euro-American men. With the notable exception of her discussions on balancing work and family and sexual harassment, the issues have also been a part of the racism lexicon.

This chapter is a significant contribution to this volume. Major shifts are indeed necessary in the way work does or does not get done in organizations. While there are things that women need to do, Esty also outlines a variety of reforms that must take place within organizational systems themselves. As the paradigm is shifting, signaling (as Marshak notes elsewhere in this volume) movement from one era to the next, the changes that Esty advocates assume greater weight and substance.

W hy bother with a special chapter on women in management? Aren't the issues really the same for all managers? In the mid-1990s, isn't writing about women managers both anachronistic and divisive? Haven't women made extraordinary progress in the last decades?

In fact, when we look carefully at the status of women managers today, what we see is disquieting. There has been a significant increase in the number of women managers in the last 20 years. In 1970, 20 percent of managers were women, while 40 percent are today. This is remarkable progress. Recent studies, however, indicate only a slight increase in the representation of women in executive positions of the nation's largest companies. Another study reports that only 2 percent of all corporate officers are women. In addition, the salaries of women managers continue to trail far behind those of men. One study reports that women managers earn about 71 cents for every dollar that their male counterparts earn.

Where are we then? Some authors, such as Sylvia Hewlett, talk about the "stalled revolution," while Susan Faludi and others talk about a backlash or countermovement. Such common terms as the "glass ceiling" and the "mommy track" reflect the continued difficulty that women managers encounter in the workplace. More recently, Deborah J. Swiss and Judith P. Walker coined the term "the maternal wall."

Felice Schwartz, in her 1992 book on corporate women, agrees that women face significant barriers and claims that there is a conspiracy of silence on the topic of women's issues. Women themselves are confused about the status quo. Some insist that competence is all that matters, that everybody has an equal chance to succeed. Others experience slow advancement in spite of tremendous effort; they begin to wonder about gender bias. Still others feel outraged or crushed by the outright discrimination they believe they have encountered in the workplace.

Despite the media blitz of articles on the topic of women managers, it seems that very little has actually changed over the last decade in most workplaces. Core work practices and career structures remain essentially untouched, and progress must be labeled modest. In this chapter, seven issues are presented, each of which affects the woman manager to some degree differently than managers who are men. Each of the issues presents a challenge to women managers, usually a challenge that cannot be avoided. The perspective of this chapter is systemic; that is, solutions to these issues lie in changing policies, practices, and systems as well as individual behavior.

ISSUE 1: UNDERVALUED MANAGEMENT STYLE

Studies show that most employees describe a good manager using words like *decisive, aggressive, logical,* and *objective*—words they also use to describe *masculine.* Women's style of leading is often captured by a totally different set of words: *participative, team player, enthusiastic, people-oriented,* and *listening.* The latter style has been used by many successful women managers, while other successful women are described using the same set of words used to describe successful men (see Hahn and Litwin, Chapter 19).

The issue for many women, especially in bureaucratic and hierarchical organizations, is that they believe that the only way to get ahead is to mimic the masculine "command and control" style, even if it means playing a role. As one woman manager put it, "My boss is easy to please, but it isn't really me and I resent having to put on a fake face."

ISSUE 2: SEXIST LANGUAGE

Sexist comments and language with a gender bias continue to be problematic for many women managers. Words like *girl, sweetie, honey,* or *dear* remain all too common in the workplace. Many women still face a barrage of sexist jokes and put-downs. The dilemma for the woman manager is how to handle these comments. If she says nothing, the comments may continue and she has not even raised the person's awareness. If she responds subtly or just looks away, the message is often missed. If she is blunt and confronts the comments directly, she runs the risk of being labeled "angry" or "militant," and it often means she will be overlooked for advancement.

ISSUE 3: BEING INVISIBLE

Women managers often report that they feel invisible at meetings even when they are with colleagues who are all at their own or lower levels. Women talk about making comments that elicit no response. Later in the meeting, a male colleague says essentially the same thing and everyone says, "What a wonderful idea." Women managers also report that they are frequently interrupted. Research studies have documented that women's comments are indeed ignored more frequently than those of men and that women are more frequently interrupted.

The recent publication of a study by the American Association of University Women indicated that gender bias is still the norm in American classrooms, where boys are called on far more often than girls. When boys shout out answers, they are listened to by their teachers; when girls do the same thing, they are told to raise their hands. When teachers are asked who has talked more in their classes, they almost always report that the girls have talked more—even when the observer has counted and found that the boys have made significantly more comments. With such discouraging experiences year after year, it is not surprising that some women managers have trouble speaking up.

ISSUE 4: BALANCING WORK
AND FAMILY

How can a person balance two primary responsibilities and two primary loyalties: a job and a family? Certainly this issue is not only a women's issue, but it is a major issue for many working women. More than 50 percent of the mothers of children under one year of age are in the workforce today. For the woman manager, dealing with both work and family needs may create conflict and stress. Often, organizational policies and practices make things more difficult than is necessary. Managerial meetings at 7:30 in the morning create problems, since this is before drop-off time at many day care centers or schools.

Regular, everyday occurrences such as snow days, school conferences, sick children, school plays, and doctor appointments can create stressful decision points for the woman manager. When women opt to attend to their family responsibilities, they may be labeled ''not serious about their careers,'' which is just about the most damaging thing one can say about a manager. When they opt to attend to their job responsibilities, women often feel enormous guilt. Many women managers report being profoundly worried about whether they are doing right by their families. Common refrains are: ''I feel guilty all the time.'' ''I feel I don't do enough for my kids.'' ''I am always behind in my work at the office and I never have any time at all for myself to, say, exercise or meditate.''

ISSUE 5: SEXUAL HARASSMENT

Although this issue is not exclusively a women's problem, again, in the vast majority of incidents of sexual harassment, it is a woman being harassed. Women managers routinely report getting pinched, poked, and propositioned. They face an onslaught of sexual innuendos. These incidents happen most frequently when alcohol is involved, such as at a holiday party or during an out-of-town meeting, but they happen at other times as well.

Women managers typically feel extremely vulnerable when they confront these types of behavior. They are only too aware that the victim typically gets blamed. Women managers with concerns about advancement or about keeping their jobs are faced with a series of difficult choices, all of which may turn out badly for them. If they speak out, their careers can be permanently damaged. Even when the instigator is terminated, colleagues' resentment can be so intense that the work environment becomes intolerable. On the other hand, if women don't speak out, they lose self-esteem and the harassment may continue. Many organizations offer no middle way—no mechanism for dealing with sexual harassment without making a formal, official complaint. (See Chapter 22 for further information on this topic.)

ISSUE 6: THE GLASS CEILING

Women managers are not reaching the higher echelons of organizations in large numbers. Although some individual women have made progress, those at the top remain predominantly Euro-American men. Women's salaries are still lower than men's, and women are frequently not offered the important assignments. One issue for the woman manager is how to handle being passed over for a promotion or an assignment when they feel they are the most qualified. Speaking out about these practices seems futile to many, who are afraid of being labeled "complainers." So the pattern continues, and the conspiracy of silence is maintained.

ISSUE 7: CAREER PATTERNS

The typical career pattern of women differs from that of men. Women's careers are characterized by discontinuity; women pass in and out of the workforce as their family responsibilities shift. In addition, women change career directions more frequently than men do and are more often "late bloomers"—that is, they come into their full stride later in life than men.

The present career structures are too rigid for all this movement. After having a baby, a woman typically would like a longer leave of absence than the usual 6 to 12 weeks' paid leave offered by most organizations. Many women would like a year or two at home with a new baby; others would like longer vacations to match those of their school-age children. Unfortunately, our organizations are still characterized by a "tournament" model of advancement: Once you leave the game, even for a short while, you are essentially no longer considered for advancement. So women managers continue to face difficult choices about how to integrate the two primary aspects of their lives. There are no easy answers.

THE SYSTEMS PERSPECTIVE

Most women continue to think about these issues as personal problems. Many articles counsel women managers on how to increase their personal effectiveness. Women managers are exhorted to "try harder." Among the critical success factors typically cited for women managers are: (1) a track record of achievements, (2) the desire to succeed, (3) the ability to manage subordinates, (4) a willingness to take career risks, and (5) the ability to be tough, decisive, and demanding. These are all *individual* traits or behaviors.

The trouble with this approach is that it locates all of the problems as residing within the women managers rather than within the organization. Instead of telling individual women to "be more competent" or "try harder," or instead of telling men to "give women a break," it makes more sense to look at organizational variables and systems for solutions as well.

The first task is to gain an understanding of which specific policies or practices are acting as barriers for women. This can be done with a short questionnaire, a series of focus groups, or, better yet, a formal audit of the organization. It is critical to learn about the organizational culture, both informal and formal, and its systems— what works for women and what does not.

Excellent questions to ask are:

- What does it take to succeed in this organization?
- What is it like for you as a woman to work here?
- What are your daily hassles and major concerns?
- If you could change three things about the organization, what would they be?
- What are the personnel policies or practices that limit you from contributing to the organization?

Several issues are likely to emerge. First, women managers want more flexible work arrangements. For support staff there are often flextime options, part-time work, and even job-sharing options, but managers' jobs are still rigidly designed. Why couldn't there be job sharing for managers, or part-time managers? Can organizations create work-at-home options and longer leaves of absence? We need to shift our paradigm.

Second, women managers frequently complain that competence is usually measured by "face time"; that is, by the number of hours spent on the job. Too often, it is those who come early and stay late that are perceived as promotable. Confusing competence with the number of hours worked is a major problem for women managers. Flexible arrangements are typically acquired by individuals negotiating a special deal for themselves. If a manager is a "star," the deal is granted. It would be far better to make flexibility available to all managers.

Third, training for women managers has usually focused on giving them basic managerial skills and increasing their assertiveness. Again, this is only part of the picture and implies that increasing skills and improving competencies are all that is needed. In addition, women managers need training in the systems perspective. They need to understand how an organization's culture and practices can work against their advancement and sense of well-being. With more savvy about systems, women managers will begin to learn about making alliances and being visible rather than assuming that if they work hard they will be noticed and rewarded. They will also understand what to do if they want to advance in the organizational hierarchy and how to create a level playing field for all women managers.

Finally, women managers need to understand that *power* is not a dirty word; it is merely the ability to get things done. Power means having access to information, support, and resources. With this perspective, it becomes clear that the staff jobs that women managers frequently seek offer less opportunity in the long term than do line jobs.

Women managers who are aware of organizational issues manage work groups and their own careers differently than those who think only in terms of individual competence. Once this system perspective is understood by women, it is often a major breakthrough. Once they consider its implications for themselves as managers, they will never see their jobs in the same way again.

GETTING STARTED: A CHECKLIST FOR WOMEN MANAGERS

1. Who are the successful women managers in this organization? What can I learn from them?

2. Has our organization issued a list of terms that are considered demeaning or sexist?

3. Do I support other women managers in meetings, making sure their comments are heard?

4. Which policy changes are needed to increase the flexibility of work arrangements?

5. Has our organization provided to all managers training for preventing sexual harassment? Does it include some standard ways for women to deal with unwelcome attention?

6. Do women managers here meet together for support and professional development? Is this supported by the organization?

7. What changes in policy and practice are needed in this organization to make it easier for women managers to move in and out of full-time work as their needs evolve?

8. How can I build more opportunity and more power into my present job?

Katharine Esty

Katharine Esty, PhD, is president of Ibis Consulting Group, Inc., a consulting firm based in Cambridge, Massachusetts, that specializes in the management of change. A social psychologist by training, Dr. Esty has consulted over the last 15 years for a wide variety of organizations on large-systems change, team building, women's issues, and diversity. Currently, her work is focused on helping organizations manage the increasingly diverse workforce and change their corporate cultures and systems to support diversity.

Chapter Twenty-One

Answers to the Mommy Track

Trudi Ferguson

Executive Summary

In order for scores of talented non-traditional workers to be fully utilized in the multicultural world ahead, society must undergo a transformation in how it thinks about who and what has value. For example, given the present state of computer technology, many professional jobs that require 10 to 12 hours a day at work can just as easily be accomplished at home. The workplace itself must be transformed.

Trudi Ferguson argues that several biases need to be reexamined. Those that govern what constitutes appropriate and inappropriate behavior in the workplace, in terms of responsibilities for child rearing, serve as glaring cases in point. Why can't a parent bring her or his offspring to an office with a well-planned infrastructure in place, including appropriate child development capability? Another part of the transformation will inevitably take place within men and what have been their accepted roles in the family structure. Ferguson debunks the mythology that women cannot successfully attend to their families and still work at a top professional level.

Transformation will also mean "changing the picture of what mothers look like to include fathers who drive car pools and take the kids to the dentist, grandmothers who perform day care, and families that eat prepared food and look at dirty dishes in the sink." The author discusses four models of success that reflect the variety and shape of some of the adjustments that must be made if the workforce is to benefit from the contributions of talented women.

From her research, which yielded the four models of success, Ferguson extrapolates a number of highly significant learnings: (1) personal learnings *within* women; (2) organizational learnings; (3) learnings *about* women; and (4) societally relevant learnings. She ends with a series of helpful tips arising from her research data, addressed in many instances to women but also carrying major implications for men. The tips and the entire chapter are a solid statement of one key dimension of social evolution in the Western world.

Society is not there yet, and it may get there "kicking and screaming," but it must get there—that is, if America is to survive and prosper. The essential underlying message in Ferguson's chapter is that the changes she discusses are ones that have to be made by both men and women.

W omen can be both *good* mothers and *top* professionals. While popular literature often suggests that truly good mothers have to choose between children and work, new models show that this is not true. Successful women in a variety of fields demonstrate that mothers can and do perform multiple roles very successfully. Often, excellence in one role can predict and instruct high performance in the other.

Success requires individual as well as corporate strategies. What do individual women have to do? How do corporations that utilize such talented women recruit, develop, and support them? This chapter offers portraits of the lives and philosophies of successful women and their organizations; it includes specific strategies to assist the individual woman and organization. It uses examples and rhetoric to resist the insidious notions that women and corporations are limited by having to make a choice.

WHAT IS THE MOMMY TRACK?

The "mommy track" is a debilitating myth that came from a 1989 article in the *Harvard Business Review* by Felice Schwartz, who made the suggestion that women could not successfully attend to their families and still work at a top professional level. She suggested that corporations offer an alternative work track—a lesser track for family women that would allow them to hold jobs but not to aspire to or achieve upper levels of contribution, power, or money. It would leave them more time for family activities, reduce work stress, and acknowledge that their primary interests were elsewhere.

Many women responded with outrage to this demeaning suggestion. It was defeating. It did not take into account the often invisible but sizable numbers of women who were already successful in both arenas. It discouraged aspiring women and gave corporations an excuse to continue the outmoded, traditional patterns of underutilizing a large part of their workforce. The mommy track is dysfunctional for organizations. The internalization of that notion for women encourages self-imposed limitations: "I can't do both. I can't have children and do this work."

But defying the limitations of the mommy track means changing the definitions of success. It means incorporating a picture of a chief executive officer conducting business at home while sitting on the rug. It means changing the picture of workplaces to include kids in the office on snow days, corporate cooks, family benefits, spousal relocation plans, executive sick leave, nannies, and child care services. It means changing the picture of what mothers look like to include fathers who drive car pools and take the kids to the dentist, grandmothers who perform day care, and families that eat prepared food and look at dirty dishes in the sink.

FOUR MODELS OF SUCCESS

Sandra Day O'Connor

Sandra Day O'Connor is the first female justice of the US Supreme Court. She also has three sons. Worried that taking time off for family would harm her career, she feared she "would lose [her] skills and would not be marketable." But she was persistent in making requests about part-time work to accommodate her need for family time and to maintain her intellectual skills.

Justice O'Connor grew up with an independent mind and spent a lot of time alone. She was raised primarily on her grandparents' ranch away from her parents and credits this with enabling her to resist more conventional notions of work and family. She developed her own internal standards and learned to take care of her own needs.

Contrary to popular mythology, which portrays guilt-ridden working mothers, Sandra Day O'Connor had little guilt. Her attitude is liberating. "I would be a bad full-time mother because all my judgmental, controlling, decision-making nature that makes me good at what I do would be directed at my children, and they would be squashed." But she also credits the same skills that help her at work with the success of her children. Knowing the importance of child care, she hired young college men who would be good role models to baby-sit her three boys. She hired a surrogate grandfather to read and play with them. O'Connor was active in arranging how the children spent their free time; for instance, she substituted band and competitive swimming for television watching.

Her children developed independence and resourcefulness because they were not being raised under her hovering wing. "The good side is that they are very independent. For example, our dog was hit by a car when no adult was there; they did the sensible thing. They found an old door and made it into a stretcher and carried the dog to the vet. I was proud of that!"

Jennifer Lawson

Jennifer Lawson is vice-president of programming at the Public Broadcasing System (PBS). One of the few top-level African-American women in this country, she deliberately chose to work for a supportive corporation that shares family values. PBS finds it charming that parents bring their kids to work. There is even a room with crayons where children are welcome. To ensure that the corporation is supportive to her (in both work and family) and to others, she has served as the ombudsperson for female and family issues. She also meets racial and gender discrimination head on. Early in her career, for instance, a colleague described her male supervisor as sexist and racist because he constantly referred to her as his "gal." Lawson told him that if he used the term *gal*, then she could use the term *boy*. This made it crystal clear exactly how she expected to be treated. In 1975 she found that her rate of pay was lower than that of a man doing comparable work. "I immediately raised that issue with my employers, saying if they didn't raise my salary I would have to quit." They increased it.

Jennifer's home-computer terminal and modem connect her to the office. "I can be the mom at home and cook dinner. When I need to work overtime, I can do it at home, so I can be a physical presence.

I believe in rituals like vacation, special holidays, special weekends, dinner together, and reading to my son before he goes to bed.

"The workplace is very important, and I worked up until the day of [my son's] delivery. . . . I went home and my son was born later that night. I took six weeks' maternity leave. Since we were in the funding cycle, I returned to work two weeks after he was born. I brought him with me and nursed him, even though there was heavy traffic. I amused friends with the Do Not Disturb sign on my office door. I have no guilt about day care because I found the very best day care center I could and I was coming home to a healthy, happy baby. I was well informed of what was going on. They even kept a log of what the baby had eaten!" Now, she says, "I take a short vacation alone to look at who I am and where I want to go . . . and what is important to me. I can focus on creating harmony in life—a mixture of work, family, and friends."

Rebecca Sinkler

Rebecca Sinkler serves as the very successful editor-in-chief of the prestigious *New York Times Book Review*. It wasn't always so. She started as the typical suburban housewife, raising three children and tending to the needs of her successful husband. When her youngest child was in school full time, Rebecca returned to work on a casual basis and was amazed to find how much she loved it. She began working long hours, working at home late into the night. Poignantly, she describes how this upset the family's dynamics and led to marital trouble. When discussing such conflict, she emphasizes the importance of understanding how a working mother's reentry can disrupt the foundations of family agreements. Happily, her family resolved the issue and rebalanced their lives through therapy, but she was willing to describe this process to illustrate that it is not simple, that it requires work.

Geraldine Ferraro

Geraldine Ferraro, the first female vice-presidential candidate, offers other insights. She was raised in an area where presidential candidates would walk through proclaiming, "This is the kind of neighborhood we have to do something about." Her father died when she was 8; her world crumbled. As an adult, she married and raised three children. So when she entered the legal profession, she was considerably older than the other graduates and encountered greater expectations of her as an "older" employee. In reality, she was worried about being rusty and out-of-date. Because of her public positions, we all learned about her husband's business practices and her son's drug problem. This raises the question of whether a woman in politics is subjected to greater public scrutiny of her family than a man.

WHAT DO WE LEARN FROM THESE WOMEN AND FROM THE MOMMY TRACK?

We learn that it can be done. Women can be both top professionals and good mothers.

We learn how important it is to find receptive organizations. PBS shared Jennifer Lawson's values; everyone understood that working women have family needs and that children might show up at work on occasion and should be treated with respect. Physician Elizabeth Blalock chose to affiliate with a group health plan, Kaiser Permanante, over private practice because as a single mother, she didn't want to add the burden of running her own medical business.

Carol Dinkins's husband was a partner in a large law firm, so she saw firsthand the rigorous requirements of hours and dedication. Having two small children, she knew she couldn't commit that kind of time. She was also aware that there were not many married women with children working in large corporate law firms. She wanted to select a legal field in which there were more opportunities for achievement, flexibility, and individuality. She found a college faculty position with regular, limited hours and no travel. Along with hard work and competence, that excellent choice resulted in her developing a specialty in a new field, environmental law, that has taken center stage in our national life and priorities in the 1990s. She is now a top expert in that field and is in great demand. Her children are also well launched, so she can devote more time to the professional life she has developed.

We learn that women make changes. Cathleen Black, the successful publisher of *USA Today,* started her career at the prestigious *New York Times.* She was thrilled to have such a job. But after several years of making no progress, she courageously left and went to work for *Ms.* magazine, a smaller publication. The magazine offered more visibility and more opportunity, but most importantly, it valued women. She left *Ms* (again, courageously) to take a flier on the position at the untested *USA Today:* Would condensed news in color really work?

Amy Roseman had worked for years to become an obstetrician–gynecologist. Yet, she says, she "loved her work and hated her life." With great resolve, she changed her life and made the time to find a mate and have two children. She was comfortably settled until her five-year-old asked why they never saw her (she was on call delivering babies every other night). Because of her family commitments, after 14 years Amy Roseman forsook her original goal of an obstetrical practice, focused on gynecology, and developed a whole new interest in the specialty of female incontinence.

We learn that women can create their own scripts. Ellen Gordon, president of Tootsie Roll, lived in New England and often brought her youngest daughter to work with her at the Tootsie Roll manufacturing plant in Chicago. Worried that her daughter was growing up in a factory, Gordon enrolled her in two schools: a New England private school and an inner-city Chicago school. This unconventional decision allowed her daughter both to be with her and to get an education.

Carol Dinkins was offered the job of deputy US attorney general in Washington, DC, but her two small children were in Texas. Not to be denied the second-highest job in her profession, she worked Monday through Friday in Washington, then took the red-eye on weekends to be with her young family.

Nancy Evans, publisher of Doubleday, tells her story: "When I got pregnant, I immediately installed a fax, hired a secretary, and developed a schedule for messengers so I could operate from home. Everybody came to my house. They loved it. And we got so much more accomplished. When you are in the office, there are all kinds of interruptions. But when they had to trek downtown to my house, they were more comfortable. You could drink a soda. There was no resistance to this for me." One of the most important components of making our lives work is not to think in stereotypes but to invent our own lifestyle patterns.

We learn to make appropriate demands. Women should not be afraid to spell out clearly what they want and need. Astronaut Anna Fisher worked for NASA and went on a space mission after the birth of her first child. Later, with two children, she decided not to "go hurling around in space." NASA was shocked when she asked for part-time status. "We do not have part-time astronauts." But why not? "You can't keep up to speed half-time. . . . We are this prestigious institution of serious, top-flight employees." Persistence prevailed, and she is now NASA's first part-time astronaut.

We learn about new pictures or models of success and family. Women can work from their home, bring their kids to work, bring in corporate cooks, and use trainers and psychologists to tend to the needs of their staffs. Single mother Peggy Noonin served as a speechwriter to Presidents Ronald Reagan and George Bush. Yet she resigned her job at the White House to write at home so she could comfort the hurts of her young son. On her bedroom computer she wrote a best-seller and composed President Bush's 1988 campaign slogan; "a kinder, gentler nation."

We learn about the use of the feminine perspective. Top women use their mothering skills in their professional lives. Madeline Kunin, the former governor of Vermont, praised the value of her 10 child-rearing years in teaching her how to run a government required the same conflict-resolution skills and the inevitable humility she learned as a parent. In another case, the first female captain of a Boeing 747 talked about disclosing to her crew the news of expected bad weather and about working as a team (family) to calm the passengers. These women did not shy away from their feminine perspective.

We learn that support is a key ingredient of success. Contrary to many popular myths, these dual-role women did find support. They were deliberate in choosing the men they married. For instance, successful television producer ("Roseanne" and "The Bill Cosby Show") Marcy Carsey avoided men who wanted her to put them through law school. Working women sought professional partners who embraced the importance of the women's professional roles. Support can be found in grandmothers, neighbors, day care, and organizations able to embrace mothers as top professionals.

Above all, we learn that this is not easy. Here are some specific tips from these women:

Work close to home.

Find ways to reduce office stress.

Make realistic financial obligations.

Negotiate reduced expectations and pay while pregnant.

Get good child care; you can't leave home without it.

Establish rituals and patterns that work for you.

Pick a field in which you have some control over your life.

Install a computer terminal at home with a modem.

Take a personal vacation every year.

Use your support system.

Believe in the long run.

Be organized.

Set priorities and stick to them.

Reduce guilt.

Make choices and don't second-guess yourself.

Set realistic goals while aiming high.

Don't care if the pot is greasy.

It doesn't have to be perfect.

Things go wrong.

Enjoy your children and family.

Buy stockings in bulk.

Forget any organization where all you see is women typing and men in the offices.

Get television trays for the inevitable dinners on the run.

Get rid of math anxiety.

CONCLUSIONS

Women can be both top professionals and good mothers. But you have to create your own new script. That script needs to have support within the family and within the organization. Create and demand that support. Change the script until you are satisfied. Look at models around you.

Managers at all levels can help by recognizing the realities of family life. Educate the workforce through gender workshops, reading lists, speakers, and sensitivity to offensive language and behavior patterns. Appoint a responsible person to advocate female and family issues. A task force can monitor the issues. Get women involved in the hiring process. Establish a formal mentoring program for career guidance. Create visible and accessible female role models. Tie retention and promotion of women to the bottom line (by monitoring the cost of turnover and alienation). Publish clear and fair maternity policies. Review child care assistance and select from referral, on-site care, sick nurse providers, executive nannies, and child-at-work policies. Explore the options provided by flexible workday schedules.

Men have more to learn. And they have to keep learning—and looking, listening, and asking. Men have to learn the realities working mothers face. They have to reevaluate their supportive roles as husbands and fathers. It may mean going over the next day's slide presentation at home. It may mean assuming primary responsibility for kids' play dates, sick care, school drop-off, or providing the mother with rest and protection on Sunday. The organizational man—managers—must understand the realities of working mothers: that these women can and often want to do both seriously and well; that meetings can't be arbitrarily scheduled at 7 AM, thus conflicting with child care; that overnights cannot always be hastily arranged because there may not be support at home; that a traveling woman might bring a nanny and a baby and still be serious about her job. The most important contribution managers and organizations can make is honest, ongoing, open discussion of these issues. Cooperation in addressing these fundamental work and life issues is crucial to *all* of us.

Trudi Ferguson

Trudi Ferguson, PhD, is an organizational development consultant specializing in organizational diagnosis, communication and team building. She is a member of the NTL Institute. Her recent work with women in organizations resulted in her 1991 book, *Answers to the Mommy Track: How Wives and Mothers in Business Reach the Top and Balance Their Lives.* She is a frequent guest on CNN and has worked with women in nontraditional roles such as telephone-pole climbers. She lives in Los Angeles and is the mother of two children.

Chapter Twenty-Two

Combatting Sexual Harassment in the Workplace: Every Manager's Responsibility

Anne Litwin

Sophie Hahn

Executive Summary

That there is no place for sexual harassment in the workplace, or anywhere else in American life, is obvious. However, the sad truth is that in many organizations it remains an ugly fact of life. Harassment of a woman by a man or of a man by a woman, or harassment between people of the same gender is in its essence the enactment of power, whether hierarchical, based on stronger physical attributes, or both. It reduces the other to an object.

As Anne Litwin and Sophie Hahn point out, it took the harassment charges brought by Anita Hill during the Clarence Thomas Supreme Court confirmation hearings to bring harassment to light across America.

The responsible manager must be fully aware of the law and of the various levels of harassing behavior. Given the evolving nature of harassment law, managers must keep updated of changes in it as they are enacted. Litwin and Hahn also point out that if harassment is reported or observed, managers may have a most significant role to play in the investigation and resolution of alleged incidents. This may include supporting a victim, recommending or implementing punishment of a harasser, or healing the workplace in the aftermath.

Many managers shiver at the thought of having to take a proactive stance in a documented incident of harassment occurring within their purview. This is understandable. Often such incidents involve people in the workforce with whom a manager may have developed a positive work relationship. It can get messy. Yet failing to act appropriately can make the situation messier still.

Such failure continuously embeds the behavior as part of the fabric of the culture of the organization—an insidious outcome. It is in this context that becoming familiar with this chapter is a critically important dimension of the manager's role. Managers who fail to take this matter seriously are managers who are positioning themselves to become involved in potential litigation procedures, to the detriment of both themselves and their organizations.

D espite a previous lack of attention to the widespread problem of sexual harassment in the workplace, the subject has long been an issue for many employees and has been considered an illegal form of sex discrimination for more than a decade.

The issue of sexual harassment first attracted broad public attention during the Clarence Thomas Supreme Court confirmation hearings in the fall of 1991. During those hearings, Anita Hill, an attorney and law professor who had formerly worked for Thomas, presented her allegations of sexual harassment and brought this previously hidden issue into the light. Today, all managers are expected to know about and work to combat sexual harassment.

Many organizations have policies defining and prohibiting sexual harassment. Sexual harassment is also against the law. Thus, every manager should familiarize herself or himself with the legal definition of sexual harassment and with the organization's own definition and policies, if any.

Because managers can be held responsible for the sexual harassment of one employee by another if the manager knew or should have known about the conduct and did nothing to stop it, they should also become familiar with and implement methods for the prevention and early detection of sexual harassment. Finally, managers may have a significant role to play in the investigation and resolution of an incident of alleged sexual harassment, including supporting a victim and recommending or implementing punishment of a harasser.

This chapter serves as an introduction to the issue of sexual harassment and the definitions, rules, policies, practices, and procedures all managers should be aware of and follow.

WHAT IS SEXUAL HARASSMENT?

Sexual harassment usually falls into one of three categories: verbal, nonverbal, and physical.

- *Verbal sexual harassment* includes suggestive comments about dress, sexual desirability, physique, or sexual orientation; jokes about gender-specific traits; sexual propositions; and sexually related threats and insults.
- *Non-verbal sexual harassment* includes suggestive or insulting noises, obscene gestures, whistling, leering, and displaying obscene pictures.
- *Physical sexual harassment* includes touching, pinching, standing or sitting too close, intentionally brushing against someone else's body, and coercing sexual intercourse and assault.

The Legal Definition of Sexual Harassment

The US Equal Employment Opportunity Commission (EEOC), the agency charged with enforcing federal laws against employment discrimination (sexual harassment is a form of discrimination based on sex), has defined sexual harassment as:

. . . unwelcome sexual advances, requests for sexual favors, and other verbal or physical conduct of a sexual nature . . . when

1. submission to such conduct is made either explicitly or implicitly a term or condition of an individual's employment or academic achievement,
2. submission to or rejection of such conduct by an individual is used as the basis for employment decisions or academic decisions affecting such individual, or
3. such conduct has the purpose or effect of unreasonably interfering with an individual's work or academic performance or creating an intimidating, hostile, or offensive working or academic environment.

As more and more sexual harassment cases are reviewed by the EEOC, state and local agencies, and the courts, the legal definition of sexual harassment may be expanded or modified. Every few years, managers should request from a local EEOC office or human rights agency or from the legal or personnel department of their organizations, the most up-to-date legal definitions of sexual harassment available.

Understanding Sexual Harassment

Sexual harassment can occur in a variety of circumstances. The vast majority of sexual harassment is done by a male supervisor toward a female subordinate. Although less common, victims can also be of the same gender as the harasser, and a man can be the victim of a female harasser.

In some instances, the harasser may not be the victim's own supervisor, but a colleague, a client, or another supervisory employee. Under the law, even an individual who has not been the direct recipient of unwelcome sexual conduct can be a victim of sexual harassment. For example, the direct sexual harassment of one worker can create an intimidating or hostile work environment for a co-worker who is upset by the harasser's behavior.

In general, the keys to the definition of sexual harassment are that the conduct is *unwelcome* and that it is of an *explicitly* or *implicitly sexual nature*.

To determine whether it would be considered sexual harassment, the severity, circumstances, and frequency of the conduct in question must be taken into account. If the conduct is severe or pervasive enough to create an environment that a "reasonable person" would find hostile or abusive, and the victim perceives the environment as hostile or abusive, then the conduct is considered sexual harassment.

For example, if a male colleague asks a female colleague for a date, in a friendly manner, this alone would not be considered sexual harassment. However, if he persists, and his behavior becomes pervasive enough to detract from her job performance, it may become sexual harassment.

Some conduct could be considered sexual harassment the first time it occurs. For example, if a male supervisor suggests even once that a female subordinate can get a raise if she provides sexual favors, and this suggestion is perceived by the female subordinate to be serious, this could be considered sexual harassment.

Conduct that is considered to be of a *sexual nature* is conduct that makes reference, explicitly or implicitly, to a person's sexuality, sexual desirability, sexual organs, or other sexual attributes. More general comments about women or men, such as "Women are too emotional to be good managers," will not be considered to be of a sexual nature, although they may be evidence of or suggest other forms of discrimination.

- *Explicit conduct* is obviously sexual. This would include, for example, touching sexual organs, asking a co-worker to perform sexual acts, or other direct sexual conduct or requests.
- *Implicit conduct* is less obvious behavior that would include, for example, looks or stares that, given the context, frequency, suggested intent, or accompanying body language, are in fact sexually inappropriate leers.

In many cases, behavior that is experienced as sexual harassment might not be considered sexual under other circumstances. As such, this implicit conduct can be the most difficult form of sexual harassment to understand.

For example, one colleague may occasionally compliment other colleagues on their clothes. This conduct can be harmless if done in a neutral and straightforward manner. But if these same compliments are delivered with sexual innuendo in the giver's tone of voice, or with a leer, or if a recipient indicates that such comments make her or him uncomfortable, and the compliments continue, then they may constitute sexual harassment. Thus, managers should always carefully evaluate the circumstances of conduct that may, when first described, seem entirely innocuous.

Managers should also take into account whether or not a power differential exists between two employees in evaluating conduct that appears innocuous. Unwelcome behavior is especially likely to be experienced as sexual harassment when one co-worker has more formal or informal power than the other.

PREVENTING SEXUAL HARASSMENT

Managers can do much to create a work environment where sexual harassment is less likely to occur and where they will be able to learn about potential problems as soon as they arise. With preventive measures in place and with early warning, managers have the opportunity to address potential harassment before a situation escalates. The following are ways to create an environment in which sexual harassment will be less likely to occur.

1. *Continually assess the work environment* for signs that a problem may exist so that corrective action can be taken. Such signs may include:
   - Open displays of inappropriate material or behaviors such as pin-up calendars, common use of sexually explicit language, or the telling of lewd jokes
   - Friction between the sexes as manifested by frequent complaints or grievances pitting women and men against each other
   - Persistent gossip that includes whispered conversations or sexually oriented rumors
   - Sudden changes in an employee's job performance
2. *Distribute and post the sexual harassment policy* and reporting procedure of your organization. If none exists, post the EEOC guidelines and elaborate specific conduct that is considered unacceptable.
3. *Educate all employees* by providing sexual harassment workshops and information.
4. *Be an example.* Show a gender-neutral attitude. Ask for feedback regularly from female and male employees about your own behavior.
5. *Be firm and consistent.* Work for changes in others' attitudes. Do not tolerate offensive jokes or comments from women or men. Provide frequent feedback to employees who need to adjust their conduct.
6. *Be personally accessible to employees* and listen to their complaints.
7. *Offer employees more than one route for registering complaints,* including routes that bypass direct supervisors, who may be the source of harassment.
8. *Respond quickly, fairly,* and with as much confidentiality as possible to any complaint of sexual harassment.

INVESTIGATING AND RESOLVING INCIDENTS OF SEXUAL HARASSMENT

If a manager observes sexual harassment or if sexual harassment is reported, that manager has an obligation to act. If the organization has a written policy, the policy and related procedures should be followed. Where no specific sexual harassment policy exists, a manager may follow a general grievance procedure.

How behavior or a complaint is handled sends a message about how the organization perceives sexual harassment. It sets a tone that has a lasting impact on future occurrences and complaints of sexual harassment. Some guidelines for properly conducting an investigation and resolving a complaint are described below. In most instances, managers should also seek the guidance of their personnel department when confronted with the possibility of sexual harassment.

1. *Interview the complaining employee,* making it clear that the complaint is taken seriously. Gather the details of what happened, including when, where, and with whom. Determine whether there were witnesses and whether the complaining employee discussed the behavior with any friends or colleagues or was seen by them to be visibly upset.

2. *Interview the accused employee.* Stay objective. Inform the accused employee that a complaint has been made against her or him and caution against any form of retaliation. It is generally not advised to reveal the name of the accuser at this point, unless she or he has agreed to be named.

3. *Evaluate whether the matter is minor enough to be resolved through a face-to-face discussion.* If so, and if the parties are willing, bring the two individuals together to try to reach agreement on what is appropriate behavior in the future. If the complainant does not agree to this session, or if the accused denies that the events occurred, then it will be necessary to proceed with a more in-depth investigation.

4. *Interview all witnesses and individuals* who may have first- or second-hand knowledge of the alleged conduct or of the complainant's reaction to the conduct. Phrase questions carefully to determine what other employees know about the situation and to protect the privacy and reputations of the employees involved.

5. *Evaluate whether employees should be separated while the investigation is conducted.* Consider whether continued

day-to-day contact between the employees involved in
the complaint is interfering with their ability to work, or
whether the accused is able or likely to engage in intimi-
dation or retaliation. If so, it is advisable to temporarily
move the accused in order to avoid the perception of retaliation against the employee making the complaint.

6. *Decide whether or not sexual harassment has occurred.* Weigh
   all the evidence. Consider the credibility of each individual. Compare the reported behavior with the definition
   of sexual harassment. Assess the level of seriousness of
   the alleged behavior. In cases where there are no first- or
   second-hand witnesses, the EEOC rules state that the victim's word alone may prevail if it is sufficiently detailed
   and internally consistent.

7. *Take action.* If you determine that sexual harassment has
   not occurred, write a detailed report explaining why. If
   you determine that sexual harassment has occurred, follow the organization's disciplinary procedures. If no procedures exist, make recommendations for appropriate discipline based on the seriousness of the behavior and
   discuss these with the personnel department before implementation. Some examples of the range of disciplines
   possible are:

   • *Mild discipline.* Manager gives a verbal reprimand fol-
     lowed by a written warning that is not included in the
     employee's personnel file.
   • *Moderate discipline.* Manager gives a verbal reprimand
     followed by written warning that is included in the em-
     ployee's personnel file. Outside counseling may also
     be required as a condition of continued employment,
     or the harasser may be transferred.
   • *Severe discipline.* Suspension, probation, demotion, or
     termination.

8. *Support and/or provide restitution to the harassed employee.*
   Tangible damage to the victim should be rectified. This
   may include invalidating poor performance reviews or delivering promotions or raises that were unjustly denied.
   Harassment victims should also be offered counseling to
   help them repair the psychological and emotional damage that is often sustained.

9. *Monitor the work environment* to prevent retaliation against either party by co-workers or from an accused toward an accuser. It often takes some time for the interpersonal relationships among all employees to return to normal. Employees should be provided with opportunities to discuss their feelings. Information and training can help the organization or department recover from the disruption of the harassment and/or the investigation.

10. *Keep careful notes* of all conversations and actions related to all phases of any investigation and resolution of all sexual harassment complaints.

CONCLUSION

Sexual harassment is damaging to the victims and to the workplace in general. It is also against the law. Managers can be held responsible for the sexual harassment of one employee by another if the manager knew or should have known about the conduct and did nothing to stop it.

Managers can do a lot to create work environments where sexual harassment will be less likely to occur. They have a duty to be vigilant for signs of a problem, to inform themselves and their employees, to act as role models, to be accessible to employees, to be a good listener, to be objective and consistent, and to respond quickly and with sensitivity to complaints.

If sexual harassment is reported or observed, managers may have a significant role to play in the investigation and resolution of an alleged incident, including supporting a victim, recommending or implementing punishment of a harasser, and healing the workplaces in the aftermath. It is important that managers know about the laws, policies, and procedures governing sexual harassment so they can fulfill their responsibilities, protect their organizations from costly legal action, and provide a respectful work environment for all.

Anne Litwin

Anne Litwin is president of Anne H. Litwin Associates, based in Boston and New York City. She has been an organizational development consultant for 18 years for a wide variety of organizations in the private, public, and not-for-profit sectors, specializing in diversity issues in the workplace. She is the creator of a workshop for the NTL Institute entitled "Women and Men Working Together." Anne Litwin is a member of the NTL Institute and is an adjunct professor in the Schools of Business and Public Administration at Long Island University. She was also the chief executive officer of a retail business for several years.

Sophie Hahn

Sophie Hahn, Esq, is studying for a PhD in industrial relations and human resources at the Rutgers University Institute of Management and Labor Relations. Her work has ranged from practicing law at a major New York firm to acting as organizational strategist for a large international entity. Focusing on issues of personnel management and development, diversity, gender, and culture in the workplace, Sophie Hahn has participated in the resolution of sexual harassment and other workplace grievances. Her current research interests include abuse, equity, and healing at work.

Chapter Twenty-Three

Sensitizing Managers to Asian-American Diversity Issues

Toy-Ping Taira

Executive Summary

This chapter is of great importance because it identifies issues that non-Asian-American managers must recognize. Stereotypes exist across the board. Those from Asia are often seen as hardworking, nonconfrontational, quiet, reserved, and deferential to others. Because of some of these attributes and the meanings that often get attached to them, Asian professionals are often given less attention by managers than they need. The fact is, as Toy-Ping Taira observes, "many Asian Americans feel that they have more assets to offer than are being used or understood."

This chapter makes a number of critically important points, the understanding of which is crucial to making better utilization of this enormous potential resource. Key toward this end will be the ability of non-Asian-American managers to move past the unspoken rule, "Know your place." This, Taira points out, is what often underlies the very polite communication between management and Asian Americans. Non-Asian-American managers interested in more effective management of today's and tomorrow's larger multiracial workforce need to demonstrate sensitivity to all people, including those who have not expressed their issues.

Many non-Asian Americans assume that all Asian Americans share common backgrounds. In truth, there is probably more diversity among Asians than there is among European Americans and other groups making up the American population. One feature that may be common among Asian workers, Taira observes, is not "losing face" and not causing anyone else to lose face. Loss of face in Asian cultures is tantamount to losing respect, and asking another for help may result in disrespect. This then constitutes a collision of cultural values that gets played out to the detriment of Asian-American professionals.

The chapter is replete with information central to the development of this talented resource base. Historically, talented Asians have almost always been confined to technical and scientific jobs in industry. Taira's chapter includes a most helpful chart that captures the way in which non-Asian Americans observe Asian behavior and the meanings and interpretations that are associated with those behaviors. This and a careful and thoughtful reading of the chapter will assist managers in moving past what may be their current beliefs and behavioral dispositions to a new place in which Asian Americans will be far more represented at all levels, but especially in management, where they have historically been unrepresented.

THE WORKFORCE OF THE FUTURE

M anagers in the United States need to better manage certain of their employees who are hardworking, skillful, and underutilized. These employees, Asian Americans, are a group that is the fastest growing in the United States, as shown in the 1990 census.

Asian Americans feel they have generally been overlooked for development and job-advancement opportunities because of cultural diversity issues. Managers must develop the sensitized behavior that demonstrates awareness of Asian American concerns to ensure the best use of human resources now and in the workforce of the future.

Asian-American Employees Can Benefit Business

With globalization of the competitive market, companies can use the diversity of employee creativity, values, pioneering spirit, energy, outlook, skills, knowledge, problem solving, leadership styles, and work ethics to gain a competitive edge.

Management Can Be Ready

Forward planning now more likely paves a successful path toward a better-prepared management style for the future. Managers can begin to find out what types of developmental training are needed to help their Asian-American employees develop the tools they need to be productive and successful and what kind of organizational and individual strategic plans can be implemented. Positive actions, job opportunities, and improved communication need to be carefully thought out, understood, and implemented.

Managers Can Reverse the Asian-American Invalidation

Most employees seek to have their work and status valued by their managers. However, there are circumstances unique to Asian Americans that cause this need for recognition to remain unmet. Asian Americans, whether US-born or foreign-born, are given less attention by managers than they need. This phenomenon of unrecognized, benign neglect can be called "Asian-American invalidation."

Many Asian Americans feel that they have more assets to offer than are being used or understood. This lack of positive acknowledgement by managers alienates many employees. They intuitively know that they, as a class, have not been supported or given advantageous positioning at the level they need to feel fully valued or validated. It is not unusual for the unspoken rule, Know Your Place, to underlie polite communication between management and Asian Americans.

Asian Americans perceive themselves as not being allowed the same job opportunities afforded other special-interest groups, even with all the capabilities and diligence they believe they have. Asian Americans in the corporate and government workplaces are generally supportive of the other groups. Asian Americans are no different from other Americans in that they justifiably do not care to be forgotten, excluded, or left behind—individually or as a minority group.

Those interested in managing today's and tomorrow's

multiracial workforce more effectively need to demonstrate sensitivity to all people, including those who have not expressed their issues.

Managers can learn to address Asian Americans' concerns by becoming more informed about and more involved in those concerns. This chapter focuses on how American managers can increase their effectiveness with their Asian-American employees.

DIFFERENCES AMONG ASIANS

Asian Americans are just as diverse as other groups of people; they should not be treated as if they were all the same. The caveat that prefaces this chapter is not to generalize too much about Asian Americans because the term *Asian* represents very diverse groups, each often very proud of its distinct heritage. Asians come from different national or ethnic origins, cultures, and countries. For example, many Asian Americans of Chinese ancestry can trace their origins to India, Vietnam, Singapore, Hong Kong, Taiwan, or mainland China.

Although most often lumped into one category here in United States, it is not unusual for Asian Americans themselves not to understand each other, since their family and personal values may originate from different Asian societies, each with its own political system, culture, familial system, technology, language, religion, tradition, belief, dress, attitudes, and behaviors. There are even major differences depending on how long the Asian American and his or her family has been in the United States.

Managers must remember to treat each employee, no matter what differences exist, as an individual and not let stereotypes and cultural generalizations get in the way of straightforward and unencumbered human interactions.

To sensitize their awareness, managers can try to understand their Asian-American employee better by first asking themselves if they are reacting to the physical differences rather than to the person within. Take the time to process any such turnoffs into an appreciation. Go the extra mile by providing employees with encouragement, support, and care in terms of training and development, promotions into managerial positions, assignments, awards, bonuses, visibility opportunities, conferences, and chances for professional and personal growth.

VALUES THAT CONTRIBUTE TO ASIAN-AMERICAN INVALIDATION

The phenomenon of Asian-American invalidation is the result of unrecognized benign neglect by managers. Historically, Asian Americans have not lobbied for recognition of their issues because of some core values that have resulted in collusion with their neglect. The most important of these values are not "losing face" (i.e., respect) and expecting rewards for hard work.

Not Losing Face

Asian Americans may reveal their problems to each other, but even then, there is hesitancy. Part of this behavior stems from the value placed on not losing face and not causing anyone else to lose face. This implies that a person should not lose respect from others and should not show disrespect for another by acknowledging weakness, asking for help, or placing others in an awkward situation and potentially causing others to lose face.

This value may also cause some Asian Americans to follow the exact instructions given on a project and not take any creative chances for fear of reprisal or criticism that might cause loss of face. To counteract that, managers can promote a safe environment for Asian Americans to feel that they can step outside the boundaries and not be persecuted. Asking questions should be encouraged.

Belief in Rewards for Hard Work

Asian Americans often seek employment in performing personal services or scientific or technical work. Most Asian cultures have stressed that hard work automatically brings rewards. More often

than not, Asian Americans have naively believed this value to be
true in the United States. Such hard work, while not demanding
much from their managers, has contributed to Asian-American
employees being treated as ''worker bees'' and to the non-Asian-
American managers' biased belief that Asian Americans are not
leaders or managers themselves.

Acceptance of Fate

The stoicism ingrained in many Asian Americans has resulted in
their hesitancy to confront any unpleasantness or to lobby for better and more fair treatment. Asian Americans have not complained
loudly enough or made their discontent known. Their stoicism
has not served them well and has not been understood in the
American culture. Many Asian Americans value the acceptance
of unpleasant events with no visible signs of passion. They believe
that such occurrences are the unavoidable result of fate.

Without advocacy and attention drawn to them, Asian Americans have hidden the frustration of being ignored and not helped,
of not being valued as a first-class citizen, and of not feeling validated. While not being seen as a problem may have been what
the Asian-American community has unconsciously wanted up to
now, the flip side has been that nothing was seen by the non-Asian-
American employer as needing to be fixed or facilitated.

No wonder managers are puzzled and experience some frustration. They cannot understand why Asian Americans are now beginning to speak out about their problems, which, to managers,
have never existed before. To them, Asian Americans have always
appeared content on the job.

WHAT ARE SOME MAJOR ISSUES?

In order for managers to fully understand their Asian-American
employees, they need to know and appreciate the issues that concern those employees.

    1. *Foreign-born Asian Americans need guidance and support to become
acclimated to the American culture.*

2. *US-born Asian Americans want to be seen and treated as equally American as US-born European Americans are.*

3. *Asian Americans believe they are not being seen nor heard.* Some Asian Americans believe that their issues and needs are viewed by the majority of European Americans as unimportant and secondary to those of other minority groups. In many Asian Americans' experience, equal opportunity programs are mainly for the benefit of other groups.

4. *Asian Americans know that the "glass ceiling" exists.* Asian Americans are just beginning to identify and share their experiences with the glass ceiling. They are allowed to be promoted up to a point—often for a scientific, technical, or service position, but not into management. Those who have tried to break through that unacknowledged glass ceiling into the managerial level have done so with varied success and with setbacks. Often, the level of frustration became so high that they retreated to their original positions.

5. *Asian Americans' historical distrust.* Many Asian groups hesitate to call attention to their issues because of past US exclusionary and discriminatory legislation against Asians. Some examples include the 1882 Chinese Exclusion Act, which denied citizenship; the Immigration Act of 1924, directed towards stemming Japanese and other Asian immigration; the World War II evacuation and internment of US citizens of Japanese origin under Executive Order 9066; and several state laws prohibiting the ownership and leasing of land by noncitizens.

MANAGING ASIAN-AMERICAN EMPLOYEES

On an individual basis, each manager can help reduce these frustrating dynamics, improve working relationships, and facilitate the professional and personal development of their Asian-American employees.

1. *Check out perceptions.* Managers can take on the responsibility of becoming more sensitive and self-aware during interactions with their Asian-American employees. Managers should try to understand what it is that they do to disempower Asian-American employees. By routinely checking out their

TABLE 23–1
Common Stereotypes and Corresponding Cultural Explanations

Observed Behavior of Asian Americans	Common Stereotypical Misinterpretations	Possible Cultural Explanation
Nonconfrontational	Passive; does not care one way or another	Values harmony; sees disagreements as being in disharmony
Quiet; reserved	Has no opinions	Values opinions of others and fitting in with group
Agreeable; dependable follower	Unassertive, no leadership qualities	Values what is good for group; can be assertive and a leader if needed for the group
Industrious	Make good "worker bees"	Values carrying their share of work; believes hard work will be recognized and rewarded
Technically and scientifically competent	No management competence or leader-type charisma	Values science as universal language crossing cultural barriers; believes leadership comes in many forms
Deferential to others	Not committed to own opinions, judgments, or preferences	Values being respectful of others; believes in 'saving face' for self and others; values age and wisdom
Very American behavior	Looks Asian; must be of different culture	Born in United States; values American heritage

perceptions with their Asian-American employees and encouraging them to do the same, managers can avoid many misunderstandings. It would improve working relationships if the managers would reconsider their first impressions and seek possible cultural explanations (see Table 23–1).

2. *Become more Self-Aware.* In order to manage diverse groups of employees effectively, managers need to have a great deal of self-understanding. This includes how stereotypes, values, beliefs,

experiences, biases, and body language affect their own level of patience and the quality of their feedback awareness.

3. *Treat Asians born in United States as having inbred American culture.* To complicate matters more, there are different levels of assimilation, depending on which generation the employee represents. An Asian American born in the United States whose great-grandparents came from an Asian country may not consciously experience and exhibit any culture except the American culture. However, to most non-Asian-American managers, they look as Asian as the recent Asian immigrant; so, without thinking, the manager may treat them both the same. This confusion does not help.

There is no doubt that many complexities exist in managing employees who may look like they represent Asian diversity issues, when in fact more cultural parallels could be drawn between the US-born Asian and the non-Asian American. It is just as irrelevant for a person to say to an Asian born in the United States that they have a friend from Asia as for that person to say to a European American born in the United States that they have a friend from Europe.

Many non-Asian Americans unintentionally demonstrate their misplaced goodwill by making such references. This demonstrates that they are reacting to the physical appearance of the Asian American, and not to the individual. The best way to avoid this situation is to ask the employees how they see themselves in terms of cultural identification.

4. *Improve your understanding of different Asian cultures.* Understanding one Asian-American employee does not guarantee the same level of understanding of another. Management and communication with Asian-American employees often run into misunderstandings not only because of cultural differences between non-Asian-American managers and Asian-American employees, but also because of the wide differences among Asian Americans themselves.

Managers should appreciatively inquire and learn about their employees on an individual basis. For example, your interaction with and understanding of an employee who is Chinese American may not be consistent with the sensitivity you need when interacting with a Vietnamese-American employee. An

TABLE 23–2
Reiterative Feedback Loop

1. Employee explains own frame of reference on issue	2. Manager repeats in own words what was said by employee	3. Employee agrees or clarifies further
4. Repeat steps 1–3 until understanding is reached	5. Manager explains own frame of reference on issue	6. Employee repeats in own words what manager said
7. Manager agrees or clarifies further	8. Repeat steps 5–7 until understanding is reached	9. Both understand real issue and work on agreeable outcome

employee from India may represent an Indo-European culture, which is very different from that of a Japanese American. Managers need to actively listen, be curious and interested, and appreciate differences.

5. *Communicate with reiterative feedback loops.* Managers should use communication techniques such as reiterative feedback loops (see Table 23–2 and Model Y in Figure 23–1) to come to an understanding about each other's frame of reference and an interpretation of what caused any misunderstanding. Managers must deal with interactive biases; that is, the preferences and cultural norms dictating how we treat others and how we want to be treated. So often managers miss the real issue an Asian American may have because they don't spend enough time and effort to try and get a true understanding. The superficial bandage effort may seem more expedient, but it is not. More time is lost through the employee's loss of motivation and reduced productivity.

6. *Facilitate formal training and development.* Managers can get more out of their Asian-American employees by capitalizing on their complete range of skills and potential. For instance, managers can assist them by giving them the opportunity to be supervisors, thus facilitating the professional and personal development they need to become leaders, managers, and administrators.

Training can be offered to help them become more empowered, self-fulfilled, and effective on the job. Training specific to the needs of the individual can be helpful; for example, speech

FIGURE 23–1
Behavioral Models Managers Can Choose to Deal with
Interactive Biases

Model X	Model Y
Manager assumes that own interpretation of situation is correct	Manager becomes appreciatively curious about employee's behavior, ideas, and perceptions; asks employee to clarify using reiterative feedback loops
Does not check out own perceptions while interactive biases come into play	
	Resists acting on own biases; first checks out own perceptions with employee using reiterative feedback loops
Allows the interactive biases and misunderstandings to continue	
Allows escalation of miscommunication	Both begin to appreciate each other's differences
Does not come to agreement with employees for a desired outcome	Both discuss desired outcomes using reiterative feedback loops and come to an understanding
Allows problem to manifest as distrust of each other	With consensus agreement, both can begin to trust each other

therapy or training in diction will minimize misunderstandings due to accents. Assertiveness training focuses on alternative ways of behaving. Management training promotes leadership and needed skills, knowledge, and abilities. Training on presentations and workshops on how to conduct meetings help make effective managers.

7. *Facilitate informal training and development.* Informal training and support can help Asian Americans as well as other employees. Sharing political and other information not generally known, encouraging and showing the Asian-American trainee the importance of networking, explaining the different career tracks,

coaching on the finer points of achieving their targeted position, and giving space and flexibility are helpful managerial strategies. Offering to be a mentor advances the employee's potential.

CONCLUSION

Managers need to create and promote a sense of belonging to the greater community, with social responsibilities toward the company and its environment. With everyone working together as a community with common goals, the Asian American in particular can respond as an integral part of the total multicultural team. Managers can perform their roles in the most effective leadership manner, behaving with very sensitized awareness. In return, they can promote higher commitment, creativity, energized performance, and increased appreciation from a potentially actualized group of employees, Asian Americans.

Toy-Ping Taira

Toy-Ping Taira is a consultant and proprietor of Potomac Change Management in Potomac, Maryland. Concurrently, she is an adjunct faculty member in the master's program of applied behavioral sciences at Johns Hopkins University. She also works as a social transformational agent in the capacity of deputy director at a major US government agency. She has worked for numerous years in high-level management and evaluation positions in both the executive and legislative branches of the US government. Her birthplace is New Haven, Connecticut.

Chapter Twenty-Four

African-American Women and Men in the Workplace: Dismantling the Glass Ceiling

Lee Butler

Executive Summary

During the 1960s and 1970s, the influx of college-educated African Americans into professional and managerial jobs in the private sector was more numerous than ever before in the nation's history. In this chapter, Lee Butler discusses this influx from the vantage point of the 1990s. He poses the question, What has happened to this group, in terms of its upward mobility in the corporations into which they were recruited?

He argues that while some few have made it to the upper reaches (policy level) of some companies, perhaps far too many have found themselves thwarted in their career-advancement ambitions and are consigned to staff jobs, where they are unable to amass the essential management skills necessary to reach corporate-level positions. It is his contention that within corporations, this is the so-called glass ceiling, an invisible sociological barrier that rarely allows people of color to move beyond it.

Butler discusses the concept of mentoring, an age-old mechanism in organizations in which a well-established manager mentors a talented mentee in the skills and knowledge necessary for the latter's continued upward advancement. It is his contention that the conventional mode for identifying junior managers for mentorship is one that does not often include people of color or women.

Butler ends the chapter with a discussion of an alternative to mentorship, a systemwide cultural-change effort that has the management of diversity at its center. This chapter, and the Wasserman, Miller, and Johnson chapter on cross-cultural mentoring, view the systemic development of people of color from two different perspectives.

The Wasserman et al. chapter looks at development from the level of the individual. Butler's chapter raises the discussion to a systems level. Both perspectives are clearly key to effective change and should not be viewed as either/or. Done simultaneously, they enhance the likelihood of attaining preferred outcomes.

This chapter's importance rests on its emphasis on changing the organization's culture. It establishes a series of guideposts for companies to follow as they move toward becoming truly multicultural systems. It also clearly establishes the fact that there are no quick fixes; it has taken organizations many years to become what they are today; it will take several additional years for them to change in a way that fully utilizes the diversity that exists within them.

THE CULTURAL AND POLITICAL CONTEXT

T hree decades have passed since African Americans first began having significant access to professional and managerial jobs in corporate America. In the 1960s, when major American industry first began to open its managerial doors to those who, at the time, were called Negroes, some conservative Euro-American onlookers felt that this marked the beginning of a great "social experiment." A 1960s *New York Times* article, in which I appeared as one of three professional or managerial African Americans, proclaimed that equal opportunity was becoming a reality.

Many of us, the beneficiaries of this so-called corporate enlightenment, became the first in our families to assume such socially esteemed positions. We felt that we had finally arrived. The investment of four years of undergraduate education, and perhaps two to three additional years in the successful pursuit of a master's degree (usually an MBA), had paid off. No more careers limited to sleeping-car porters, public-sector employees, teachers, and the like. The sky was the limit! Or was it?

Outside the walls of many of these corporations, urban areas were in turmoil. The civil rights movement was in full bloom.

The rhetoric of the brothers on ghetto streets held that African Americans could not be relevant if they were working for "the man" in corporate America. Yet some corporately employed African Americans, committed to labor and usually in staff or lower-level managerial positions, took solace in the fact that their lifestyles were vast economic improvements over those of their parents.

After the 1968 assassination of Dr. Martin Luther King, many of us began to take a closer look at our new found success and to raise serious questions as to whether we were indeed pursuing the proper course. Those of us who stayed through the 1960s saw new issues emerge as the 1970s drew nigh, and with them the presidencies of Richard Nixon, Gerald Ford, and Jimmy Carter.

Equal opportunity rhetoric was giving way to the sporadic enforcement of affirmative action in companies. However, unlike the 1960s, there was little significant cultural and political context in support of African Americans in corporate America throughout the 1970s. While the Carter administration may well have been supportive, it was being eaten alive by the politics of Washington.

The specter of federal support for fair hiring and promotion policies all but came to a standstill in the 1980s with the presidencies of Ronald Reagan and George Bush. The Bush campaign was reminiscent of old-time campaigns for sheriff in the Deep South. Exhortations about crime in America were personified by pictures of an African American man found guilty of a heinous crime and controversially released from prison.

Yet as the 1980s ended, another realization began to preoccupy many in the private sector. While the Reagan and Bush administrations provided little or no political or cultural context for those who came to be called people of color and women, a Hudson Institute study forced many decision makers to start paying attention in ways that they had not in the past. The study by this esteemed public policy research institution found that there were not going to be enough native-born Euro-American men to man (pun intended) all professional and managerial positions by the year 2000.

The cultural and political context then yielded to a much more potent economic reality. Washington didn't have to push the matter solo any longer. The "bully pulpit" had moved from politics to economics, from politicians to business leaders. If American industry was to thrive, it would have to change its ways of doing business. One key area was in the way it utilized workforce differences based on the racial and gender identities of its workers.

In the 1990s, women and people of color now hold more professional and managerial positions than ever before in the nation's history. The issue has also changed in nature. While there are organizational dinosaurs still stuck in the 1960s, the more predominant issues for well-prepared African Americans are: "Now that we're in the door, where do we go from here?" "What about the glass ceiling?" Examples are legion; here are but two:

1. Mel is an African-American male with an undergraduate degree from a state university. He is a gifted and talented home builder, working as an assistant superintendent, a somewhat lofty-sounding title. He has been with this organization for 10 years. He has more education, experience, and training than almost everyone hired by the large East Coast builder. However, his primary responsibility is to train newly hired, virtually all Euro-American workers in his company. He trains them thoroughly, for within a short time most of his charges are functioning well in their roles. Over the past eight years, Mel has seen virtually all of his charges move on to higher-level positions in the company, making much better pay than he. Embittered, Mel has begun drinking heavily; his marriage is in trouble; he is in trouble.

2. Sheila has been employed by one of the major tobacco companies in America for about 15 years. She has a master's degree from an Ivy League institution. However, throughout her tenure on the job, she has never been able to crack the barrier between staff and line positions. In her staff role, she has worked in almost all of the middle-management positions that the company has available, and then some. Some staff positions have even been created just for her!

   Embittered by all this, she refuses to complain openly about her situation, fearing that it would endanger her politically within the company. Yet her opportunities to reach the upper levels of management will depend on whether there is sufficient fortitude and commitment to move her into a line position, where she has closer product access, and therefore far better opportunities for advancement. But a line position would mean that she would be responsible for the work of others. She would be in a power position relative to workers, many of whom would be male, many of whom would be Euro-American.

THE CULTURAL BARRIERS WITHIN

The glass ceiling, that semipermeable membrane between the middle and upper levels of management, allows access only to a small percentage of African-American men and women. These same corporations take pride in proclaiming the open-door, equal-access nature of their organizations. To a degree, this assertion is true. Many companies actively recruit people of color and Euro-American women; many are armed with ample evidence to support their assertions. On the other hand, elaborate rationales and justifications are usually trotted out to explain the limited upward mobility of *these same individuals.*

For example, one often hears that slow to no movement upward is due to factors existing within African Americans themselves. Euro-American organization managers tend to perceive the lack of progress as a function of the unpreparedness of African-American lower-level managers; "they aren't ready yet." This is a tactic so frequently employed that for at least two decades it has become known as *blaming the victim.*

FORCES WITHIN ORGANIZATIONAL CULTURES

In order to understand the behaviors swimming around the issue of difference, it is also essential to understand and appreciate the idea of organizational culture. Organizational culture means the *established ways of thinking and doing things.* Therefore, it follows that the culture of an organization plays a major role in how its participants believe, think, and solve problems in areas related to race and gender—in a word, *diversity.*

Existing policies and procedures take a back seat to how the organization acts. Organizations reflect the larger society. Unlike policy, cultural decision outcomes are difficult to impossible either to track or, more fundamentally, for organizational participants— sometimes both African-American and Euro-American—to acknowledge. This gives meaning and substance to the term *glass ceiling*. Everyone knows it's there, but you can't see it. And therefore, attempting to prove its existence may call the state of one's mental health seriously into question. Is this paranoia, or what?

From a cultural perspective, it is a major move for an American organization to open its upper reaches to people who are different than those who have always been there. Typically, rationales used to justify and explain the lack of progress in this domain mirror the system dynamics that occur at the company's lower levels. And it is here, at the lower levels, that we discover both Mel and Sheila.

Upper-level managers are therefore "correct" when they point to the lack of solid line experience and background among African-American men and women to justify their lack of upward mobility in the company. Unacknowledged are the roadblocks that guarantee that African Americans will fail to have the essential background and experience for upper-level posts!

MENTORING: THE BUMPY ROAD LESS TRAVELED

A critically important dynamic that is firmly and deeply embedded in many organizational cultures is who gets mentored and who does not. Mentoring has historically been the way organizations identify lower-level Euro-American men suitable for upper management. The process is an informal one, often based on friendship or a desire to see a particular individual succeed. Clearly, all Euro-American men are not fortunate enough to have a mentor. But those who do benefit in substantial ways.

Mentoring provides important information on how to present oneself in the organization. It can "grease the skids" by creating opportunities to shine. Since some mentoring takes place off the job in informal social settings such as tennis courts and golf courses, invitations to participate are extended only to those who share common cultural habits, patterns and, most importantly, *access*. This social process has traditionally excluded those who are different in race or gender.

Recognizing the pervasiveness of the mentoring phenomenon, many thoughtful organizations have put formal mentoring programs in place that pair savvy Euro-American managers with male or female people of color. The success of such programs varies. Many Euro-American managers confidentially argue that mixed outcomes are all one can expect. But mentees are historically, and frequently voluntarily, chosen quietly and invisibly by well-placed, upper-level managers. They are chosen because they are liked, often because the mentor sees attributes in the mentee that correspond to the way the mentor sees himself. That is, the mentee is aggressive, has style, and is a "take charge kind of guy."

Indeed, a mentor (sometimes called a "sponsor") may even be someone quite unknown to the mentee but performs the mentorship by clearing away various obstacles that stand in the way of the mentee's success. *Liking* the person quickly evolves into *wanting* that person to be successful. When one's mentee succeeds, it is a jewel in the crown of the mentor and a further embodiment of his power in the organization.

If we are to understand what is happening with Mel and Sheila, we have to understand that the success of a particular mentee and the continued credibility of his or her upper-level-management mentor are quite often intimately tied together. The fact that so many Euro-American male mentees become successful follows from this systemic reality: It is almost guaranteed! The perceived risks entailed in taking on either a Mel or a Sheila as mentees are often far too great for a disproportionately large number of Euro-American corporate-level executives.

Herein lies the curious nature and cultural complexity in establishing a *formal* mentoring program for African-American men and women to combat a historically *informal* process. Upper-level managers who opt to become mentors are taking risks. They will also be required to fight fires that they would never be required to fight if the mentee were a Euro-American man. Mentors must go into the relationship fully aware that they will have to work much harder in this situation than they did before under similar circumstances.

Simple operational priorities that under normal conditions would move ahead, unencumbered by obstacles of any significance, suddenly become major storms.

The cultural barriers within organizations must be acknowledged forthrightly. They make it unlikely for people who are different in race or gender to crack the upper-managerial reaches. The behavior of seeking similarities rather than differences—based on race and gender—must be overcome. It can no longer be used surreptitiously as a basis for determining whether or not someone is eligible for a corporate-level position. Seeking these "comfort zones" based on racial, ethnic, and gender similarities may be the undoing of many companies in the difficult years ahead.

DISMANTLING THE GLASS CEILING

The major part of dismantling the ceiling is not in the establishment of formal mentor/mentee relationships. It is in a conscientious and dedicated systemwide program to *transform* the very culture that obstructs the success of those formal relationships. The task of including difference in a long-standing organizational practice of *exclusion* is difficult. This is especially true when the established practice of exclusion is a deeply entrenched norm. It will be difficult. It will not be impossible. The most powerful rationale available, as a basis for changing who is *included,* is the recognition that organizations *must* pursue revised practices in order to ensure that the best possible candidates for particular positions are being moved up. In these terms, organizations adopting a total quality orientation must have in it the management of diversity as a high strategic priority.

There will be opposition to this change. The familiar rhetoric says, "The company is instituting a *social* program that is discriminating against Euro-American men." This is one of the more benign reactions. Others will be more strident. Yet dismantling the glass ceiling is especially important now, when, as Robert Marshak points out in this volume, the entire planet is moving through a major paradigm shift. The disease is far more deadly than the cure because, left unattended, the disease is fatal!

Changing an organizational culture so it functions effectively in the area of total quality means, by definition, that it has learned to incorporate *difference* as a standard of doing business. How can this be done? Here are key strategic issues in dismantling the metaphorical glass ceiling:

- *Set clear policies and goals for the upward development and advancement of all highly talented and high-performing managerial employees.* Make explicit that the reformulation of existing policy is manifestly intended to include women and people of color. At the same time, the words ''all talented and high-performing employees'' send the message that the organization is not explicitly targeting women and people of color for advancement at the exclusion of Euro-American men. Be aware nevertheless that one response to the initiative will be precisely that. Consequently, it is important to have a well-thought-out strategy in place early on to combat this response.

- *Acknowledge past organizational failures* and note that this is a priority action agenda item tied strategically to the organization's future viability. This step should be one that grows out of a consensus-driven system change effort.

- *Recognize the sociocultural complexities within the organization.* Spend the needed time to identify those points in the system where there may be difficulties. Hold meetings with all managers from these areas. It is essential that corporate-level officers act as highly visible role models reflecting the expectations of others at all levels in the company. Any behavior on the part of this group that is seen as halfhearted support will be interpreted, perhaps correctly, as lip service.

- *Meetings should be part of a comprehensive total-quality, diversity-focused cultural change effort.* All relevant managerial and support staff must participate in all components of the effort. Companies have to recognize that a change of this magnitude is not a quick fix.

- *Remember that success takes time*, perhaps 10 years. Early results, however, will begin to surface after two or three years.

- *Lasting change will take place only when old behaviors and practices are uniformly seen as aberrant.* Old ways of operating will quickly reassert themselves if change strategies are prematurely relaxed.

- *Current norms that embed racism and sexism must be resisted in the new culture.* True change will have occurred in the organization when resistance to the old ways carries the same energy that propelled resistance to the new ways during the early stages of the change process. Only then has the organization been transformed.

- *Remember that some key corporate-level managers will be cool toward the change effort in its initial stages.* This is natural. It should be expected.

- When obstacles are worked through, *there is a net increase in energy within the critical mass, pushing in the direction of change goals.* Careful, well-developed strategies can overcome resistance.

- *Remember that everyone engaged in the change process is learning.* Together they comprise a learning organization. Collusion with the old ways is how the old system occurred. Colluding with the new norms may well be the path to entrenching the new one.

- *Recognize that high-quality outside assistance is crucial.*

CONCLUSION

These suggestions convey the essential elements for successful, long-term cultural change. By focusing on identifying resistance and by slowly gaining acceptance for the change effort, important work can be done in the early stages. Inadequate attention to the politics of the change process will make success difficult, as will premature initiation of a formal diversity/total quality program initiative. But it can be done.

Lee Butler

Lee Butler, PhD, is currently chief executive officer of the Delphi Network, Inc., located in Baltimore, Maryland. Prior to starting Delphi with his wife, Toni Dunton-Butler, Lee served in a variety of positions, mostly in universities. At the University of Maryland at Baltimore, for instance, he served as the director of planning and organization development; at the State University of New York at Buffalo, New York, as a faculty member; and at a Buffalo community college, as a chief campus administrator. He has also been employed in the private sector with Westinghouse and the Western Electric Company. He is a member of the NTL Institute and has served on its board of directors.

Chapter Twenty-Five

Hispanics in the Workplace

Cresencio Torres

Executive Summary

In his concluding remarks in this chapter, Cresencio Torres observes that "the time has come for American companies to recognize the value of a well-balanced workforce that includes Hispanics. Because Hispanics will represent an increasing proportion of the labor force, organizations must learn to effectively utilize their human resource capital. They must acknowledge the need to attract, develop, and retain Hispanic employees at all levels." With these observations, Torres's chapter assumes an important place in the overall discussion of diversity and multiculturalism.

The enormous growth in the size of the Hispanic population in America makes it the fastest-growing "minority" group. It also makes this population impossible to ignore as a key element in the iterative stages of growth of the American workforce. Torres correctly points out the utter confusion that exists among Euro-Americans about who is a Hispanic. His answer to the question, in broad terms, is that there is as much or perhaps more diversity *within* the Hispanic community as there is between it and the Euro-American community. Yet there are ways in which there are shared values among Hispanic groups that differ from those that exist among European Americans.

For example, values differ in areas such as the importance of family versus individuals, time, relationships, authority, and what is and what is not appropriate in the workplace. It is only through a full and continuous exploration and understanding of these value differences that a diverse workforce can result, one that yields positive organizational outcomes.

Torres examines some critical issues for managers from both an individual and an organizational perspective. He moves on to look at some critical issues for organizations and some strategies that they can use to overcome them. His final discussion acknowledges the transactional nature of systems change. Here he lays out what he sees as issues for Hispanics, in terms of values, requisite knowledge, and political considerations.

In its 21st century march toward becoming a multicultural society, the American workforce will incorporate larger and larger numbers of Hispanics. The transactions that will inevitably have to occur between the dominant society and this and other minority groups will determine the shape of the United States as a multicultural society. Changes in values on both sides, for the so-called minority populations and the majority European Americans, will have to be a centerpiece of the process. This chapter outlines some of the contours of this change process for one of the key groups engaged in it.

H ispanics represent a critical part of the labor force that has yet to be recognized or effectively utilized. This chapter provides managers and their organizations with important information concerning Hispanics in the workplace. It defines and identifies the four groups that are considered to be Hispanic, according to the US Census Bureau; examines the critical issues they face in the workplace; defines strategies for overcoming organizational barriers; shares methods with which Hispanics can increase their chances of success; and discusses implications for managers and organizations. The time has come for this country's corporations to realize there is a value in attracting, retaining, and developing a well-balanced labor force.

DEMOGRAPHICS

The need for greater Hispanic participation in all sectors of organizational life represents a shift created not by the choice of American corporations but by the magnitude of changes in the United States workforce. By the end of this century, Hispanics will be the largest minority in the United States, representing a projected 29 percent of the labor force.

The number of Hispanics within the United States rose from 14 million in 1980 to 22 million in 1990, an increase of 53 percent. California's Hispanic population alone rose by more than 3 million (or almost 70 percent) in the past decade, growing from 4.5 million in 1980 to 7.7 million in 1990. Texas experienced a 45 percent increase; New York, 33 percent; Florida, 83 percent; and Illinois, 42 percent.[1] Clearly, contemporary managers must understand that Hispanics encompass a labor force that has yet to be fully recognized or effectively utilized.

Hispanic workers today are asking American corporations for an equal opportunity to compete in the workplace; a culture in which performance is assessed against unbiased, business-based standards; and a corporate commitment that demonstrates respect for the Hispanic employee. Since values are the social principles or standards held by individuals in society, it is important to understand some of the existing differences between Hispanic and Euro-American values.

THE IMPORTANCE OF A NAME

The term *Hispanic* describes people of Spanish origin. The US Bureau of the Census also uses it to identify persons with Spanish surnames. The term *Latino* identifies persons of Latin American origins and is sometimes used interchangeably with the term *Hispanic*. Hispanics, by definition, are not a race of people. They are a group of people that includes whites, blacks, Native Americans, and every possible combination of these groups. Not all Americans with Spanish surnames consider themselves Hispanic because of different family lineages. But because of their surnames, they are often assumed by European Americans to belong to a minority group; this may be offensive to them.

Hispanics in the United States have roots in four geographic areas: Mexico, Puerto Rico, Cuba, and Central and South America. Each of these areas is described below.

Mexicans

Historically, Mexicans controlled large sections of the western part of what is now the United States for hundreds of years before

Europeans took most of the land by conquest. In 1848, Mexico signed the Treaty of Guadalupe Hidalgo, ceding to the United States the vast territory now known as California, Arizona, New Mexico, Nevada, Utah, and portions of several other states. Under this treaty, Mexicans would become US citizens if they remained in the ceded territory for more than one year. Most did. But between 1850 and 1930, Mexican Americans experienced greater brutality from European Americans in the Southwest than African Americans did in the South.

The United States would have taken more Mexican land if large numbers of Mexicans had not been occupying it. At that time, European Americans believed in the superiority of their institutions and in the implied assumption of racial inferiority of Mexicans. The fear existed that this "alien race" would cause much difficulty if it were part of American society. Mexicans were regarded with the same scorn as Native Americans and were often not differentiated from them.

Today, job discrimination keeps the per-capita income of Mexican Americans the lowest in the United States. Health conditions and services in many areas remain poor. In some schools, Mexicans are still treated as second-class citizens and are often assumed to be illegal (or undocumented) aliens, whether or not they are, in fact, American citizens. With the increased numbers of undocumented immigrants around the country, this has become an even greater problem for Mexican Americans and other Hispanics.

Puerto Ricans

The second largest Hispanic group in the United States has Puerto Rican roots. This population has a unique status. Because Puerto Rico was once a US colony, Puerto Ricans are US citizens, even if they were born on the island. Like other immigrant groups, Puerto Ricans came to the United States seeking better lives and opportunities. Since World War II, many have settled in the United States, primarily in the Northeast.

The Puerto Rican population is a mixture of both black and Spanish populations. As a group, they suffer greater discrimination than all other Hispanic groups because many are dark-skinned. Puerto Ricans moving to the United States are often shocked by their abrupt confrontation with majority prejudice based on skin color. In Puerto Rico, distinctions between people are based on class, regardless of skin color.

Cubans

The history of the Cuban community in the United States is relatively brief. The vast majority of Cubans (700,000) live and work in the Miami area. Many immigrated around the time of Castro's revolution. They were mostly white, were middle- or upper-class, and had been associated with former Cuban ruler Batista, the leader overthrown by Fidel Castro. This well-educated, urban, high-status, primarily white-looking Hispanic group received a much warmer reception than did Mexicans and Puerto Ricans.

There are two distinct groups of Cubans in the United States today: those who immigrated during and immediately following the Cuban revolution, and recent immigrants who left Cuba in what have been termed "boat lifts." The earlier immigrants are, on average, more highly educated and skilled, and have done well in the United States. Many were professionals or business people in Cuba; they brought their skills and resources with them to the United States. The more recent immigrants do not have such advantages and for that reason have had a much more difficult time making it. Because they are the lightest, in terms of skin color, of the groups described, Cubans are most likely to identify with the conservative sector in the United States.

Central and South Americans

Another growing segment of the Hispanic population in the United States comes from Central and South America. By virtue of being from so many different places, their common thread is that they are *not* Mexican, Puerto Rican, or Cuban. Beyond that, the differences are extensive; it is impossible to make generalizations. Recent immigrants from Central and South America may be from either privileged or disadvantaged backgrounds. Because legal immigration is restricted, it is likely that many are both illegal and poor.

In summary, it is crucial to understand that there are four groups identified as Hispanic. Two facts are important to consider at this point: (1) each Hispanic group differs from the others, and (2) it is impossible to draw generalizations that fit all four ethnic groups because of their differences. What binds the groups together, from a historical perspective, is the Spanish language and culture. This is not to say that they all speak Spanish the same way or share the same culture today. Rather, each group holds a distinct world view. However, the Hispanic groups do share some common values that are different from those of European Americans.

HISPANIC AND EURO-AMERICAN VALUES

Because values can and do conflict in the workplace, managers who understand Hispanic values in relation to Euro-American values will be better prepared to motivate, lead, and inspire their Hispanic employees. Insufficient information about Hispanic groups or ignorance about how Hispanic values differ from Euro-American values contributes to frustration, misunderstanding, and conflict in the workplace.

The following values are for the most part true for either Hispanics or European Americans. They are not inclusive of all values but illustrate some of the differences.

Hispanic Values	*Euro-American Values*
• The family is more important than the individual.	• The individual is more important than the family.
• Time is vague and relative.	• Time is precious and precise.
• Relationships are based on a process orientation.	• Relationships are task oriented for material reward.
• Authority is respected.	• Authority is often questioned.
• Music, family, and food are welcome additions to work settings.	• Music, family, and food are rarely a part of the work environment.

These sets of values are neither right nor wrong. They represent differing perspectives that can be equally beneficial to organizational thinking.

Some problems that arise between Hispanics and Euro-American managers in the workplace come from the belief that one set of values is better than another. The reality of this paradox is that each set of values is correct for each group, and that each set of values can contribute to any given situation or circumstance. Failure to understand and appreciate different values results in and reinforces negative stereotypes.

CRITICAL ISSUES FOR MANAGERS AND ORGANIZATIONS

The average Euro-American manager has long been ignorant of Hispanic concerns, and the traditional workforce doesn't really know anything about Hispanic groups. European Americans do not realize that workers with different backgrounds have significant contributions to make to organizational success.

At the individual level, a lack of awareness is common in many workplace settings. It presents barriers that inhibit Hispanic success at all levels of American business. Maintaining these beliefs and their associated behaviors often means that Euro-American managers react negatively to Hispanics. Some of the stereotypes frequently held by European Americans are as follows:

- Hispanics all share the same cultural heritage.
- Hispanic men are macho and their women are subservient.
- Hispanics are lazy.
- Hispanics are volatile and emotional.

Whether the manager's response is overt or covert, the result is the same—discrimination against Hispanics.

But rather than viewing the increase in the numbers of persons of Spanish origin as a threat, a more positive view recognizes that employee diversity provides a competitive advantage. Overcoming these attitudes can best be done by Hispanics and European Americans working together to move beyond the roadblocks of misunderstandings and stereotypes.

Critical Issues for Euro-American Managers

- Understand the dynamics of individual and institutional racism.
- Understand the difference between equal employment opportunity and affirmative action.
- Manage diversity as a vital resource.
- Learn to value and respect Hispanic employees.
- Find common ground on which to build relationships of trust and mutual respect.
- Test assumptions in cross-cultural communication.
- Learn how Hispanics and European Americans differ in expectations, in values, and in attitudes toward family and work.

These issues suggest that managers must receive continuing training in (1) understanding differences, (2) cross-cultural communication, and (3) developing effective cross-cultural working relationships. In addition, training programs should be designed to give managers methods to better evaluate minority performance and potential and to prepare them for managing career-development and other planning requirements.

Critical Issues for Organizations

At the organizational level, discrimination in recruitment, hiring, retention, development, and promotion are critical problems faced by Hispanics. These areas of institutional racism must be confronted. Other concerns include the issue of qualification, the exclusion from informal work groups, the perceived need to be better performers, dual performance standards, and the lack of mentors, sponsors, and role models.

Another key obstacle encountered by most Hispanics is the organizational structure itself. The current trends toward mergers and downsizing suggest that there will be even fewer opportunities for advancement in the future. Hispanic employees may be ready for advancement just as the positions disappear. This is a reality that Hispanics as well as other minority group members must recognize and be prepared to face.

ORGANIZATIONAL STRATEGIES FOR OVERCOMING BARRIERS

First, American businesses must make a commitment to demonstrate their valuing of Hispanic as well as other minority employees. This can be done by making diversity appreciation a basic component of the organization's culture, values, and operating principles. In other words, valuing all employees should be a part of the fundamental competitive strategy, not handled as a peripheral program that has a beginning and an end.

Second, organizations must ensure that all their internal systems align with their diversity goals. This involves examining the organization's:

- *Strategies*, or methods used to achieve goals
- *Structures*, or the functions that can support diversity
- *Systems*, or the practices, policies, and procedures employees use in their day-to-day duties
- *Skills*, or the talents and abilities possessed by the workforce that give the organization its distinct competitive advantage
- *Style*, or the everyday managerial behavior that is a prime indicator of the corporate culture and a major determinant of the work climate
- *Staffing*, or the profile of the employee body
- *Shared values*, or the core beliefs that employees hold in common, which serve to guide their actions

Organizations must understand that the options for increasing or decreasing each variable are dependent on whether or not they support diversity. This approach is both cost-effective and a smart business move.

Third, organizations must maintain specified goals and timetables for all departments with respect to the hiring and promotion of Hispanic and other minority employees. This includes the development of performance criteria and rewards and penalties for managers working directly with diverse employees. These programs and policies will help the organization meet its equal employment opportunity and affirmative action strategies.

Finally, organizations must ensure that Hispanics and other minorities with high potential have access to mentors and coaches who can assist in their career development.

The following list of activities can improve the overall organizational work environment for Hispanics and their colleagues:

Recruitment and Hiring

- Ensure top leadership's organizational commitment to maintain this as a public priority.
- Reevaluate hiring and recruitment practices.
- Target schools with a predominantly Hispanic population.
- Develop an in-house pool of Hispanic resources.
- Ensure that the personnel officer is committed to hiring Hispanics.
- Have Hispanics sit on recruitment committees.
- Use Hispanic networks to recommend new hires.
- Establish Hispanic internship programs.

Retention

- Actively reach out to Hispanics on the job by using peers as resources, coaches, and mentors.
- Develop effective Hispanic support networks.
- Ensure appropriate career-planning opportunities.
- Assign mentors to new recruits.
- Ensure adequate coaching for Hispanics on a career path.

Development and Promotion

- Ensure human resources follow-through.
- Advertise in-house career opportunities.
- Support and track upward mobility.
- Network by grade and level and exchange information on criteria for success.
- Develop a success image of Hispanics in the workplace.
- Provide training in self-development and leadership.

- Ensure that Hispanics are represented on promotion boards.

These strategies and activities will help organizations give Hispanics and other minorities the opportunity to compete on a level playing field. In addition, they demonstrate a value and respect for all employees.

The actions recommended above are best initiated by a multifaceted approach. For example, rather than relying just on one intervention (e.g., training) to impact the attitudes and behaviors of managers and non-Hispanic employees, a total systems approach (examining all aspects of the organization that can contribute to the improvement of the diverse workforce environment) will increase understanding throughout the organization.

CRITICAL ISSUES FOR HISPANICS

Finally, to be successful in business, Hispanic employees must first know what kind of contribution they want to make to the organization. They need to have a dream that can be translated into both short- and long-term career goals. At the same time, it is necessary that they learn realistic goals about how far and how fast they can move in any given career path.

Hispanics must become aware of the obstacles they face and learn to overcome adversity. They must learn to compete, to negotiate, and most important, to want to win. The important thing for Hispanic employees to remember is to maintain active control of their own environments and to find ways to do what must be done to ensure success.

A summary of strategies is presented for Hispanic employees to understand and use to ensure that they maintain their integrity while striving to achieve success in the workplace.

Values

- Know your own value set and what is important to you.
- Accept and respect yourself.
- Concentrate on your strengths but recognize your weaknesses.

- Get a clearer picture of your dream and talk about it.
- Set realistic short- and long-term goals based on your dream.
- Learn to turn negatives into positives.
- Don't take no for an answer.

Knowledge

- Understand Hispanic cultures and individual heritage.
- Understand what the differences are between Euro-American culture and Hispanic culture in the workplace—learn what is valued and important.
- Know the skills, training, and experience needed for the position you want to obtain.
- Develop your oral and written communication skills.
- Obtain a balance between technical and nontechnical training.

Political Considerations

- Know what you are worth and what rewards others in similar circumstances are receiving.
- Stand up for yourself without letting it get in the way of your effectiveness.
- Beware of obstacles that may hinder advancement.
- Know what you are willing to do and not do to get ahead.
- Make it easy for people to like and respect you.
- Know your constituents, their needs, and how to influence them.
- Create networks both within the Hispanic community and outside of it.
- Learn how to sell yourself.
- Learn to be a team player.
- Learn how to use your own personal power.

These are actions that Hispanic employees can take immediately to create a healthier personal work environment. They are not ends in themselves, but methods for creating a desired future state that may not presently exist in the workplace.

CONCLUSION

The time has come for American companies to recognize the value of a well-balanced workforce that includes Hispanics. Because Hispanics will represent an increasing proportion of the labor force, organizations must learn to effectively utilize their human resource capital. They must acknowledge the need to attract, develop, and retain Hispanic employees at all levels.

ENDNOTE

1. US Bureau of the Census, *Demographic Changes in the United States: 1990.* (Washington, DC: US Government Printing Office, 1990).

Cresencio Torres

Cresencio Torres, PhD, is an organizational change consultant who works with managers in educational and cultural change efforts aimed at valuing employee diversity and developing leadership. Dr. Torres is presently a program associate with the Center for Creative Leadership in La Jolla, California. In addition to this work, his writing appears in professional journals and trade magazines. He is a coauthor of *Self-Directed Work Teams: A Primer, Teamworking: The Official Guide for Team Development,* and *The Tao of Teams* (all published by Pfeiffer & Company). He is a member of the NTL Institute.

Chapter Twenty-Six

Diversity Skills in Action: Cross-Cultural Mentoring

Ilene C. Wasserman
Frederick A. Miller
Martha N. Johnson

Executive Summary

Mentoring as an informal cultural process in organizations has been a norm for as long as formal organizations have existed. In it, typically a senior manager, historically a white man with power in the structure, decides to take a younger white male under his tutelage. More often than not, the essential focus of the mentoring is the provision of assistance to the junior-level manager in negotiating the various elements of the organization's cultural apparatus. Through mentoring, highly successful careers have been built. Indeed "fast-trackers" have often been positioned for rapid movement as a consequence of a mentoring relationship (see "African-American Women and Men in the Workplace," Chapter 24).

Here, Ilene Wasserman, Frederick Miller, and Martha Johnson discuss the often complex aspects of cross-cultural mentoring. They argue persuasively, as have others in this book, that the management of diversity is and will remain a key business issue. Successful mentoring across race and gender lines nevertheless has many complexities embedded in it. The authors present us with five key steps toward successful mentoring. Among other notable suggestions, the authors cite the importance of learning to communicate across cultures and genders in ways that build mutual comfort. They point out that this brand of mentoring often serves as an important learning experience for both parties, the mentor and the mentee.

At the turn of the next century, only a little more than 11 percent of new workers entering the labor market will be white men. If American organizations are to survive in the near and long term, they must become adept in the management of diversity, an essential component of which is the establishment of viable, nurturing cross-cultural mentoring relationships. Without them the now normative glass ceiling for women and people of color will continue to be a major obstacle. Should this happen, high turnover rates within these two demographic groups are likely as they search for better opportunities—in one business setting after another.

The biggest losers will then be American industry. Managers must adjust their personal attitudes and beliefs if they serve as barriers to productive mentoring of those who are different in race, gender, or both. America's economic survival may well depend on the effectiveness with which this business objective is achieved.

I n the monotony of organizational life, few mentoring relationships assume the mythic proportions of Merlin and King Arthur. Yet mentoring legends shape much of what happens—and doesn't happen—when we try to establish mentoring processes, particularly cross-cultural ones. Think of the lore: stories of Casey Stengel and Billy Martin; political tales of Sam Rayburn and Lyndon Johnson; anecdotes about Charley Beacham and his protégé, Lee Iacocca. Stories like these help form our ideas about mentoring. Yet, these legends steer us poorly. Most notably, none of them includes people of color or white women.

This is, after all, the era of Workforce 2000. Between 1988 and 2000, the US Department of Labor forecasts, white males will account for only 11.6 percent of the net addition to the labor force. Organizations are quickly learning that tapping our cultural diversity is both a necessity and a competitive skill. The challenge now is to assure that all people are valued and have opportunities to make their fullest contributions.

But this is tough work. Mentoring will be critical. It helps connect organizational generations and develop, guide, and retain talent. However, it must respond to current workforce demographics: a mentor pool made up largely of white men and a group of people to be mentored more and more likely to be culturally diverse. Organizations now need consciously to support mentoring relationships between people of different genders, races, and nationalities. How can that be done?

STEP 1: CREATE THE BUSINESS CASE

Building momentum for cross-cultural mentoring requires first identifying the benefits to the organization. Nothing damages a process more than the lack of clear connections to managers' daily work or to the goals and strategies of the organization. Therefore, senior management and people who might become mentors and mentees need to address this question: What are the business benefits to be realized from successful cross-cultural mentoring?

The human resources staff can support this. First, they often facilitate the analysis. How might such mentoring support:

- Management skills needed in the 1990s?
- Efforts to expand and capture markets?
- Productivity?
- More creative teams?

Second, human resources can supply useful data so that the business rationale can include information about the environment and the employees as well as the organization's plans and expectations. What, for example, are the demographics? What are the costs of recruiting and training? Are people skillful in valuing cultural differences? Anchored with facts and an analysis of future needs, the business case will build ownership and excitement for cross-cultural mentoring.

STEP 2: ATTEND TO THE PROCESS OF FORMING RELATIONSHIPS

For any mentoring process, there may be difficulty in orchestrating a match between two people; that is human, unique, and inevitably personal. Cross-cultural mentoring presents particular challenges in this regard.

"We did a quick-and-dirty job in creating our mentoring program," says the employment manager of one Indiana equipment manufacturer. "We asked the recruiting team that went to each college to adopt the new hires from that school. Mentoring relationships developed; among them were cross-cultural ones."

"We believe the key is exposure," says the chair of a midwestern food company. "The organization needs to provide opportunities for exposure—events, job rotation, workshops—where people can meet and form relationships."

Others emphasize that mentors must not carry the full burden of initiating the relationship. Mentees must also take some initiative. This is similar to the university, where faculty are available after class or during office hours, but the students are still responsible for signing up for a conference.

Whatever the design and approach, cross-cultural mentoring cannot be left entirely to chance. Mentoring across gender, race, and nationality lines will rarely occur spontaneously, often because there are barriers against reaching out to someone who is different. It requires deliberate action.

For the human resource professional charged with starting a cross-cultural mentoring process, the key is the organizational culture. How structured and formal is the organization? Would people welcome or rebel against assignments? Can the organization incorporate mentoring into work plans or incentives? Since cross-cultural mentoring challenges certain norms about working relationships, the chances of success improve if the initial concepts accommodate the prevailing organizational norms.

STEP 3: OVERTURN MYTHS AND CLARIFY EXPECTATIONS

With some disappointment, Louise Kelley shares her story of being mentored by a man 10 years her senior: "I learned a lot. He encouraged me to take a management job and introduced me to the top guys, including the chairman. There was excitement in learning, sharing, and problem solving together. That resulted in caring about and liking each other—all on a very professional level. But he was a man and I was a younger woman, so we always kept our guard up. We were never close the way he seemed to be with the men he mentored."

Louise's story illustrates how cross-cultural mentoring requires us to shed old beliefs about relationships. Mentoring legends have not served us well. They suggest that a mentoring bond should be a close friendship, including spending personal time together after hours, taking trips, sharing meals, and meeting each other's families. Though not necessarily valid, these can complicate matters when relationships are cross-cultural. Clearly, Louise had a solid, helpful, supportive mentor. It is unfortunate that she did not have anyone to help her understand and value her experiences in the context of cross-gender mentoring.

Poorly conceived expectations create anxiety for people contemplating a cross-gender mentoring relationship. A male mentor can sense and experience extra risks in dealing with a female mentee: Will people link us romantically? Do I want to mentor her *because* I am attracted to her? What will she assume if I help her more than I do others? Will she think she owes me something in return? Will we become too attracted to each other?

Such anxieties commonly arise when people are unsure of what to expect or how to act. The best way to deal with these fears is to discuss them. Talk them over with a human resources professional or with others who have experienced cross-gender mentoring relationships. Get together with other potential mentoring pairs, explain anxieties, and test expectations. Once their concerns are public, people can find support and courage for cross-gender mentoring in the context of their organizational culture and social codes.

Likewise, cross-racial relationships can be stymied by unclarified expectations. Jim, an African-American account manager at a major utility, was pleased that the chief financial officer (CFO), a white man, had agreed to mentor him. "But our meetings are so awkward and formal," Jim complained to a friend. "He doesn't have any feel for me. He suggested I join Toastmasters to practice communicating my ideas! Was he criticizing me? Am I failing? Was he supporting me?" Jim did not understand that the CFO thought Jim needed to present his ideas more forcefully. In addition, the CFO had failed to share with Jim a comment from another manager, indicating that Jim had been misunderstood at a recent briefing. The CFO, for his part, did not want to be patronizing to an African American and tried to avoid doing so by talking around the issues and suggesting third party resources. Each had expectations that the other did not know about: the CFO expected to point Jim in a direction and let someone else give him feedback, while

Jim expected "straight talk" from the CFO. Both needed a way to explain and negotiate their expectations. Their racial difference made this more difficult.

Probably the greatest single ill-formed expectation in cross-cultural mentoring is in regard to its purpose: What do people expect to get out of the relationship? Mentoring between white men has traditionally had a clear agenda. The senior-to-junior relationship is based on a patriarchal tradition. The tacit agreement is that the senior man teaches the junior one how to advance in the organization. "My mentor," remarks Lyle Marks, a white PhD candidate, "fits the classical model. He had me collaborate with him on research projects. He arranged for me to be hired on the institute staff. He shares his thinking with me and encourages my ideas." Such mentors offer protection, assist in promotions, teach the mentee how to be successful, and develop a close personal friendship with the mentee.

The agenda changes for cross-cultural mentoring: A white male mentor cannot fully advise a mentee on what it will take to succeed. Success for a white woman, a person of color, and a person from another country each requires different skills and tactics to handle the stress, feelings of loneliness, pressures to assimilate, and less informal access to lines of power and information. The mentoring pair must learn to communicate and trust one another, often not as large a challenge for two white men. The latter might sense a warmth, a "chemistry," between them early on in their acquaintance. They might feel easy and comfortable with each other socially before their relationship takes shape as a mentoring one. Across gender, color, and national differences, however, there is less likelihood that a relationship will begin with such ease and familiarity, although a relaxed camaraderie can certainly build as the relationship progresses. "Chemistry" will not necessarily instigate or fuel a cross-cultural mentoring relationship. Such mentoring will more likely begin in a purposeful and even awkward manner. Its motivations and rewards might instead be the joy and excitement of discovering each other's perspectives and worlds, the thrill of creating a new model of cross-cultural interactions, or the liberating sense of breaking through barriers long confronting people of color, white women, and those from other countries.

Furthermore, in the patriarchal model the teaching is from senior to junior; in cross-cultural relationships the learning flows back and forth. "As the mentoring continued," claims one white man, "it felt as if we were switching places at times. I was learning from her what it was to be a Hispanic woman here and what inner resources she needed to handle the stresses, the misperceptions, the 'rubs.'" The mentor in a cross-cultural relationship has the chance to examine the world of a person traditionally shut out of the system. As the mentor explains the norms and standards of the organization, the mentee can interpret their impact in a different light; together they can define success. *Both must expect to learn for the relationship to be a success.*

Not surprisingly, in cross-cultural mentoring, signals are easily crossed. People with different backgrounds or styles need to sort out their expectations consciously. A group sharing process can help. A third party can be useful. Human resources professionals will often need to provide counsel and direction for a mentoring duo to learn mutual understanding. Debunking myths and clarifying expectations are critical in seeing the mentoring relationship off to a healthy start.

STEP 4: BUILD SKILLS

Our society seems absorbed with building skills to support better relationships. Parenting classes, customer relations seminars, and team-building retreats serve as examples. Likewise, mentoring relationships are not automatically healthy and productive. Skills play a large part. Successful cross-cultural relationships have good communications. Yet these skills are not automatic for two people from different backgrounds. Vocabulary, intonation, and slang are cues we easily understand from people like ourselves. Conversely, those cues can be mistaken across cultures. The sheer act of speaking to each other across cultures can be formidable. "I had to write her a memo," says Hal Danden, a white human resources director, describing his first gesture toward a potential mentee who was an African-American woman. "I wasn't sure I could explain face-to-face what I was hoping for in a mentoring relationship. As a white man, I'm not always comfortable having those conversations. So, I wrote it out."

Skills-building does not stop with good communications. Mentors can also benefit from matrix management and networking skills. Such skills are used by product managers as they pull various resources together, make connections, and act with confidence to support a new endeavor. This is not unlike the attention a mentee needs, particularly in a cross-cultural relationship. Mentoring white women, people of color, and people from other countries requires many of these same management skills. There is no proven formula for success. What support do they need? How can these supports be knit together? A mentor's challenge is strategic and so are the skills needed.

Increasing the sophistication of mentees is also important. They must understand what skills they need to cultivate to be successful in the organization. The human resources staff can help mentees figure out how to seek those skills and when to look to a mentor—or someone else such as a manager or a peer—for support.

STEP 5: CONTINUE THE SUPPORT

How cross-cultural mentoring relationships begin is crucial. But the real test is their endurance. After crossing the early hurdles of matching, communications, and skills building, the work takes on a new shape. Often, the mentee's manager needs attention. A successful mentoring relationship can cloud responsibility lines. A manager might feel threatened by the mentee's relationship with the mentor and wonder if the pair is spending their time talking about him. Whatever the twist, the entire trio needs to talk and work together on the relationship.

Another tension occurs when the organization views the relationship with suspicion. The idea of cross-cultural mentoring might seem OK, but as the relationship unfolds, it can put pressure on the social and cultural norms of the organization. "I think our relationship put us at risk with the organization," says one mentor. "There were no other cross-cultural mentoring pairs, and we stuck out." Being the only such mentoring pair can create a stigma, which can be handled with education and support for more mentoring.

In a third example, the master scheduler of an automotive production facility observed, ''I believe that no matter how much my accomplishments were my own doing, management gave my mentor, Jack, the credit. I was discounted. I think that our relationship undercut my professional reputation in the organization. I was still not seen as bright enough to be so successful.'' She and her mentor needed to be sensitive to this skepticism and figure out ways for her to receive her due.

Cross-cultural mentoring offers a special challenge. As organizations work to connect people across genders, races, and nationalities, deliberate, thoughtful, and honest effort is necessary. Such action nurtures a broader range of talent, making the organization more attractive for a diverse group of people. Significantly, cross-cultural mentoring nurtures the skills for valuing and tapping cultural diversity in an organization, skills that can only be developed by patiently building bridges between two people, one relationship at a time.

Ilene C. Wasserman

Ilene has been a management consultant for over 15 years. She holds an MSW and an MA in counseling psychology. She has been with the Kaleel Jamison Consulting Group since 1988, where she directs numerous projects in corporate, university, community, and religious institutions. She also maintains a private practice, where she assists individuals and groups in career management development, planning, and effective interpersonal communications. She has held leadership positions in the community, including president of the Greater Philadelphia Health Assembly, and member of the board of directors of the Family Planning Council of Southeastern Pennsylvania.

Frederick A. Miller

Fred Miller has been president of the Kaleel Jamison Consulting Group since 1985. His career in organizational development began in 1972, when he was a manager with Connecticut General Life Insurance Company (CIGNA). Since joining the Kaleel Jamison Consulting Group in 1979, he has been involved in a variety of large-systems change efforts in Fortune 100 companies. Fred is known for his engaging and supportive educational approach, for consulting partnerships with senior managers, and for innovative cultural-change strategies. He is a member of the NTL Institute, where he served on the board of directors. Currently, he is a member of the board of directors of Ben & Jerry's, Inc.; the Organization Development Network; and the Institute of Developmental Research (IDR).

Martha N. Johnson

Martha is currently serving the Clinton administration as the chief of staff to the deputy secretary of the Department of Commerce. Prior to that, she worked in Presidential Personnel in the White House. Her career began in manufacturing and recruiting at Cummins Engine Company. She then joined an executive research firm that specialized in recruiting candidates from diverse backgrounds. She became director of communications for the Kaleel Jamison Consulting Group, where she worked on the business case for cultural diversity. Martha Johnson holds a master's degree from the Yale University School of Organization and Management.

Chapter Twenty-Seven

People with Disabilities: Emerging Members of the Workforce

Jan Nisbet

Jo-Ann Sowers

Executive Summary

Diversity often refers to race, ethnicity, gender, and age. Yet a growing percentage of the labor force in the United States consists of our disabled neighbors. The legal and moral challenges that will confront managers in the immediate future require new ideas about the skills, abilities, and capabilities of workers with disabilities. Jan Nisbet and Jo-Ann Sowers provide a straightforward presentation of the issue and of how managers can meet these demands. The worker with a disability needs the same level of attention, supervision, training, and performance assessment as does any other worker.

This chapter presents an overview of the key terminology used in Public Law 101-336, the Americans with Disabilities Act (ADA). As we become more comfortable with making reasonable accommodations, managers will learn that these new employees produce at levels equal to other workers. As more organizations report the results of their efforts, managers will also learn to utilize the services of state and county governments, just as they use the services of local employment agencies. And as the other employees learn to work side by side with a person with a disability, they will overcome a reluctance to engage that person. Thus, effective teams emerge where contributions are judged by performance, not by disability.

Nisbet and Sowers present four action steps to assist managers in meeting this social, organizational, and legal mandate. We must continue to recognize that organizations should hire people who can do the job and that managers should not establish different expectations, since "different" almost always means "lower." Managers must recognize the need to provide training to meet the employee's unique needs. This is exactly the same as providing training for other employees to bring their skills up to the level expected by the organization. Attention must also be given to integrating the employee into the system. Mentoring is a path to success and a benchmark of effective management. And, finally, if the employee fails to meet expectations after meaningful support, training, and accommodation, then the employee should be terminated—just like any other employee would be.

This chapter builds on the foundation that diversity means many things. All organizations will confront the implications of the Americans with Disabilities Act. Some will do so reluctantly; others will embrace the opportunity to grow and to lead. Nisbet and Sowers give helpful advice for those who want to rise to the occasion.

Communities need to strengthen themselves by incorporating excluded people. It is important to understand how important it is for communities to be supported in their work of incorporating and developing capacities of people who have been excluded.

John McKnight, *Northwestern University*

BACKGROUND

The recognition that the workforce is becoming more diverse has traditionally resulted from the increasing numbers of ethnic minorities striving for economic success in America. Persons with disabilities are slowly being recognized as important contributors, although they are continually under- and unemployed. Until recently, it was assumed that most persons with disabilities were not capable of entering and being successful in the workforce. These individuals either remained at home or attended sheltered programs designed for persons with disabilities. The societal costs of maintaining both these individuals and programs, plus the loss of tax dollars that could be contributed by these persons, has been high. During the past decade federal and state programs have begun to encourage human services agencies and other organizations to provide individuals with disabilities the opportunity to gain employment. Seen first as part of a social experiment, these individuals quickly proved their competence and their capacity to be valued and productive members of the workforce. Today hundreds of thousands of persons with disabilities are successfully working beside their nondisabled co-workers, contributing to their own support, and paying taxes.

There is a shared private and public interest in the employment of people with disabilities. Limited resources, an underdeveloped workforce, and global competition have generated an understanding of the benefits of employing persons who are currently dependent on entitlements and welfare. That is, when fewer resources are expended on public entitlements, more funds can be targeted toward developing and maintaining a competitive workforce. More and more, society recognizes the wasted human resources resulting from the high unemployment and underemployment of persons with disabilities. In fact, less than 20 percent of individuals labeled "significantly disabled" are employed; there is room for improvement.

As public attitudes shift from pity to higher expectations, persons with disabilities are increasingly entering the workforce. A guiding principle of employment has been that, with support, adults with severe disabilities can participate in the workforce as productive and contributing citizens. This is the message that is routinely conveyed to employers.

But at the same time, employees with disabilities must remain eligible for participation in a number of programs—public assistance, special medical benefits, and employment and other support services—whose guiding principles might be radically different. The dilemma that results is one of compromise. A person must be labeled "severely disabled" to acquire one type of support, yet "too disabled to work" to acquire another; both supports are necessary for employment. Thus, many remain members of the 80 percent who are under- and unemployed. In addition to these work disincentives, which force persons not to work to maintain the health benefits typically covered by Medicaid, other barriers to employment include poor training opportunities, a reliance on segregated work centers for jobs, and a historical bias against persons with disabilities.

In response to the unacceptable employment status of persons with disabilities, the federal government has encouraged states and regions to provide "supported employment," defined as "competitive work in an integrated work setting for individuals who, because of their handicaps, need ongoing support services to perform that work."[1] Supported employment strategies that rely on the human services system rather than on employers and co-workers are commonplace but generally unsuccessful. More recently, strategies that focus on supporting employers and co-workers to train and supervise persons with disabilities have been articulated and demonstrated successfully. For example, at Microsoft Corporation, Puget Sound Employment Services works with a team of co-workers to develop support strategies for a woman with a disability. The support is provided at different times during the day by each member of the work team. If the intent is to develop supportive work cultures for all of its staff, including those with disabilities, then all members of the team should be involved in learning how to support one another.[2] This approach differs from a "job coach" or outside expert, who is not a team member but provides training and support with the expectation that the support will fade. More progressive training and support strategies focused on improving the ability of employers and co-workers to provide support to diverse members of the workforce will more readily be utilized throughout the private and public sectors as a result of the Americans with Disabilities Act (ADA).[3]

THE LAW

The passage of the Americans with Disabilities Act on July 26, 1990, was based on the historical discrimination against persons with disabilities in both the private and public sectors. Regarding employment, the law requires that, beginning July 26, 1994, employers with 15 or more employees abide by nondiscrimination practices in job application procedures, hiring, firing, advancement, compensation, training, and other terms, conditions, and privileges of employment. The ADA also applies to recruitment, advertising, tenure, layoff, leave, and fringe benefits. The law is meant to protect both individuals with disabilities and persons who have a relationship with individuals with disabilities.

The definition of those considered covered under the ADA is

threefold. The first part applies to persons who have "substantial" impairments, which must limit major life activities, in seeing, hearing, speaking, walking, breathing, performing manual tasks, learning, caring for oneself, or working. For example, a person who has seizures, uses a wheelchair, or has a visual impairment would be covered under the law. Persons with acute illnesses, fractures, or sprains would not. The second part of the definition includes people with mental illness or a long-term illness such as cancer. Finally, the third part of the definition protects people who are perceived as having substantial limitations but in fact do not. One example would be individuals who have unusual facial characteristics or have been disfigured in some way.[4]

Although the definition of the term *disability* has been of interest to some, most employers are concerned about the part of the ADA that refers to "qualified individual with a disability" and "reasonable accommodation." Both elements are specifically defined within the law. A "qualified person with a disability" has legitimate skills, experience, and education and can perform the *essential functions* of the job. The essential functions requirement is designed to prevent discrimination based on a person's inability to perform incidental or peripheral job functions. If individuals are considered qualified and can perform the essential job functions except for limitations caused by their disability, the employer must provide reasonable accommodations. For example, a person with a disability who has difficulty moving her arms but holds a master's degree in computer programming must be considered for a job as a programmer. If she is considered qualified, the employer would have to provide her with the modified computer keyboard she would need to perform the job.

Most reasonable accommodations that fall into the category of devices are inexpensive, and many are commercially available. Other accommodations may include modified work schedules to meet transportation requirements, assistance in obtaining necessary materials, built-in personnel supports for personal needs such as eating and using the bathroom, and modified training and supervision.

The law specifically recognizes that reasonable accommodations should not result in "undue hardship" for the employer. Undue hardship is defined as "actions requiring significant difficulty or expense in relation to the size, resources, and structure, or the employee's operations." In general, larger and more profitable organizations would be required to expend greater effort and expense.[5] It is important to note that many resources exist to assist businesses in employing persons with disabilities. For example, every state has a department of vocational rehabilitation (or similar title) that is required to assist persons determined to be eligible to secure employment. These agencies can provide the training necessary to perform the job.

LESSONS FROM OTHER ORGANIZATIONS

Positive experiences of employing individuals with disabilities have taught the human services field and the corporate world some important lessons about what contributes to success.

Lesson 1. There is a higher rate of long-term job success achieved by those employees with disabilities hired by companies who took primary responsibility for training and supporting them than by those employees who were trained and supported by an outside vocational service agency.

One approach commonly used to help persons with disabilities obtain employment is to have a vocational service agency take the primary responsibility for training a new employee with a disability. The company then relies on the vocational agency to resolve any employee performance difficulties that may arise on a long-term basis. Other companies have indicated a desire to take responsibility for the training and supervision of their employees with disabilities in the same fashion as with any other employee. Employees trained by outside agencies have often experienced difficulties both in successfully performing their jobs over time as well as in being accepted into the social fabric of the workplace.

The presence of the person from the outside agency robs the supervisor of the opportunity to be viewed by the employee as the source of control and accountability for job performance. It also takes away the supervisor's opportunity to learn how to work with and supervise the employee. Co-workers also naturally have difficulty viewing their colleague as an equal or to establish personal relationships. On the other hand, employees trained by their supervisors and co-workers establish regular working and social relationships with these individuals. The supervisor and co-workers learn how to train and support the employee and get to know the employee through these experiences.

Lesson 2. Through experience, companies (and human services agencies consulting with companies) have come to recognize that the training and supervision techniques that are effective for persons with disabilities are typically not very different than those effective for all employees.

Those companies that were more committed to providing all employees with high-quality training, education, and supervision are most likely to be successful in providing the necessary supports to employees with disabilities. For employees with a disability to be successful in a new job, they may need a mentor—a co-worker who is experienced at the company to serve as a role model. The new employee may also need a supervisor who will provide encouragement and corrective feedback. In addition, the employee will benefit from a team of supportive co-workers. Mentoring, coaching, and work teams are all recognized as innovative organizational and management interventions. The Marriott Corporation and US Bancorp have made such commitments in their personnel, organizational, and managerial practices regarding hiring, training, and supporting persons with disabilities.

In addition, many companies report that their training and supervision of all employees have benefited from the techniques they have learned through the consultation provided by a vocational service agency in connection with an employee with a disability. These agencies may assist a supervisor in learning strategies, such as task analysis, job restructuring and adaptation, systematic instruction, and productivity monitoring, that they can then implement with other employees to improve work performance and efficiency.

Lesson 3. Those organizations that understand and value the need to train and manage a diverse workforce succeed as employers of persons with disabilities.

It is estimated that over 85 percent of these entering the workforce during the 1990s will be women and minorities including numerous racial groups, older workers, and people with disabilities. Forward-planning organizations proactively identify and implement personnel strategies to effectively manage this new workforce. The available workforce mirrors a shift in the customer base to one that is highly diverse. This includes 43 million American customers with disabilities. Organizations need employee input to attract and accommodate this expanding customer base.

Lesson 4. People with disabilities have proved to be competent and valued employees.

Companies that have provided employment opportunities to people with disabilities rate them as equal to other workers, based on their productivity, quality of work produced, work attitudes, and work habits. It is that clear.

Lesson 5. The cost of accommodations and training has been low. In fact, the vast majority cost less than $500.

Employers have also found that costly job-site accommodations can be paid for by their state's vocational rehabilitation agency. There are also a number of resources that can be utilized by a company to pay for any training costs that significantly exceed the amount that would be spent on other employees.

NEXT STEPS

In addition to the lessons learned through successful employment experiences, specific suggestions that can guide managers when hiring a person with a disability are as follows:

Action step 1. Hire an individual, not a program or a "client with a disability." The extent to which employees will be successful at a job will depend on how well they are suited to the job duties and work environment of a particular company.

Many employers who provide an employment opportunity to a person with a disability often leave the decision for the selection of the employee to the vocational service agency. In no other situation (except possibly when hiring a temporary employee from an employment service) would a company abdicate its responsibility for employee selection to an outside person or agency. It is important that both the company and the vocational service agency work closely together to identify the best person for the position. This means the employer must provide the agency with detailed information about the job duties and expectations. In fact, the vocational agency should take the time to actually observe the job over a period of several hours or even days.

Based on this information, the agency should then identify a candidate whose skills, abilities, and interests match the job requirements. The employer should interview the applicant and learn, with the help of the agency, as much as possible about the person. The company should then make the decision about whether or not to hire this individual.

Action step 2. Take responsibility for training.

All new employees will require some training in order to learn their job. Since many firms assume that they will provide this training, there should be no difference with a new employee who has a disability. A consultant from a vocational agency can provide suggestions about which strategies and modifications might make it easier for the person to perform the job. If the accommodations are costly or if the employee needs substantially more training than other employees, then the employment consultant can facilitate financial reimbursements to the employer for these expenses.

Action step 3. Help the new employee's co-workers feel comfortable with the person, and help the new employee fit in.

Perhaps one of the most important things for any employee is to feel accepted by new co-workers. It is a fact that many if not most individuals feel uncomfortable being around a person with a disability. This discomfort occurs because most individuals simply have not had the opportunity to associate with people with disabilities; they may be unsure of what to say or do. The vocational agency's employment consultant can help the employer make the co-workers feel comfortable and teach them how to interact with the new employee. This may include explaining the person's disability and suggesting any special assistance the person may need. However, the primary message that needs to be conveyed is that co-workers should treat the person in the same manner they would treat any other employee.

The new employee should also be given direct assistance in feeling comfortable and fitting in with the social environment. Entering a new job and getting to know co-workers who have worked together for a long time can be difficult for any new employee. A person with a disability may feel self-conscious and thus find it more difficult to meet co-workers. Providing this person with a mentor—a co-worker who is respected by others, who will make a special effort to get to know the person, who will assist with introductions, who will share coffee breaks, and who will define the organization's social customs (for example, "That's the supervisor's seat at the break table—don't sit there!")—can be a real help to a new employee with a disability.

Action step 4. If the employee doesn't work out, don't blame it on the disability.

There are few organizations that have not had at least one employee in the last year who didn't work out and had to be terminated. Typically, a manager will not generalize from the characteristics of the failed employee to other prospective employees. For example, if the failed employee was a male, the employer would not decide never to hire another male; if the employee was 40 years old, the employer would not vow never to hire another person who is 40 years old. However, employers often decide after hiring one employee with a disability who did not work out that no person with a disability will be successful at the company. Each person with a disability is an individual and different than every other person, with or without a disability. Because a particular employee with a disability does not work out at a company does not mean that another employee with a disability would not be successful.

One of the primary fears of many managers when considering hiring a person with a disability is what they will do if the person does not work out. The answer is, "What would you do for any other employee?." A good employer will work with any employee to help solve a work problem. A good employer will also make reasonable accommodations to permit the employee to maintain employment. However, any good employer will also terminate any employee whose problem can not be resolved or reasonably accommodated. Some employers are concerned about the legal liabilities they may face if they fire an employee with a disability. However, if the employer has attempted to help the employee remove the performance problem and has made reasonable accommodations, the company should not face legal liability and the vocational agency should support the decision.

CONCLUSION

Local, state, and national employment initiatives designed to enhance the employment of persons with disabilities are now supported by the Americans with Disabilities Act. This bill was not meant to scare employers or put them in a protective or defensive stance. Rather, it is a piece of civil rights legislation designed to encourage employers to recognize the productivity of citizens with disabilities and the importance of their contributions to the workforce. The ADA must be interpreted and is compatible with the ever-changing workforce culture that emphasizes innovation, training, small program units, self-managing teams, service over self-interest, and consumerism.

ENDNOTES

1. Federal Register (Washington, DC: US Government Printing Office, 1991): p. 30546.
2. *Stewardship: Choosing service over self-interest.* San Francisco: Barrett-Kohler. Aug. 19, 1991. 56(160).
3. Americans with Disabilities Act, Public Law 101-336, 101st Cong., sess. 2 (26 July 1990).
4. Wehman, P. *Life beyond the classroom: Transition strategies for young people with disabilities.* Baltimore: Paul H. Brookes Publishing Co., p. 232.
5. Wehman, p. 233.

Jan Nisbet

Jan Nisbet, PhD, is director of the Institute on Disability and an associate professor in the Department of Education at the University of New Hampshire. She received her PhD at the University of Wisconsin. She has been conducting research and writing for the past 15 years on topics related to school restructuring and reform, the transition from school to adult life, supported employment, and inclusive adult lives. Dr. Nisbet is also president of the executive board of directors of the Association for Persons with Severe Handicaps (TASH), a national organization focused on improving the lives of persons with severe disabilities and their families through research, training, and advocacy.

Jo-Ann Sowers

Jo-Ann Sowers, PhD, has worked in the field of vocational rehabilitation since 1973 and received her doctorate in rehabilitation from the University of Oregon. She has directed numerous employment assistance programs, as well as consulting with school districts, related to the vocational preparation of students with disabilities. Dr. Sowers has conducted research to identify strategies and approaches to enhance the employment success of persons with disabilities and has published widely in this area through professional journals and books. She is currently the project director of a federally funded project whose purpose is to build the capacity of businesses to hire, train, and support individuals who experience disabilities.

Index